THE DENTIST AND THE EMPRESS

The Dentist and the Empress

THE ADVENTURES OF DR. TOM EVANS
IN GAS-LIT PARIS

Gerald Carson

HOUGHTON MIFFLIN COMPANY BOSTON
1983

Chapters 10 and 11 contain material that appeared in somewhat
different form in *American Heritage*, volume 31, June / July 1980.

Library of Congress Cataloging in Publication Data

Carson, Gerald.
The dentist and the Empress.

Bibliography: p.
Includes index.
1. Evans, Thomas Wiltberger, 1823–1897. 2. Dentists—
United States—Biography. 3. Eugénie, Empress, consort
of Napoleon III, Emperor of the French, 1826–1920.
4. France—Queens—Biography. 5. France—Social life
and customs—19th century. I. Title.
RK43.E93C37 1983   944.07′092′4 [B]   82–15632
ISBN 0-395-33122-6

Printed in the United States of America

V 10 9 8 7 6 5 4 3 2 1

for
LETTIE,
who shared

———————

It used to be said,
"Paris is the Heaven of Americans."

DR. THOMAS W. EVANS (1823–1897),
court dentist to the Emperor Napoleon III

Contents

Illustrations

Preface

I HAVE SPENT a bit more than three years in the company of a remarkable American, the dentist Thomas W. Evans, celebrated in his own time throughout Europe, almost unknown in his native land. Highly competent and innovative in his profession, a born diplomat with a genial personality that charmed the courts of Europe when royalties were still in flower, Dr. Evans figures twice in mainstream history, through his unshakable loyalty to Napoleon III and the beautiful Empress Eugénie, and through his considerable diplomatic services to the United States during the American Civil War.

Dr. Evans also had a very good time during the brilliant if shaky years of France's Second Empire, an era when life in Paris was illuminated by wit and gaslight, in step with the rhythm of the waltz, faintly perfumed by the aroma of Parma violets. I have tried to do justice both to the man and his social environment. For most of my material I am indebted to those who have gone before me and to other persons and institutions gratefully named in the acknowledgments. I have corrected some errors and possibly made a few new ones.

And now, would you like to meet Evans, American dentist, diplomat, boulevardier, Commander of the Legion of Honor, of Paris, France?

G.C.

NEWTOWN, PENNSYLVANIA

THE DENTIST AND THE EMPRESS

1

Golden Dreams in West Philadelphia

THE TUILERIES PALACE was ablaze with the light of hundreds of candles and gas lamps. It was the night of a court ball, a brilliant accent on the social season in the Paris of the Emperor Napoleon III, when the imperial flag flew over the central dome of the Pavillon de l'Horloge, indicating that the sovereigns, the Emperor and the Empress Eugénie, were in residence. The age demanded thrills and prosperity. The Second Empire, fairly under way, provided glitter and show, military reviews and full employment, rising prices on the Bourse, a state religion for the devout, swirling crinolines from the ateliers of Worth, Alexandrine Roget, and Bobergh for ladies of the world and half-world, gossip of juicy Bonaparte mésalliances for the delectation of the old aristocracy of the Faubourg St.-Germain. It was the best of times for elegance, upward mobility, honorific titles, band concerts, openings at the Opéra, with bread and circuses for the urban proletariat.

As women guests in décolleté gowns and diamonds, gentlemen with expansive white shirt fronts, sashed diplomats in court dress, ascended the grand staircase between impassive rows of Cent-Gardes with drawn swords, dazzling in sky-blue tunics and mirror-bright cuirasses, high black boots and gleaming helmets, they arrived at the two-story-high Salle des Maréchaux, glowing with flattering candle-light, its walls hung with portraits of the marshals of France. One woman guest turned to a friend and inquired about an attractive stranger, finding her obviously a person of breeding, a tall brunette but delicate in features, with gracious manners, indeed quite *distinguée*. The speaker hazarded the guess "She must be an Américaine." The reply was "Yes, and only to think of it, how horrible — she is the wife of a dentist."

A few moments later the lady noticed that the Emperor had approached and shaken hands cordially with a short, well-groomed, rather square-cut man. He stood very straight, not wishing to lose an inch of his stature. He had gray-blue eyes, regular features, a well-formed nose. There were side whiskers, a mustache, and a curling mass of thick hair, which framed a full forehead and round face. Teeth — white, even. In dress and general appearance, the object of their survey appeared to be a good bourgeois, who looked a little bit like William I of Prussia or the statesman Léon Gambetta, but, as one French scholar has written, "an amiable, pleasant William or Gambetta."[1]

As the two men chatted, the inquirer asked again, "And who is that man the Emperor is talking to so affably?"

"Oh," came the reply, "that is Evans, the American dentist, husband of that lady. He was pointed out to me last week at Lord Cowley's. He is the dentist to whom they say the Emperor is greatly attached."

The final comment: "Well, at least he must be a gentleman. Those American dentists, it seems, are something wonderful."[2]

The couple under scrutiny were indeed Americans, Dr. and Mrs. Thomas W. Evans. They were newcomers to Paris, but already moving up socially and professionally because of the doctor's extraordinary skill, polished manners, and winning personality. Wealth, a secure social position in the hierarchal society of the European world, a clientele of noble and royal patients, had been Evans's dream from his boyhood days in West Philadelphia. The ballroom comment identified the young dentist's problem. There was a certain condescension toward his occupation. But his presence on the guest list of the Tuileries also marked out his opportunities, which he grasped so successfully that he became the most famous dentist of the nineteenth century in Europe, known in court circles from Windsor Castle to St. Petersburg as "*the* American dentist" and, more intimately, as "Handsome Tom." The two ladies, incidentally, who observed the Evanses at the court function later became patients of the doctor, as did his recent host they referred to, the British ambassador, Earl Cowley.

When Tom Evans was eight years old, he had watched a pharmacist attempt to fill a tooth for his sister Anna, and decided that he could have done it better. Young Tom's mechanical bent and precocious manual dexterity were already manifested in a hobby. He made jewelry, rings, and breast pins in silver and gold for his three sisters, seals for school friends, a watch case for an aunt, all in his home workshop. And often after the end of his day as a pupil at a common school in Philadelphia, he stopped at the shop and manufactory of Joseph Warner, silver- and goldsmith, in Greenleaf's Court, a small street between Fourth and Fifth streets below Market. There, Warner manufactured instruments for practicing dentists and scientific appliances for the Franklin Institute, and constructed gold and silver plates and wire springs for artificial teeth. He was an intelligent and honest man, always affectionately remembered by Evans, and most obliging except when he had an attack of the gout. To the boy looking in the window the premises were holy.

"Old Jose" was delighted to see a small boy so deeply interested in the melting and rolling out of precious metals, the drawing of wire, and delicate work done with the soldering iron. Forgetful of time, Tom often got a scolding when he arrived home late, and sometimes he was sent to bed without his supper. No matter — Tom Evans was, as his life unrolled, twice blessed. He found his calling early in the profession of dentistry, which brought him fortune, fame, and an opportunity to practice enlightened philanthropy. And it threw him into associations, which he treasured, with kings, emperors, czars, and the titled nobility of a Europe still organized in accordance with the dynastic and territorial lines laid down by the Congress of Vienna in 1815.

Evans's beginnings were modest. He was the descendant of Welsh Quakers who migrated to Pennsylvania in 1682. Born in a red-brick-front house at the corner of Chestnut and what is now Thirty-seventh Street in the Borough of West Philadelphia, on December 23, 1823, Tom was the third son of William Milnor and Catherine Anne Wiltberger Evans. The father was a retired army major; the mother, the daughter of John Christian Wiltberger, a silversmith. The family was large, the fortune small. But there were aspirations toward gentility, which Major Evans displayed in some rather clumsy maneuvers to shape his son's future.

When Tom was fourteen, and already capable of making dental instruments or preparing a cavity, Warner agreed to take him into his business as an apprentice if his parents would consent. The major objected. He wanted a lawyer in the family. Having chosen Tom for the role, the father spoke disparagingly of seeing his son become, as he said, "a tooth-a-cary — might as well be an apothecary." But Tom resisted. "I had no taste nor talent for that profession," he wrote later about the legal profession, "nor ambition to rise in it, but was faithful to my first love." As a last resort, Major Evans took his son to Dr. George McClellan, anatomist, surgeon, founder of the Jefferson Medical College, now Thomas Jefferson University, in Philadelphia, and father of the Civil War general George B. McClellan. Evans *père* begged his help in diverting Tom from so mean a calling as "being a toothpuller . . . which he must know was beneath him." But Dr. McClellan, after reflection, advised that Tom be allowed to follow his bent.

One more try: Tom was taken to Dr. Emile Gardette, dentist and son of a French surgeon who had come to America at the time of the American Revolution, and lived next door to Dr. McClellan. Of this interview, Dr. Evans later wrote laconically, "Same questions, same answers," although Gardette did express some doubt as to young Evans's future success, since he was not French and "it is they who make the dentists." Dr. Evans remarked with satisfaction, in looking back, "how strangely this has been reversed for it is America that has made the profession — lifted it from the trade or art I found it in France when I came there."[3]

So Thomas Evans was apprenticed to Joseph Warner. With Warner, Tom Evans cheerfully did the grunt work — operating the bellows, cleaning up benches — then, moving ahead, learning to do fine gold soldering. And he read such books on dentistry as he could obtain, studying the character of each tooth, its relative position and its name.

"I figured to my mind," Evans wrote, "my name on a silver plate or perhaps a brass one — Thomas W. Evans, Dentist. At night I dreamed of this plate on the door, of people coming to have their teeth filled, new ones made for them . . . and even in those childish days I thought perhaps I might some day be called Doctor . . . I made up my mind I *could* be . . . I began to operate upon the teeth of sheep . . . dogs and cattle." Young Evans drilled holes in the animals' teeth, then filled them with tin-foil amalgam and, sometimes as an extravagance, with gold foil. "I had no teacher," he noted, but "used my common sense."

Despite his youth, Evans found some people with sufficient confidence in him to allow him to work on their mouths. Years later he recalled in particular a bartender employed in a hotel on Market Street for whom he filled fifteen or twenty teeth even before he ever had had a lesson or seen the inside of a dentist's office. Years later, when the doctor visited America wearing the rosette of France's Legion of Honor, "this gentleman sought me out . . . I found nearly all my fillings there as good as new."

Among the leading dentists of Philadelphia who frequently called at Joseph Warner's shop was the eminent Dr. John de Haven White. Dr. White was impressed by the mental quickness, the promising skills, the willingness to go the extra mile, the pleasing manners, of the goldsmith's apprentice. In 1841 he accepted Tom Evans as a private student. The preceptorship system of training still prevailed. In fact, the first dental school in the United States, the Baltimore College of Dental Surgery, "the cradle of American dentistry," founded in 1839, produced its first graduates in the year when Evans began his studies under Dr. White. The degree conferred by the Baltimore College was Chirurgiae Dentrium Doctor, translated as Doctor of Dental Surgery, or the now familiar initials D.D.S. The new concept of dentistry, which Evans embraced wholeheartedly, was to view the mouth and teeth not as something apart from the general physiology, but as an integral part of it, subject to the same biological, mechanical, and pathological laws as the rest of the body. This was new doctrine, and it pointed up the need for medical as well as mechanical training. Therefore, Evans, while working under Dr. White, attended lectures on anatomy, surgery, and physiology at the Jefferson Medical College, though no record is extant today showing that he graduated as a medical doctor. A fellow student, who became a lifelong friend of Dr. Evans's, was Samuel Stockton White (not a relative of Tom Evans's preceptor), who devoted himself to the manufacture of "indestructible" porcelain teeth and founded the S. S. White Dental Manufacturing Company, once the largest dental supply company in the world.

In 1843, in accordance with the custom of the time, there being no system of licensure, Dr. White and the Jefferson Medical College issued Evans a certificate, or diploma, permitting him to practice "the art and mystery of dentistry." Thus, Evans never was a doctor in the modern sense of the term. But he later received honorary degrees, and his professional success validated his use of the title.

Also in 1843, Tom Evans fell in love with and married Agnes Josephine Doyle, the attractive daughter of a Philadelphia merchant. Evans practiced for a few months in Baltimore, then moved to Lancaster, Pennsylvania, to gain experience and confidence before finally settling down, "or, as I had determined, going to Europe sooner or later." At Lancaster he joined as a partner in the practice of Dr. William Van Patten, with rooms on the second floor of the Kramphs Building at the corner of North Queen and Orange streets, opposite the post office.

After a brief association with Dr. Van Patten, Evans struck out for himself. On April 1, 1846, he bought advertising space in the Lancaster press, announcing that he was locating permanently in Lancaster. Nor did he wait for patients to come to him. Like the country doctor of the period, the young dentist hired a horse and buggy and took his services to the places where they were needed. Already his technique was impressive. Improvising when necessary, he could take a simple excavator, with its tiny spoonlike end, break off the point, and use the remaining end to push filling material into a prepared cavity. He could make an impression tray out of pasteboard and red sealing wax. His perception as to the quantity of gold needed for a cavity was uncanny; never was any material lost. But Evans was still a young man with the romantic drive that placed him in imagination among the notable personalities of an aristocratic civilization. Through them he would enjoy the emoluments of professional success. He would introduce not only dentistry of a high order but equally the dentist.

"I determined at an early age to make a high reputation, to gain celebrity, position and fortune," he wrote to his parents after he was established in Paris, "not from any selfish motive or personal aggrandizement further than is justifiable." His career would be "founded upon industry, activity, and having for its object to benefit mankind . . . I have lived feeling that every minute is precious."[4]

In Lancaster Dr. Evans established a solid reputation as a specialist in the manipulation of gold foil. When he submitted a series of gold contour-filling operations to an exhibition of arts and manufacture at the Franklin Institute in 1847, he was awarded a silver medal by a jury of dentists and doctors for "natural teeth plugged in the mouth . . . in a superior manner, and by a new method."

Among those who saw Evans's exhibit was Dr. John C. Clark, a retired Philadelphia physician living in Paris but then visiting in Philadelphia. Clark had been alerted by a colleague, Dr. Cyrus Starr Brewster, a native of South Carolina but with a thriving dental practice in Paris, to find an assistant, a young man who, in the words of Theodore Evans, a nephew of Dr. Tom's, "would present well as a dentist." Clark was greatly impressed with Tom Evans's improvement in the art of plugging, that is, filling decayed teeth. He made some inquiries that led him to Lancaster. The local druggist told Evans, speaking of Dr. Clark, "He asked me if I knew a smart young dentist who could do fine gold fillings and would like to go to Paris." He did indeed know such a person.

There were interviews between Clark and Evans, who warmed to the proposal. Among its attractions: Dr. Brewster was overworked and feeling the weight of the years. But he drew a fashionable clientele to his *cabinet* in the Rue de la Paix near the Place Vendôme. It would not escape Evans's notice that Dr. Brewster enjoyed the patronage of King Louis Philippe and his court. The upshot of the matter was that Dr. Clark recommended young Evans to Dr. Brewster and received the reply, "Bring him with you on your return trip." Evans, for his part, recognizing that world figures were scarce in Lancaster, decided to go. "I saw a chance," the young dentist told his bride; "it is a sin to let it pass." A brother, Theodore Sewall Evans, also a dentist, would take Tom's place at Lancaster, where he stayed until 1852, when he joined Thomas in Paris.[5]

So, on November 10, 1847, the Evanses sailed for Europe on the steamer *Bavaria* with a nest egg of five hundred dollars. Evans knew nothing of France or of Paris, had no understanding of the French language. But he had boundless confidence in his professional competence. Fourteen days later the Evanses landed at Le Havre, took the boat train for Paris, and drove to the Hôtel de Normandy, Rue de la Paix, the gas-lit street of the luxury trades, of fashionable dressmakers, jewelers, and dentists. Dr. Brewster's office was nearly opposite the hotel, at Number 11. Meeting the next day with Evans,

Dr. Brewster asked to see the case of contour fillings that had won the award at the Franklin Institute, watched him work on a patient, and came to an agreement with him. Dr. Evans moved to modest quarters at 39 Rue de l'Arcade, back of the Madeleine, "for his means," the nephew Theodore wrote later, "were none of the greatest." However, the young dentist toiled at his French, labored diligently at the dental chair, and by June 1848 had recouped his savings. The partnership, called Brewster and Evans, lasted only until 1850. After many personal and professional differences with Brewster, Dr. Evans moved his residence and office to an apartment at 15 Rue de la Paix on the first floor (the second floor in American usage) and so escaped from the rather draconian contract Dr. Brewster had imposed on him. Dr. Evans planted his standard, his nephew wrote, as "a devoted defender of the rights of gold fillings," declaring " 'gold only gold' for front teeth." The doctor would place a leaf of gold in his left hand, then crush it with his right, tear it up, and roll it into pellets, as he often did with bread at the dinner table. Then, with extraordinary dexterity, there came a quick movement — one, two, three — and the cavity was solidly filled.[6]

Somewhat belatedly, the *Dental News Letter* announced, in October 1848, "We now have another American dentist (a Philadelphian) in Paris. We are speaking of Mr. T. W. Evans whose examples of orification won him a medal."[7]

Dr. Evans arrived in France just in time to witness the Revolution of February 1848, which dethroned Louis Philippe, who had reigned as King of the French, a title that is not at all the same as King of France. Louis Philippe was a good man but tedious. He had the eyes and nose of a Bourbon, but he lacked tradition. Louis Philippe was expendable. So the Citizen King, with pear-shaped head and bad teeth, out of urgent necessity cut off his whiskers, fled from the Tuileries, and caught a public cab in the Place de la Concorde. Got up like a stage Englishman, he wore an old hat, shabby coat, blue spectacles, a toupee, and carried a cotton umbrella. As plain "Mr. Smith," the King was smuggled out of France by the British consul at Le Havre, gained the shores of England without luggage, and lived and died quietly at Claremont in Surrey as the guest of Queen Victoria.

Charles Godfrey Leland, a genial Philadelphian with a gargantuan taste for life who wielded an accomplished pen and even mounted the barricades himself, described with relish the political situation he found in France. "We dined under a Monarchy, supped under a Regency, went to sleep under a Provisional Government, and woke up under a Republic — not to mention about two hours when we had just no government at all."[8] Out of this upheaval came a republic, known as the Second. It brought to the presidency Charles Louis Napoleon Bonaparte, the bachelor Prince and nephew of Napoleon I, under a constitution filled with contradictions certain to provide a deadlock between the Assembly and the executive. Furthermore, the constitution could not be changed. There was no recognition in its provisions of the possibility that the country might "welcome as a deliverer the man who could cut the cords that could not legally be loosed."[9] Prophetic words. In deference to the suffrages that had called him home from exile in England, Louis Napoleon (he dropped the "Charles") moved symbolically into the shabby and relatively modest Elysée palace instead of the royal splendors of the Tuileries. But in the estimation of knowledgeable observers he was not likely to stay there.

If Thomas Evans was shocked by the volatile character of French politics and the sight of blood on the barricades, by the swift transition from Gallic gaiety and courtesy to the menace in the old revolutionary song "Ça ira!" he left no record of his impressions. But he was unhappily surprised at the low esteem in which dentists were held. They were unregulated, uninhibited, and grouped in the public mind, not without reason, with midwives, cuppers and bleeders, itinerant tinkers, and barbers. Street-corner tooth-drawers, garbed in fantastic costumes like sorcerers of old, wielded the forceps *al fresco* along the quays of the Seine to the edification of onlookers while the howls of the victims were drowned by a timely beating of drums and clashing of cymbals. As had been noticed long before, "The haphazard pulling out of a tooth is an easy enough thing: the only requisites for doing this are impudence and the audacity natural to the . . . charlatan." With reason, the French had an old saying: "The teeth leave when the dentist arrives."

Victor Hugo describes the wandering tooth-drawer through his character Babet in *Les Misérables*. Babet, thin, shrewd, with a copious flow of words, had been a barkeep, a clown, and a showman. He equipped himself for the practice of dentistry by setting up a booth at fairs, with a trumpet to announce his presence, and a placard that read, in part: "Babet, dental artist, member of the Academies . . . extirpates teeth, removes stumps left by other dentists. Price, one tooth, one franc, fifty centimes; two teeth, two francs . . ."

It was a long-standing custom in Paris for dentists to hustle for patients. As far back as the eighteenth century big wooden or iron molars hung on brackets over the dentist's door, and drawings on the walls of his house pointed the way. James Jackson Jarves, American author, editor, critic, and pioneer art collector, has left a vivid description of the offensive advertising he saw on one of the principal streets of "Paris, the magnificent" around 1856, notably by chiropodists; but the dentists, he said:

> bear away the palm in practical illustrations of their art. They have elegant gilt frames set with glass, in which are displayed artificial jaws with bright red gums and milky white teeth, others in every variety of loss, decay, and repair, row within row, like the anatomy of a shark's mouth, all opening and shutting in different degrees of velocity and emphasis, by some concealed mechanism, the whole forming the most complete exhibition of gnashing of teeth to be seen this side of "outer darkness." Above are wax heads which revolve every minute on pivots, showing alternately a ghastly, sunken-jawed toothless face, and the same lineaments freshened and filled out with a new set of grinders spotless from the maker's hands. The effect of this, under the reflection of a powerful gas-light, is easier imagined than described.

The French, Jarves added, "are a practical people at the bottom of their gallantry. They make their wants or wares known in the most straight-forward manner."

One Parisian dentist-showman in particular was worthy of comparison with Phineas T. Barnum. His name was Georges Fattet. Fattet surrounded himself with black servants in gorgeous uniforms and commissioned caricatures of himself to be published in the *Charivari* and other comic newspapers. He himself wore silken robes when he officiated at the dental chair, and when he appeared in public he mingled the elegant with the macabre by traveling in a carriage shaped like a huge denture, which bore him through the streets of the City of Light to the blare and flourish of trumpets.[10] All this was part of the French popular culture that Dr. Evans, an alien, proposed to change. A formidable undertaking.

In Paris Evans found that even reputable dentists still sat below the salt. They made house calls and were expected to enter the residence of a patient with any social position by the back stairs, like the butcher boy, seamstress, bootmaker, or coachman, since use of the front stairs implied equality with those the dentist called on. Furthermore, even the best practitioners were kept at a professional and social distance by the medical doctors, who did not admit that dentistry was a branch of their profession.

"They excluded surgery from their ranks as long as they could," Dr. Evans recalled. "The jealousy was so great that they prohibited their patients from having the most simple operations performed without their consent and generally their presence . . . in fact, they wanted to control the entire case." To them, "a dentist was a man to pull aching teeth and to cleanse dirty ones . . . I am speaking generally . . . [but] this was what I found upon coming to Paris."[11] The family physician, that is, was determined to keep down specialists who might diminish his influence with Monsieur or Madame.

From the beginning, Dr. Evans firmly rejected any tutelage of this sort. "I asserted my independence modestly but insisted upon acting as I thought best in those cases confided to me." Soon the American found himself accepted on his own terms. His reputation grew, and his practice increased to the point where he was overwhelmed with demands for his services. Because he burned with a hard, gemlike flame not only to advance his own standing but also that of the profession at large, the doctor "refused to . . . be treated as one who needed to be told what I might do or what I ought to do." If patients did not accord him the respect he felt due his calling, Dr. Evans politely sent them elsewhere. The effect, he said, was "wonderful."[12]

The first royal patient to call for Dr. Evans was Maximilian II, King of Bavaria, who in 1850 asked that he come to Munich. That would have taken three days and nights and worked havoc on Dr. Evans's engagement book. A gracious compromise was made to meet halfway at Aix-la-Chapelle. Evans saved teeth that the King had despaired of. Soon the doctor became the dentist for all the Bavarian royal family and was on such a footing with Maximilian that the King offered him a decoration.

"I was young and inexperienced in those matters and thoroughly American and did not wish in the least," Evans remembered, "to accept . . . an order of chivalry [that] might affect my much-treasured Americanism." So the young dentist asked the King to let him inquire about any laws of the United States bearing on the acceptance of a foreign order.

Dr. Evans wrote for guidance to the former United States senator, Secretary of State, and future President of the United States, James Buchanan, whom he had known in Lancaster. Buchanan replied that there is nothing in the U.S. Constitution that prohibits the acceptance of a decoration by a private citizen if no title of nobility is attached to it.

The doctor's scruples were satisfied, and he became a Knight of the Order of St. Michael of Bavaria. Other similar honors — stars and ribbons, crosses and sashes, blazons and the brilliants of heraldry, something like two hundred in number — followed over the years. But none was of a character to ennoble the recipient. Dr. Evans wore the emblem of one or another of these honors on special occasions, especially in the country that had bestowed it. For, as Dr. Evans observed tactfully, it "would not be kind or decorous not to wear them in the presence of the giver." He regarded these honors, he said, "as given to the profession through me."[13] The willingness of one of Europe's royals of high consideration in the great world to place himself under the care of the young dentist within three years of his arrival in Europe, and to adjust to the American's convenience, provides impressive evidence of the standing he had already achieved and tells us something about the charm of his personality and the range of his practice.

In sharp contrast to the low estate of dentistry in nineteenth-century Paris, French dental procedures had once led the world. As early as 1614 and 1699 ordinances were passed in France requiring dentists to pass an examination. Names still remembered from the eighteenth century include Pierre Fauchard, who marked off dentistry from general medicine in a seminal book, *Le Chirurgien dentiste ou traité des dents* (1728); Nicolas Dubois de Chemant, who turned out satisfactory dentures made of porcelain and was granted a patent on his method by Louis XVI; and Gustov A. Plantou, who introduced the artificial teeth, made of porcelain, into America at Philadelphia shortly after the Revolution. Other French dentists who brought professional standards to this country when the French expeditionary forces arrived were Joseph Jean François Lemaire and Jacques Gardette, father of the Gardette already mentioned, who counted George Washington among his patients.[14]

The French Revolution was a disaster for dentistry. Only a license, easily obtained by any citizen, with no requirement as to professional training, was needed for the practice of medicine, surgery, or dentistry. The result was near anarchy in all areas of medicine until Napoleon Bonaparte proclaimed a new law of medical regulation to curb the quacks, effective March 10, 1803 (19 Ventôse, Year XI on the French republican calendar). But, curiously, dentists were not covered by the law until the far distant date of 1892, when Dr. Evans's career was substantially finished. During almost all of the nineteenth century, then, the dentist was the only professional person whose practice was not regulated in France, "where everything is regulated." A private Society of Dental Surgery in Paris did try through litigation to create standards based on judicial decisions, but its efforts were no match for the problem. Dr. Evans, because of his personal prestige, his royal connections, his abiding interest in improving "all that concerns my profession," proved to be more effective than the society in influencing public attitudes toward the art and science of dentistry during the last half of the century.[15]

Chance played its part in the doctor's rise. It was Evans's great good fortune that Prince Louis Napoleon, President of republican France, had extremely delicate teeth, sensitive gums, numerous cavities, much anxiety and fear of pain, and suffered "absolute torture" from toothaches. This susceptibility also plagued his mother, Queen Hortense, wife of Louis Bonaparte, once King of Holland.[16] Sheer coincidence brought the young American dentist to the attention of the head of the Second Republic, and intertwined the subsequent lives of the future Emperor of the French, Dr. Evans, and the ravishing Andalusian beauty, Mlle. Eugénie-Marie de Montijo de Guzman.

2

A Versatile American Meets a Man of Destiny

In the spring of 1850, Dr. Brewster made an extended trip to the United States. One day in July an urgent message reached the office at 11 Rue de la Paix, requesting that Brewster come immediately to the Elysée palace. Dr. Evans, still Brewster's partner, responded to the call. He found the President in extreme pain; the trouble was in a lower molar, right side. "I was lucky enough to remove the pain at once," he wrote to Dr. Brewster, and added that Napoleon had said, "You are a young fellow, but clever. I like you."[1]

Louis Napoleon expressed the wish to see the dentist the next day, and from that time on until Napoleon's death Dr. Evans attended him frequently, sometimes as often as twice a week. Their relations became friendly and confidential, because Bonaparte found the American to be discreet, a man of sound judgment, an amusing exemplar of what he regarded as New World pragmatism; and he enjoyed talking with Evans in English, since the Prince-President spoke it fluently as a consequence of his forced residence in England during the reign of Louis Philippe. Perhaps another consideration was that, although Dr. Evans acquired a good command of French, he was never able to master the French accent. Indeed, Louis Napoleon himself spoke his native French like a German from Augsburg.

It is not straining the metaphor to say that Dr. Evans enjoyed Napoleon's unusual consideration because he conducted his whole life in accordance with a precept he followed professionally: "If the bottom of a cavity is not properly cleaned, the best high polished filling will fail."[2] The fundamentals were always sound in Evans's relationship with his highly placed sponsor. Once, at a large luncheon at the Tuileries after a morning when Napoleon had been importuned for all sorts of favors, he complimented a countess because she had, as he recollected, never asked him for anything, which set her apart from all who were present. Then he corrected himself. "No," he said, turning to the dentist. "Evans has never asked anything of me for himself." The genial doctor responded, "I hope, Your Majesty, that it will always be thus."[3]

ome

Louis Napoleon was the nephew of Napoleon the Grand and the third son of the great Napoleon's next-to-youngest brother, Louis, a cranky, morose man who became King of Holland as Napoleon I's surrogate, and Queen Hortense, daughter of the Empress Josephine. It was an unfortunate marriage, forced on the contracting parties by Napoleon for dynastic reasons. When Charles Louis was born, in 1808, he was fourth in the line of succession in the Bonaparte dynasty, but by 1848, following the death of his two older brothers and Napoleon I's only son, the Duc de Reichstadt, he was first in line for the heritage of Napoleon I in case the French turned out King Louis Philippe. Louis Napoleon (recall that he dropped the "Charles") had a shrewd understanding of the times; he knew that the French people were sighing for peace and prosperity but also for *la gloire,* and he clung to an almost mystical belief that it was his destiny to fulfill the national desires.

The Prince-President looked like a Frank rather than a Corsican Bonaparte. His head was large, with features strongly accented. His eyes, small and pale blue, under drooping lids that veiled his thoughts, brightened when he was amused and radiated a sense of power when he was aroused. His face was lengthened by a goatee, and was broadened by a heavy chestnut mustache, stiffly waxed by a pomade called Hungarian. His complexion was blond. The legs were too short for his body, but Louis Napoleon was a superb horseman and made an imposing figure when in the saddle. Because of the stormy marriage of his quarreling parents, there was much speculation, encouraged by his uncle Jérôme and cousin, Prince Napoleon, and accompanied by some closely reasoned mathematics, that the King of Holland was not Louis's father; but the name of no other putative father has been brought forward.

Prince Napoleon, known familiarly by the diminutive Plon-Plon, was the son of Jérôme, the youngest brother of Napoleon I and former King of Westphalia. There was ill feeling against Louis Napoleon among members of this line, since Louis stood ahead of them in the Bonapartist succession. On one occasion during an altercation of some warmth between Louis Napoleon and Prince Napoleon over the latter's tangled personal finances, Plon-Plon, who greatly resembled their great common ancestor, lost control of himself and flung the insult: "You have nothing of the Emperor about you." "You make a mistake," replied the Prince-President with perfect composure. "I have his family about me."[4]

Most scholars and all modern works of biographical reference have recognized Louis's place in the Napoleonic line, in harmony with the Latin maxim cited by the historian and littérateur Maxime Du Camp: *Pater est quem nuptiae demonstrant* (The marriage shows who the father is). In the end, Louis, the former King of Holland, after indulging in "a slander of half a life-time," acknowledged in his will that Louis Napoleon was his son.[5]

There was a succession of reconciliations, separations, and often bitter litigation between Louis's parents, so that he was, in effect, without a father and enjoyed a bit too much of an adoring mother. Expelled from France by the victorious Holy Alliance after the disaster at Waterloo in 1815, the lovely and wealthy former Queen Hortense and her son wandered over Europe and lived for a time at Augsburg, in Bavaria, where Louis attended the *Gymnasium* and learned to speak French in the German manner. For a summer home, Hortense purchased a small, romantic château in Switzerland called Arenenberg, in the canton of Thurgau, on the shore of Lake Constance, and made it a kind of shrine, commemorating the glories of the First Empire. Here, Louis grew up in its mystique, convinced "that a Bonaparte had only to land in France with a handful of men and the whole nation would rally to him." He had some conspiratorial adventures in Italy touching on the temporal power of the Pope, which he opposed in the interest of Italian nationalism. Switzerland honored the Prince with a captaincy in the Bernese artillery, where he learned enough of gunnery to write a manual on the subject, and published a pamphlet on poverty and a political treatise with a distinct Bonapartist flavor.

When the Duc de Reichstadt, who from the Bonapartist point of view was Napoleon II, died in 1832, Louis assumed the burdens and the hopes of pretender to the throne of France. He tried to claim his heritage in a clumsy putsch at Strasbourg. Easygoing Louis Philippe, underestimating his man, let Louis off with a light punishment. He sent him to America with a modest viaticum. There, he tasted high and low life in New York City, visited Niagara Falls and Washington Irving, and came to believe he understood America, before he was recalled to Europe by the imminent death of Queen Hortense. He arrived, however, too late to see his mother.

Once more he tried to dislodge the Orléanist monarchy in an abortive descent upon Boulogne from Gravesend with sixty tatterdemalion followers and an eagle tethered to the mast of his ship, though some sources insist it was a disheveled vulture. Again — failure. The 42nd Line Regiment, stationed at Boulogne, refused to rise, and there was some shooting. This was too much. Louis was captured and sentenced to imprisonment for life in the fortress of Ham, a dark, dank structure in the low-lying, misty part of Picardy. The castle was a singularly unattractive remnant of the Middle Ages and quite unhealthful.

Here, for five and a half years, Louis Napoleon walked on the gloomy ramparts, cultivated a small garden, wrote articles on miscellaneous topics, and studied to such good effect that he could say later to his friend Evans that Ham had been his university *("J'ai passé par l'université de Ham")*. From time to time the prisoner was allowed to receive visitors, and he had for further consolation the company of Alexandrine Eléanore Veugeot, his bedmaker and ironer. Louis gave la Veugeot lessons in speech and grammar, and she in turn gave him two sons. Freedom to resume the pursuit of his star came in the spring of 1846, when Louis escaped to England, where he became a hero to the general public, a romantic figure in the press, and a favorite in the upper levels of society. His final and successful chance came two years later, when the Orléanist monarchy was extinguished by the Revolution of 1848.

France, now republican under a provisional government, became increasingly aware of the existence of another Napoleon. Louis stood for the belief that the ideals of 1789 had been inherited and carried out by Napoleon I, the events that occurred between 1804 and 1814 being conveniently forgotten. It was poor history but good propaganda. And Louis Napoleon drew strength from the elevation of his uncle as folk hero. At once the imposing Emperor and beloved Little Corporal, Napoleon's picture hung in the peasant's cottage over the marriage bed, beside that of Christ and the Virgin. His remains rested after 1840 in the Dome Church at the Invalides. In the costume of Caesar he reigned from the top of the Vendôme column. His image was everywhere in engravings, in sculpture and battle paintings, on bottles and medals. The legend came through in the gay and lilting songs of Pierre Jean Béranger — "Les Deux Grenadiers," and "Le Vieux Drapeau" — and in innumerable stage dramas with a heroic protagonist, the man of St. Helena — HIM, LUI, CELUI.

When the provisional government was replaced by a permanent Constituent Assembly and a constitution, Citizen Louis Napoleon Bonaparte was elected first to the Assembly and then, on December 10, 1848, to the presidency of the Second Republic. The term was for four years, but the incumbent was prohibited by article 45 of the constitution from succeeding himself. This quick elevation was an extraordinary dénouement for a man who had bungled two attempts against the throne, at Strasbourg and at Boulogne; who was an insurgent, a conspirator, and a pamphleteer; who had spent only a third of his life in France, half as a child, half in prison. No matter. Sometimes a lack of success is worth a halo. In the words of the *Journal des Débats,* "This is one of the greatest tributes ever paid to glory. The man was little known . . . The name was enough."

But one does not elect princes as presidents of republics if one is serious about preserving republican institutions, and Napoleon's republicanism soon wore thin. In July 1851, Louis Napoleon proposed a revision of the constitution that would have allowed him to continue in office as President for ten years, but a hostile and suspicious Assembly rejected the idea, along with a return to universal suffrage, though it was known that the country wanted both. Already a certain pomp and ceremony surrounded the President. His coach was emblazoned with the imperial arms. Footmen of the Elysée wore the green livery of the great Napoleon; so did the palace detectives. The British ambassador noticed that at a presidential ball "the same etiquette was observed towards the President as would be towards royalty . . . A chair of state was placed for him and he occasionally paraded the rooms, way being made for him as for a sovereign."[6] The civil code became once more the Code Napoleon. The imperial eagles returned to military standards, and dazzling social events revived memories of the First Empire. The Second Republic became a conscious rehearsal for the Second Empire. Although Louis Napoleon was properly called President of the Republic, his right also to call himself a prince had been recognized by the Great Powers when Europe was rearranged after Waterloo. In society and among ardent Bonapartists, Louis was addressed as "Your Highness" and "Monseigneur." He was often literally the man on horseback, imposing in the uniform of a white-plumed general of the National Guard. Significantly, the portraits of Napoleon at Versailles were now labeled *Napoleon I*.

With his presidential term due to expire in May 1852, Louis and his entourage at the Elysée decided to make the throw. It would be Caesarism or the prison at Vincennes: *Aut Caesar, aut nihil.* A model coup d'état, a splendid technical success, moral considerations aside, followed on December 2, 1851. It was the anniversary of the battle of Austerlitz and the coronation of Napoleon I, a day rich in historical associations for the French nation. Under such circumstances, horoscopy can be helpful. The army stood fast for the future Emperor. Deputies of the right were escorted to the Vincennes prison, where they had an excellent dinner, wax candles, and a fire, and the governor bowed. The deputies of the left were hustled to the less attractive premises of the Mazas prison, in the Faubourg St.-Antoine, a lofty red building with a tall tower enclosed in high walls. Here, each legislator exchanged his name and sash of office for a number. Blood was shed along the boulevards to prove convincingly that times had changed, and two days later France had another Bonaparte securely exercising dictatorial powers. One understood that it would not be long before republican appearances would yield to imperial realities.

The triumph was suitably celebrated. Thurlow Weed, the New York politician and journalist, who was in Paris at the time of the December 2 coup, heard the Te Deum sung on New Year's Day at Notre-Dame, which gave the sanction of religion to the events that made Louis Napoleon Emperor in all but name. Weed felt "interest and some repugnance" as the seizure of power received the benediction of an archbishop, and walked back to Mme. Joseph's pension to clean off the candle grease that had dripped impartially from thirteen thousand wax candles upon gorgeously costumed diplomats and the party of republicans from America.[7] American opinion at home was highly critical of the coup. Horace Greeley, of the *New-York Tribune,* howled at Louis Napoleon, and George Templeton Strong, a well-placed New York lawyer, Trinity Church vestryman, and Columbia University trustee, recalled unfavorable memories of the Prince in New York and confided to his diary that constitutional government in France had succumbed to "the first kick given it by the first ambitious man of moderate abilities who had a popular name."[8]

A new constitution, promulgated on January 24, 1852, bestowed the presidency on Louis Napoleon Bonaparte for ten years. The Republic was as good as dead. The following November the Senate passed an act ordaining the Second Empire, with Louis Napoleon governing as Napoleon III, and giving him the power of appointment to fix the order of succession in the imperial family.

A carefully orchestrated plebiscite confirmed the establishment of the Second Empire. It was a change in name only. The government had been authoritarian since all resistance had been swept away by the coup. The considerable cost in lives — the official figure was six hundred, including noncombatants — the transportation of several thousand disaffected citizens to Cayenne or Algeria, the violation of the President's oath and the constitution, were accepted as regrettable necessities. France had, as they said, been "saved."

The royal Tuileries had remained uninhabited from the time of the Revolution of 1848 until December 2, 1852, when Napoleon entered the château as Emperor, passing under the arch of the

principal entrance, inscribed AVE CAESAR, IMPERATOR! The palace
was an architectural treasure and a historic monument to French
history, but it was not a convenient residence. Many passages had no
external light or ventilation, so lamps burned day and night. Different floors were connected by narrow, winding stairs. The sanitary arrangements were primitive, water being brought up in pails,
and in the upper regions, inhabited by the servants, "the air was
positively pestilential," according to Anna L. Bicknell, governess to
the daughters of the Duchesse de Tascher de La Pagerie. However,
the orange trees bordering the walks gave off a delicious perfume,
and the parterres, gardens, and chestnut trees were perfectly
groomed.

There was a legend attached to the palace concerning a Little
Red Man (Le Petit Homme Rouge), who appeared periodically
and gave the Tuileries a sinister reputation because he came to
announce the downfall of a dynasty. But Napoleon III was not dis-
turbed. At night long ago in the gardens of Arenenberg above
Lake Constance he had heard voices telling him that he would
restore the glory of the First Empire and rule over France. So he
went to the Tuileries.[9]

The northern courts — Russia, Prussia, and Austria — little liked
the notion of a Bonaparte, a rebel against the hereditary Bourbons,
claiming to rule through the will of the people. Czar Nicholas I
was furious, since the numeral III established a claim to legitimacy,
implied a dynasty, slapped rudely at the Powers who had proscribed
the Bonapartes in 1815. So Nicholas refused to follow protocol in
calling Napoleon "brother," going only so far as to address him
as *"Mon cher ami."* Queen Victoria was watchful but determined
to keep on good terms with France, and signed herself "Your
Imperial Majesty's good sister."

But the Paris Bourse reacted with enthusiasm to a government
headed by a man who had read Adam Smith's *Wealth of Nations.*
There was rejoicing in the streets and a gala performance at the
Opéra, where Mlle. Rachel, reigning dramatic actress of France,
declaimed a poem written for the occasion on the congenial theme
of peace, since the new Emperor had declared, *l'Empire c'est la
paix.* One should not, of course, take literally the promises of
sovereigns or their ministers. With hindsight, which is one of the

emoluments of historians, later chroniclers can see that the violent beginning of the Second Empire, and the wars it engaged in, prepared the way for the disasters that marked its closing scenes.

Napoleon's power was based precariously on varied and inconsistent expectations, the holding together and balancing of divergent interests, the peasants, the new class of industrialists and speculators, the urban poor, the army, and the Roman Catholic party. So the Emperor presented the army with imperial eagles, offered the provinces new departmental roads, granted valuable railroad concessions to influential figures in the financial world, and pursued a tortuous course on what was called "the Italian question." Meanwhile, the Tuileries echoed with the gay excitement of a luxurious social life, which, Napoleon pointed out, speeded up the circulation of money so that the benefits of royal government trickled down through all levels of society. It is an economic theory that has had a long and tenacious life among the propertied classes. Decree followed decree, ordering often socially useful projects. A new era was opening, and there was a generous distribution of honors and decorations. Even the Grand Emperor had not dared to bestow the medal of the Legion of Honor on his favorite actor, François Joseph Talma, but Napoleon III saw France with new eyes and dared to make his dentist, as we shall shortly see, a chevalier.

While Napoleon III's version of Caesarian democracy never attained the ruthless efficiency of our twentieth-century police states, its general characteristics must have presented Dr. Evans, given his perspective as an American and an avowed supporter of American political institutions, with some painful reflections. But this is surmise. We do not know, although there is a hint in the recollections set down by his dentist-nephew Theodore that he condoned the coup as a necessary evil. "My impressions," he told Theodore, "were that he had the game all his own way and would soon be Emperor."[10] This sounds rather jaunty, but a more serious reaction to the use of force to abolish the constitution comes through in a remark of the doctor's, suggesting that the coup was a burden from which Napoleon could not escape. "It is well known," he wrote, "to those who were intimate with Napoleon III that the coup d'état of the 2nd of December was an act for which he had no admiration, and to which he never referred except to excuse it."[11] The French republicans, at any rate, never forgot or forgave. "An aura of illegitimacy," Samuel M. Osgood, an American historian of the Second Empire, concluded, "surrounded his rule to the very end."[12]

An element of self-interest in Dr. Evans's attitude cannot be ruled out. In the mid-nineteenth century, physicians and dentists of good repute could not prosper in Paris through the fees paid by the general public. To succeed in the upper ranks of their profession, French society being what it was, they needed more than brains or skill. Prestige was essential, as represented by smart clothes, a residence on a good street, a well-tended beard, a private carriage, friendship with an aristocratic family, or an official appointment, such as physician or dentist to a bishop, and a carefully chosen hobby for the leisure hours. Dr. Evans fitted the pattern. He dressed correctly, paid especial attention to his thick hair and sideburns, presented himself as a man of culture who collected art and maintained a stable and aviary. For a patron he had the best — the Emperor himself. Dr. Evans also enjoyed the cachet of the Americans' recognized superiority in dentistry, and his American citizenship put a distance between him and the quarrels of political factions or the rivalries between the old aristocracy and the new. Dr. Evans's political posture during the Second Empire was at any rate consistent with the counsel offered by James Jackson Jarves in his *Parisian Sights and French Principles, Seen Through American Spectacles:* "There is but one safe and honorable course for Americans. To cherish their own institutions, and leave to their neighbors the task of reforming their own."[13] Dr. Evans expressed much the same idea in his later years, when the Third Republic was firmly established: "I have no political prejudices, and every country has a right to decide upon its own political affairs."[14] Often he rolled over vexing issues by saying that they were for the historians to decide.

When Napoleon III set up his imperial household, Dr. Evans was appointed surgeon-dentist by official decree. The appointment was made on February 3, 1854, but it dated back to January 1, 1853, the date when he entered on his functions. The rank was equal to that of other physicians in the *service de santé,* headed by Napoleon's faithful old friend and confidant, who had been with him in prison at Ham, Dr. Henri Conneau. Dr. Evans was entitled to wear a resplendent uniform for official ceremonies. It consisted of a straight blue coat with a collar and facing of black velvet, embroidered with purple and gold silk, white breeches, or, on less formal occasions, long trousers with a band of velvet also embroidered in gold and purple. There was a cocked hat with black plume to complete the picture and, yes, a sword. In his buttonhole, the doctor wore the red ribbon of the Legion of Honor, which in France certified success. There was an annual retainer of six thousand francs, and Evans received other marks of esteem, such as a scarf pin mounted with a large diamond.

"This stone," the Emperor told him, "I had taken from the hilt of a sword belonging to my uncle, Napoleon I";[15] and the dentist hurried off to show the gift to his wife.

Even before these evidences of favor, Dr. Evans had attracted so large a practice that he found it necessary in 1852 to bring over to Paris Theodore Sewall Evans, his brother who was a capable dentist, and he also had a number of French dentists working in his busy office.

Dr. Evans was usually summoned for dental duties, or just for companionship, by Charles Thélin, servant to Queen Hortense, later valet, private secretary, and ultimately treasurer to Louis Napoleon; for out of democratic, middle-class West Philadelphia had emerged, in the person of Tom Evans, a natural-born courtier. If in his aim of establishing a hereditary dynasty the Emperor looked backward, it is also true that as a man of the future he had a clear intention of moving France forward toward the kind of industrial development that was transforming the United States. Dr. Evans noted, as did other observers, that Napoleon III did not care for art or poetry. His visits to the Salons were mere official formalities, although he did respond to statues or paintings of well-endowed young women, such as Alexandre Cabanel's *Nymph Abducted by a Faun,* a canvas that the Emperor liked so much, he bought it. It has also been luminously disproved that Napoleon responded to music. He had a special distaste for the song "Partant pour la Syrie," although the tune was composed by his mother and the song became a kind of unofficial anthem of the régime, invariably played to salute his entrance at public ceremonies. Possibly the Emperor was wearied by the constant repetition and the awkward fact that the hymn celebrated the bravery of Queen Hortense's lover, Auguste Charles Joseph, Comte de Flahaut de la Billarderie, worldly natural son of a bishop who became famous as the statesman Talleyrand. If music could not be avoided, Louis Napoleon's taste ran to polkas, waltzes, and *des tralalas militaires.*[16]

The mind of Napoleon III was eminently practical. He liked to pore over maps and atlases with his reading glass. At one time, Dr. Evans wrote, he had a lathe set up in the Tuileries. The walls of his study showed the marks of bullets that he and Major Claude Etienne Minié, French infantry officer, instructor in the military school at Vincennes, and inventor in 1849 of the Minié rifle, had fired in their experiments together.[17]

The Emperor liked to chat with the dentist about industrial advances in the United States, such topics as a well-informed American could make interesting: the new factories, the streetcars, telegraph lines and the transatlantic cable, military hardware, hospitals and sanitary advances. The doctor observed, "The Emperor had that broad way of looking at things, those liberal ideas, that love of progress which enabled him to appreciate the greatness of our rapidly growing country."[18] It is worth noticing in this connection that Cyrus H. McCormick, who invented and perfected the McCormick reaping machine, was made an officer of the Legion of Honor by Napoleon III as a "benefactor of humanity" and of French agriculture.

In his developing relationship with Napoleon III, Dr. Evans, who had a "feel" for investments, may have made some suggestions as to Napoleon's personal finances, although he always denied it. However that may be, Evans found himself among the select few who had access to the ruler of France under the most private circumstances. He was certainly not one to encourage gossip when, late in 1848 or early in 1849, the President of the Second Republic, his patron and friend, brought over from London the most beautiful horse and most beautiful woman to be seen in Paris.

3

Miss Howard: Love's Labour's Lost

TOM EVANS was one of an intimate group in Paris that was the first to know the English beauty. The lady, who was installed as Louis Napoleon's official mistress, answered to the name Miss Harriet Howard. She was blond, with classical features, graceful carriage, and shoulders well adapted to set off the décolleté gowns of fashionable life. Dr. Evans encountered Miss Howard, or Mme. Howard, as she was often called by contemporaries, as a patient, not in his office but discreetly at her home. "The first time that I went to the house," the dentist said with great delicacy, "it was to attend to Mme. H. The Prince had said to me that *he would be obliged to me if I would go to her because, if she were to come to me, it might give rise to ill-natured gossip.*

"Later, as I continued attending Mme. H., I sometimes went to visit her in the evening."[1]

Soon the American doctor, whose engaging personality and pleasing appearance earned for him the familiar name Le Bel Evans, became one of an inner circle of trusted associates who gathered around Louis Napoleon and his lovely English companion. Louis Napoleon had a gate cut in the garden wall of the Élysée palace. From there it was only a few steps across the Avenue de Marigny to the back door of a small but handsome mansion at 14 Rue du

Cirque, where the bachelor President enjoyed the blessings of domesticity without the responsibilities of marriage. The Prince was bound to his mistress by appetite and affection, by force of habit, and by the fact that she had financed his campaign to convince the French nation that he should be the chief magistrate of their new Republic. Louis Napoleon often deceived her, it is true, with pretty women who exchanged their favors for a decoration or a nomination, and he had a special weakness for the demoiselles of the Comédie-Française. The tragedienne Rachel, for example, procured for handsome Arsène Houssaye, with his fan-shaped beard and commanding presence, the post of director of the Comédie-Française; to him the President said, in substance, Don't thank me; thank Mlle. Rachel.[2]

The management of what Napoleon himself called his *menus plaisirs* — his little diversions — was under the high direction of the Comte Félix Bacciochi, a cousin of the Prince-President, who, as Adrian Dansette has observed, negotiated the honor of women who often did not have any.[3] Louis Napoleon's inability to control his erethism remained a constant in his career, with profound consequences for his health, his marriage, and the political future of Europe.

In addition to Dr. Evans, the small circle, really an intimate little court, with Miss Howard at its center, included Victor Fialin, later elevated to Duc de Persigny, a rough customer but absolutely reliable, a born soldier of fortune and daring risk-taker, and the Fourth Marquess of Hertford, most Parisian of Englishmen, owner of the charming Bagatelle in the Bois and faithful friend of Harriet Howard. He was frequently accompanied by Richard Wallace, a young man of uncertain parentage. But Wallace was, at any rate, enormously rich and gave Paris a hundred fountains, as well as generous humanitarian assistance in 1870, when the city was under siege.

Others often present were Charles Thélin, whose devoted service was well remembered after the establishment of the Second Empire; Dr. Henri Conneau, who had shared the rigors of Ham with Louis Napoleon and stage-managed his ingenious escape; Jean Constant Mocquard, the private secretary; Edgar Ney, whose illustrious name was an echo of the First Empire; Colonel, later General, Emile

Félix Fleury; and Charles, Comte de Morny, grand seigneur, daring speculator, dandy, Voltairian skeptic, who had organized the successful coup d'état that made Louis Emperor, happiest of bastards in being the illegitimate son of Queen Hortense and the Comte de Flahaut, the general and diplomat. Morny had business interests that reached from a beet-sugar factory to shares in Dr. Louis Désiré Véron's newspaper, *Le Constitutionnel,* and combined, as one French wit suggested, *"le chic et le chèque."* Somewhat to the annoyance of his illustrious half-brother, Morny wore a large hydrangea flower in his buttonhole (in French, *hortensia*) to remind the world of his royal distaff line of descent.[4]

This, then, was the group, with women conspicuously absent, that turned with a kind of tropism toward the seat of power. Dr. Evans relished his position as a friend of the house. His hostess appreciated his professional services and his company and the opportunity to chat with him in English, since she never learned to speak good French. The doctor, always referring to her circumspectly as "Madame H——" or "Madame Henriette," has left a description of her salon. There Louis Napoleon, wrote Dr. Evans, "loved to take a cup of tea, or to sit during the whole evening sipping a cup of coffee, or smoking a cigarette, his black dog, Ham, sometimes at his feet and sometimes on his knee." While the President of France sent wreaths of smoke to the ceiling, his *amie,* Miss Henriette, lovely in a black velvet gown, her only jewels a collar of flawless diamonds, caressed a beautiful Angora cat. Its splendid tail was ornamented with green ribbons and waved graciously when the sapient feline sensed that she was the object of general admiration.[5]

At the military reviews, Miss Howard's carriage, with a horse painted on its doors instead of armorial bearings, always occupied a good spot. The lady must have had a sense of humor, since the horse, substituting for the usual heraldic device of the nobility, announced to all her humble but precocious start in life. Once, when Miss Howard accompanied the President to Tours on official business, there was a public dust-up over her presence and prominence. Louis Napoleon made a spirited reply: "I admit that I am culpable for seeking in illegitimate ties an affection of which my heart is in need." Then, after referring to the burdens of governing, his lack of family and intimate friends in France, he concluded, "I may be pardoned, I think, for entertaining an affection which does no harm to anybody."[6]

ҩ

Miss Howard was born Elizabeth Ann Haryett. Her father was a shoemaker at Brighton. Later, at an unknown date, the family moved to Great Yarmouth, in Norfolk. As Bess grew up she proved to be an expert horsewoman and a great reader of romantic novels, the Bible, and an expurgated edition of the plays of William Shakespeare. When she reached the age of Juliet, she declared that she wanted to become an actress. The parents, puritan in sentiment though Church of England people, were horrified. They wanted no Juliet, Ophelia, or Desdemona in the family. So pretty Bess ran away to London with a horse dealer, who offered to advance her theatrical career at the cost of her virtue. She assumed the surname of Howard, hereditary family name of the dukes of Norfolk, who held the highest peerage of England, and made up a forename from Haryett: Harriet.

If Harriet's beauty was great, her dramatic talent was small. She received only minor parts at the Haymarket Theatre. The climax of her short career occurred when she appeared as the Third Apparition in Act IV, Scene One, of *Macbeth*. Wearing a crown, carrying a tree, she had only one speech of five-lines, which included the prediction:

> Macbeth shall never vanquish'd be until
> Great Birnam wood to high Dunsinane hill
> Shall come against him.

Later in her adventures the lines came to have a special meaning for her: that "a Napoleon is invincible."[7]

In 1841 Bess, or Harriet, left her steeplechaser for a major in the Second Life Guards, Francis Mountjoy Martyn, who had a huge fortune. The major publicly acknowledged her as his hostess and defined her position in a contract that bestowed on her the financial arrangements of a wife, including a magnificent bank account at Baring Brothers, the great banking house. The trustee who looked after Harriet's investments was Nathaniel William John Strode, financier and landowner, one of whose properties was — here mere chance again seems stretched to the limit — Camden Place, which Dr. Evans rented for the Empress Eugénie when she fled from France, and where Napoleon III died in exile. Harriet, at first taken for quality because of her exalted surname and evident wealth, now had a splendid house in St. John's Wood, horses, carriages, and a well-drilled staff. "Never," wrote her biographer, Simone André Maurois, "was precocious immorality more sumptuously embowered."[8] When a child arrived, he was given the name Haryett and passed off as an afterthought of his mother's parents.

Miss Howard was not received in the best society, but she was welcomed at Gore House, Kensington, by Lady Blessington, widow of the First Earl of Blessington. The countess was a beautiful Irishwoman, witty, charming, generous, extravagant, the center herself of many scandals. Her late husband was a cousin of Major Martyn's. The Blessingtons had lived lavishly on the Continent in a comfortable *ménage à trois* with the elegant and handsome Alfred, Comte d'Orsay, and after the death of the earl, his wife and epicene friend continued to live together in England. There were cosmopolitan dinners for London virtuosi and the broad-minded wing of fashionable society. Writers were welcome in Lady Blessington's drawing room, since she was herself both patroness and practitioner in the field of literature, her best-known work being a record of conversations with Lord Byron.

In June 1846, Major Martyn took Miss Howard to a brilliant reception at Gore House, where her beauty created a sensation. When d'Orsay, who was strongly Bonapartist in his political sympathies, introduced her to the guest of honor, who she noticed was addressed as Monseigneur and Son Altesse Impériale, he advised her to make her best curtsy. Drawing on her Shakespearean resources, Bess performed as though she were being presented to Richard II or Henry VIII. The personage was short, with a high forehead, eyes veiled in mystery. His presence was commanding, his manner dignified but winning, his accent Germanic. The distinguished visitor was Prince Louis Napoleon Bonaparte, head of the Bonaparte family and Pretender to the throne of France.

The Prince told Harriet about his dreams, adventures, and difficulties, the star that he had followed in his tortuous career. It all seemed to her to be positively Shakespearean, wrote Simone André

Maurois, ". . . as he evoked his uncle and his destiny."[9] Soon they were lovers, with the English demimondaine eager to risk her last jewel in Louis Napoleon's cause; in fact, she put up about $5 million in today's money in support of his presidential campaign and his subsequent seizure of France by force.

After Louis Napoleon hurried home from the United States in 1837, too late to see the dying Queen Hortense, as was mentioned in the previous chapter, he took up residence in Switzerland again. Then, in response to menacing military gestures from the French government toward its small neighbor, Bonaparte, to the relief of the host nation, retired gracefully to London. Now well funded for the first time, and something of a figure on the international scene, Napoleon established himself in a fine house in Carleton Gardens. He engaged the best cook in London. His clothes were made in Savile Row. His carriage doors were emblazoned with imperial eagles, and Benjamin Disraeli introduced the Napoleonic aspirant to the French throne as "King Floristan" in his political roman à clef, *Endymion*. London society, the clubs, and the newspapers took a lively interest in the young French prince who rode in the park, drove elegantly to the opera with his equerries, and was invited to the great country houses for the shooting. The heir to the Napoleonic heritage made it clear, even to the point of being tiresome, that he would yet wear a crown.

Following the aborted descent upon Boulogne, which gained for the Prince almost six years of damp imprisonment, Louis Napoleon appeared once more in London, in May 1846, after his escape from the castle of Ham. The Prince for a while entertained the idea of a British consort to share his future. There was a pretty Miss Seymour; a rich Miss Burdett; a Lady Clementina, daughter of a lord; a beautiful Emily Rowles, who had once lived at Chislehurst in Kent and was ready to have him until she heard of the blond Miss Howard, who combined a spotted character with great riches and was elegantly established in Berkeley Street. By an almost unbelievable historical coincidence the former Rowles residence was Camden Place.

დ

As in a game of musical chairs played on the international political scene, Louis Napoleon and King Louis Philippe exchanged places as a consequence of the Revolution of 1848. The Citizen King suddenly became the refugee in England, and the Pretender, by virtue of Napoleonic hagiography and shrewd propaganda, the sovereign of France. But for all the overwhelming 5,424,226 votes he received in the election, the Prince-President felt isolated. He wrote to his friend the Earl of Malmesbury, then Foreign Secretary of England, that he felt absolutely alone. His supporters didn't know him. He didn't know his supporters, and few had even seen him since he arrived from England. There were irreconcilable factions that would still have liked to see him clapped into the prison at Vincennes. The Chamber of Deputies was suspicious and hostile. But, he added, on a more cheerful note, the army and the people were for him, and so he did not despair.[10]

It remains a constant of human nature that no matter what blessings descend upon us, we long for some other good that remains beyond our reach. Miss Howard yearned for respectability. Indeed, from the time when she fell deeply in love with Prince Louis, and supposed that her future would be joined with his, she led an exemplary life. Jean Mocquard, Lord Normandy, the British ambassador, and Count de Bark, the Swedish minister, received her. But Princess Mathilde, first cousin and official hostess of the President, called Harriet his English chain, and tried to pretend that Bess didn't exist. The noble ladies of the old aristocracy of the Faubourg St.-Germain followed suit, though their husbands, susceptible to power and beauty, were more tolerant.

Mathilde may perhaps be charged with pique, since her name had once been linked romantically with that of her cousin until his blunders at Strasbourg and Boulogne, and later she enjoyed hugely her role as hostess. The Princess was not puritanical and would have made no objection to Louis's having a mistress, providing the choice was hers. Mathilde was a wit, quite *spirituelle,* and objective enough to have said "Had my uncle not been Emperor, I should probably be selling oranges on the quay at Ajaccio!"[11] But her uncle *was* Emperor. So Harriet Howard felt the weight of the moral laws governing unconsecrated consorts of sovereigns and the unwritten laws of caste.

In 1852 Louis Napoleon, who hated domestic scenes, was forced to disclose to Harriet that dynastic considerations came first in his philosophy and that she had no prospect of becoming his Empress.

She had been appearing more and more openly at his side at public events, when there was a railroad to be opened or colors presented, a road or hospital to be dedicated in some provincial region. At Saint-Cloud Harriet made a home for her son and Louis Napoleon's two bastard sons from the years at Ham. So it was not unreasonable that she dreamed of robes decorated with Napoleonic bees, a crown upon her head, while she ostentatiously added to her costumes a large bouquet of Parma violets, the Bonaparte flower.

At first, disbelief. Then the hope of being at least the permanent mistress, to hold the ground already ceded to her. She was encouraged in this illusion by a faithful group, including Dr. Evans. There were terrible scenes, which lasted until she could accept the fact that her romance was over. Perhaps she was convinced when she found that the prefect of police had searched her house for documents that might be inconvenient to the Emperor; when Napoleon paid off her loan with interest; and when he gave her a handsome pension and a title, Comtesse de Beauregard, taken from the name of a château near Versailles that she had purchased. There, in retirement and loneliness, she cultivated her flowers, did tapestry work, and dressed for dinner, descending the stairs in her great crinolines and all her pearls. Like the wife of folklore who kept the lamp in the window for the wandering husband, Miss Howard maintained a state bedchamber, with white marble bath, where no one ever slept. Old Léon, once a servant at Beauregard, told a young scholar fifty years later, "I believe Milady had created the most beautiful apartment she could for the Emperor . . . He never came."[12]

As part of an agreement made to straighten out their tangled affairs, Harriet took a husband, Clarence Trelawney, who came from a good family. The arrangement was possible because Miss Howard was rich and still beautiful. But Trelawney made no effort to have her accepted as his wife. All that the couple had in common was mutual contempt. Once, twelve years after Napoleon III had extricated himself from the liaison and found his Empress, Harriet, driven to see him again, even at a distance, went to the Opéra in all her jewels, taking a box in the first tier, almost opposite that of the sovereigns. It was the winter of 1864–1865, and she had cancer.

All evening she gazed at the imperial box, looking for the last time, she knew, at the man she had loved so passionately. Charming prince no longer, Napoleon showed the wear and tear of responsibility, of disease and venery, the features so puffy that he might have been a complete stranger. The countess died soon after, on August 19, 1865, still hoping against hope. She had never meditated on the fate of Josephine, the wife of Napoleon I, or understood that she, too, would be discarded for reasons of state, the certain loser once the issue was drawn between love and power. Harriet could have said, with Jane Austen's Anne Elliott, that women's privilege "is that of loving longest, when existence or when hope is gone."[13]

4

An Emperor Needs a Wife

THE PRINCE-PRESIDENT understood that his projected Empire
was fragile and that a suitable marriage and an heir were essential
to future stability. Those around him urged haste, but it was not
easy for him, as Dr. Evans saw it, to "break away from old attach-
ments," meaning the devoted if prosaic Mme. Howard. There were
formidable problems ahead. All the pedigreed royalties of Europe
regarded Louis Napoleon as a parvenu, an adventurer, a gambler
who had enjoyed an extraordinary run of luck in becoming President, then Emperor. And he was a Catholic; at least he complied
with the formal observances of the Church, though he did not
necessarily regard the Church — Dr. Evans speaking — "as the
keeper of the keys of heaven."[1]

Louis Napoleon first renewed his suit to his cousin Princess
Mathilde Bonaparte. But Mathilde again refused him, a decision
she later regretted. At this delicate moment Napoleon III demonstrated, as he did on many other occasions, his inclination to use
informal and unofficial emissaries. He sent Dr. Tom Evans to sound
out discreetly the possibilities of marriage with Princess Caroline
Stéphanie, granddaughter of the late Gustavus IV, deposed and
exiled King of Sweden, and of the Grand Duchess Stéphanie of
Baden. Caroline was tall, nicely plump, and mannerly, the descendant of the ancient Vasa line of Swedish nobility. Dr. Evans

had seen much of this Princess at the court at Carlsruhe, then the capital of Baden, and was well liked by the ruling family of the duchy. Napoleon questioned Evans closely about Caroline and her suitability as a wife for him. "He wanted my opinion . . ." the dentist wrote, "which he knew he would get from me honestly and specifically . . . so to me he entrusted the task of finding out the real sentiments of the lady toward him."[2]

Dr. Evans went to Carlsruhe, ostensibly to practice his profession, to explore the matter with the Princess. He found that the idea of marrying Louis Napoleon, or at least the prospect of becoming Empress of the French, delighted the lady. All went well, and as the doctor prepared to leave she said gaily, "*Au revoir. A Paris.*" Louis Napoleon himself made a quick visit, which turned out well, and all seemed to be settled. But surprise — the scheme was collapsed by higher powers. Dr. Evans speculated that the opposition came from Francis Joseph, Emperor of Austria, who paid the displaced Swedish royals a small pension and applied pressure in the right places to reverse the decision. The Austrian Emperor, it seemed, remembered well what happened to two Austrian archduchesses married to French rulers. First there was Marie Antoinette, who perished on the guillotine; then Marie Louise, daughter of Francis I of Austria, the unhappy second wife of Napoleon I, who was estranged from her husband after his first overthrow in 1814, and fled back to Austria permanently with their son. The failure of Napoleon III's match with the Swedish Princess did not, however, affect Dr. Evans's standing with the court of Baden, where he retained the title of official dentist for the rest of his life.

Napoleon III was humiliated by the pointed slight but took his defeat philosophically. Miss Howard, who had been rusticated during the negotiations with Caroline, returned triumphantly to Saint-Cloud. Next, Morny thought of Her Serene Highness, the Princess Adelaide of Hohenlohe-Langerburg, aged seventeen, daughter of a half-sister of Queen Victoria, and hence one of Queen Victoria's many German nieces. The Emperor asked Lord Malmesbury, then British Foreign Secretary and a friend of such long standing that he had visited Bonaparte during his imprisonment in the fortress of Ham, to sound out the Queen on the subject of the proposed union. The Comte Alexandre Walewski, French ambassador at the Court of St. James's, acted for the prospective bridegroom. Again religion interposed a difficulty, Adelaide being a Lutheran. But with grave matters of state riding on the issue, affecting the relationship between France and England, it was felt that a sudden conversion to the True Church was a reasonable expectation and could be managed.

When the subject was opened up, Queen Victoria was annoyed. The more she thought about it, the less she liked it. As for Princess Adelaide herself, the more she thought about it, the better she liked it. Her mother, Princess Feodora, considered that it was all "a very disagreeable business," but acknowledged that "poor Ada . . . would rather like" to be an Empress. The Queen's attitude ultimately hardened. In the end Ada concluded, with a good deal of advice and persuasion, that she lacked the strength of character, the cleverness, or the ambition to accept so high and perilous a position. Queen Victoria was greatly relieved that dear Ada had been "saved from *ruin* of every possible *sort,*" and she alluded unfavorably to Napoleon's moral character and imperial prospects. Within a few years her opinion of Louis Napoleon was to improve spectacularly.[3]

Meanwhile Napoleon III was playing a double game. He was drawn to Adelaide for political reasons, although he had never seen her, but he was pulled in another direction by his inclinations. When the happy Comte Walewski returned to Paris to announce the favorable momentum of his mission, he was stupefied to learn from Lord Cowley, then the British ambassador, that the French Emperor had given up his efforts to capture a wife who was in the *Almanach de Gotha,* and was head over heels in love with a beautiful and spirited Spanish girl. The search for a bride within the magic circle of royalty was therefore suspended. The Spanish lady was ten years older than Ada, wonderfully good-looking, very smart in the fashion sense of the word, and one of the chief ornaments of the Spanish colony in Paris.

Mlle. Eugénie-Marie de Montijo de Guzman was named after St. Eugénie, an early Christian convert of noble lineage and great beauty, who was beheaded during the reign of the Roman Emperor Valerian for donning men's garments and becoming a monk. Eugénie was the descendant of a dozen grandees, though not of royal blood. Her Latin beauty was the more striking for containing a British strain through her mother, Doña Manuela. Manuela's father was William Kirkpatrick, a Scot with American citizenship, who had prospered in the sherry trade at Málaga, converted to Roman Catholicism, and become a leading figure in the social life of Málaga. Eugénie's father was known as the Count of Teba until he inherited the Montijo title and fortune from an older brother. He had soldiered under Napoleon I and sympathized with Louis Napoleon's coup of December 2, 1851. The loyalty of the father to Napoleonic memories was a powerful influence on his daughter when Louis Napoleon came into her life as a suitor. Moreover, she was ambitious and uplifted by the perspective of the future that opened before her. To her romantic feeling that there was still a Napoleonic destiny to be worked out was added more than a touch of superstition concerning herself. Legend has it that a Gypsy predicted she would become a queen, as had happened formerly to Josephine de Beauharnais. Such a message from the world of the spirits, even though not sanctioned by the Church, would carry weight with the Montijo.

Chaperoned by her enterprising mother, Eugénie had acquired the poise and outlook of a woman of the world and moved easily in the rather mixed society of the new Empire. Contemporaries and modern historians of whatever political persuasion who have written about her are unanimous in praise of her person, the fineness of her patrician features, her long legs and slender waist, her sparkling, deep blue eyes, her red-gold hair, which suggested to some observers the Venetian palette of Titian's paintings. When she walked, it was as though she rolled on wheels, so smoothly did she advance; it was a glide that has never been equaled. The Countess of Montijo and her daughter, who often used the name Countess of Teba, lived at 12 Place Vendôme, not far from Dr. Evans's office. He knew them well, since both were his patients.

> She possessed a singularly striking face [the doctor wrote of Eugénie], oval in contour, and remarkable for the purity of its lines; a brilliant, light, clear complexion; blue eyes, peculiarly soft and liquid, shielded by long lashes and, when in repose, cast slightly downward; hair of a most beautiful golden chestnut colour, a rather thin nose exquisitely moulded, and a small, delicate mouth that disclosed when she smiled teeth that were like pearls.

Her figure was above the average height and almost perfect in its proportions — the waist round, and the neck and shoulders admirably formed — and, withal, she possessed great vivacity of expression and elegance in her movements, together with an indescribable charm of manner.[4]

There is no question but what the Countess of Teba was one of the most beautiful women of the nineteenth century.

Eugénie's formal education was sketchy. She had received as much instruction as the nuns at the fashionable Convent of the Sacré-Coeur in the Rue de Varenne could give her. There she made her first communion. Manuela, strongly focused on the pleasures and opportunities of this world, was thoroughly alarmed at her daughter's ardent religious faith, but Prosper Mérimée, the polished Parisian author, Voltairian skeptic, and lifelong family friend, assured her that Eugénie was not the girl to turn into a nun, and took her off to a confectioner's. He also taught Eugénie how to fire a pistol and introduced her and her adored sister, Paca, to M. Henri Beyle — the author Stendhal — who spun for the little listeners romantic tales of the prodigious drama of the First Empire, in which he had played a considerable part.

There was also a brief interlude at a boarding school in England and, finally, an English governess, a good creature with sheep's eyes, named Miss Flowers. Eugénie never learned to write perfect French and in maturity regretted the gaps in her knowledge of history. At thirteen she was a handful with a reddish pigtail, wore embroidered white drawers that came down below her skirt, and wrote precocious letters to M. Beyle, filled with politics and war. Mérimée's mother, seated in her easy chair, surrounded by her cats and birds, declared, "She will be pretty." The rest of Eugénie's education came from fashionable spas, the season in London, the political salons in Paris, under the tutelage of her well-traveled mother, who argued, "Life is the best teacher." So, although she had no systematic education in the academic sense, Eugénie had mingled with statesmen, the rich and the clever, the famous, and those who were on the move. She was ready for ceremonial duties.[5]

Grown to young womanhood, the countess was, at the time the Second Republic arrived, in the full flower of her blue-eyed, auburn-haired loveliness. She was a free spirit, confident, articulate, restless, imaginative, reaching for something not yet defined. She was dressed by the best dressmakers, used a little rice powder, and with the lightest touch of the pencil traced a line over her eyelashes. It was a part of her persona. She would not have recognized herself without that shadow.

The Countess Eugénie danced, laughed, ate sorbets, was quick with a quip, and knew how to open and close a fan. Many rich and noble suitors had paid her court, only to be refused. By the standards of the time it would soon be too late for marriage. "Eugénie Montijo was sufficiently near an adventuress," wrote the British historian F. A. Simpson, "to make her a bad choice for an Emperor who was himself an adventurer."[6] Yet she would never consent to be, as events were to demonstrate, a royal mistress.

There are many conflicting accounts of how Louis Napoleon and Eugénie met. They were introduced, so one story goes, by the Rothschilds. If one is persuaded by frequency of repetition, the pair met at a dinner party given by Princess Mathilde in her residence at 24 Rue de Courcelles while Napoleon was still President. One version is quite specific. The date was December 31, 1849, and the occasion was a celebration of the New Year. Seeing that her cousin was about to leave at eleven o'clock, Mathilde advanced the hands of the clock and cried, "Midnight, everyone embrace." The Prince made a rush for Eugénie, but she took evasive action.

"It is the custom in France," he told her.

"It is not the custom in my country," the countess replied with Andalusian dignity and bewitching coquetry.[7]

Another variant on the theme of how the couple met moves the date to 1850, but with Princess Mathilde still at the center of the action. Mathilde believed she was destined to be the first Princess of the blood should the Empire follow the Second Republic, as all Bonapartists assumed would soon be the case. The succession was assured in the person of Louis Napoleon's able but difficult relative, Prince Napoleon. She thought an affair with Eugénie might eliminate the English threat, Miss Howard. So at a dinner party at Mathilde's, Louis Napoleon saw a young woman with a radiant complexion under reddish-gold hair, wearing a pale blue frock, "generously décolleté," talking with the marine painter Théodore Gudin and others.

"And who is she?" the Prince-President whispered. Mathilde replied carelessly.

"A newcomer, belonging to an Andalusian family, Mademoiselle Eugénie de Montijo."

"Ah! But you must present her to me."[8]

Soon Eugénie was sinking down in an exquisitely perfect curtsy, and the Prince took her in to dinner. Mathilde had thought of the Montijo as frivolous, but as Eugénie talked confidently and without embarrassment, the Prince listened with eyes half-closed, twisting his mustache, looking at the finely bred face, the faultless shoulders, the slender pale hands. If indeed this is a correct account of what happened, Mathilde may well have felt too late an unpleasant presentiment that perhaps Eugénie de Montijo was overqualified for the light diversion she had had in mind. Later she wept with rage as events unfolded.[9]

It has been said, and often repeated in American dental journals, that Dr. Evans was the deus ex machina who brought Louis and Eugénie together. The dentist was not one to underestimate his role in a romantic and historic episode that developed into a brilliant marriage, but what he says on the subject is restrained. He had a part, according to his recollection, but it was inadvertent. One day when the Countess of Teba was waiting in Dr. Evans's office for her appointment, a patient who was a friend of the Prince-President arrived, greatly pressed for time. The countess waived her position as the next patient and allowed him to precede her. This act of graciousness made such an impression on him that he asked Dr. Evans who she was. Soon after, the Montijos were being invited regularly to the Elysée palace.[10] This chance encounter in the doctor's outer waiting room developed over a period of time into the unqualified statement, made by an early-nineteenth-century historian of Americans in Paris, that "it was through Dr. Evans that Napoleon first met Eugénie Montijo."[11]

The best evidence is, however, that Félix Bacciochi, presidential and later imperial social secretary, and master in charge of Louis Napoleon's more intimate pleasures, obtained an invitation for Manuela and her daughter to a presidential reception at the Elysée. Perhaps Mérimée opened the matter with the President's social secretary though this is conjecture. Doña Manuela mentions this reception in a letter to her daughter Paca, which can be dated the evening of April 12, 1849, because she refers to current events, especially the première of Meyerbeer's opera *Le Prophète*. This was more than two years before Dr. Evans made the acquaintance of the Spanish family.[12]

Within a month Doña Manuela and her daughter were invited to one of Louis Napoleon's soirées at his palace, and a few weeks later there was a little dinner laid for only four — the ladies, the President, and the Comte Bacciochi — in a secluded little house near Saint-Cloud. The Prince-President was thinking of Eugénie as a new toy. He proposed a stroll through the park as the light was fading. Bacciochi could detain the mother on one pretext or another. But Eugénie took charge.

"Monseigneur," she said, "my mother is here."

Civility, she pointed out, called for his offering his arm to the elder lady. This he did, reluctantly, while Eugénie "followed at Bacciochi's side on what became a somewhat formal parade."[13]

There were no more presidential invitations after that, and the restless Manuela and her daughter were elsewhere in Europe for the next two years. On their return, in September 1852, they found the empire re-established by *senatus consultum,* by plebiscite, and by decree, and Baron Georges Eugène Haussmann, with a huge program of public works in hand, was making Paris a new city. The acquaintance between the Prince and the supple Eugénie was resumed at a quickened pace. In November there was a hunt at which Eugénie distinguished herself, and the Emperor offered her as a gift the bay horse she rode so dashingly. Those whose business it was to know such things knew he was seriously in love and hoped that his objective was seduction. In December Eugénie received marked attention from Napoleon at a ball held at Saint-Cloud. Eugénie made the first of many appearances in the private diary of the Austrian ambassador as a person of political consequence. The Elysée set felt its privileges and position threatened if there was to be an empress and sent an emissary, the Marquise de Contades, to persuade Eugénie to accept the Emperor as a lover. "Remorse," the marquise suggested, "is better than regret." To which Eugénie replied coolly that she would have neither.[14]

She could, of course, have ended all speculation by rejecting Louis outright. But she was fascinated by the possibilities that opened before her. Furthermore, as she herself said, "I had the religion of

Napoleon in my blood." She had learned the catechism as a child, and M. Beyle had told her the wondrous legend of the eagle returned to France from a Mediterranean exile, his fall on the plains of Belgium, his final torment on a rock in the South Atlantic. If Napoleon III had a sense of destiny, so too did she. For Eugénie, the game was all or nothing.

The symbolism was not lost in an anecdote that was passed around. While at a house party at Compiègne that proved to be crucial, the Emperor had, like Romeo, looked up at her window.

"How do I reach you?" he asked with a sigh. She, a Spanish Juliet, replied, "By the Church, Sire."[15]

In January 1853, the complications of the drama were resolved rapidly. Eugénie was publicly snubbed at a court ball by the wife of the Foreign Minister, and the Emperor was aroused. He no longer thought of dalliance but of acquiring an empress. A formal request was made to Doña Manuela for her daughter's hand, accepted, it goes without saying, and announced on January 22, 1853. Napoleon defended the imminent marriage in a wide-ranging and spirited speech. He declared that Eugénie "will be an ornament to the throne, and in the hour of danger one of its bravest defenders."[16] The words proved to be prophetic. Many in government, in the diplomatic corps, in the Bonaparte family, with the exception of Prince Napoleon, who remained unreconciled, and including Manuela's numerous creditors, quickly reorganized their thinking and behavior to fit the new conditions. Court functionaries bowed low, very low, and noted that Princess Mathilde's place would no longer be to the right of the dais but on the left side. When Harriet Howard heard the news of the engagement, she raised a glass of champagne, so very slowly, and said:

"I drink to their happiness."[17]

5

The Wise Virgin

Dr. Evans rose on a frosty January Sunday and made his way in winter sunshine to Notre-Dame. It was the day for the religious ceremony in which Napoleon III and Eugénie Montijo would become man and wife in the eyes of the Church. The doctor was present as an invited guest. The civil ceremony had taken place the evening before, January 29, 1853, in the great Salle des Maréchaux at the Tuileries, when the contracting parties signed the famous register of the Bonaparte family prepared by Napoleon I, attended by a cloud of witnesses, including old Jérôme Bonaparte, who bowed only to his nephew, and Prince Napoleon, who bowed to neither bride nor groom.

The Sunday ceremony was given over to spectacle and bright hopes for imperial happiness. Napoleon had all the qualities that make for a good husband, except faithfulness. He needed, as he explained to Mathilde, to have his *"petites distractions."* But he inquired with particularity as to whether Eugénie was a virgin. He had heard a good deal about her, some of it scurrilous and libelous, but did not have the precise information he wanted. Eugénie told him that her heart had spoken, and more than once, but she was still as he wished her to be *("Je suis toujours Mlle. de Montijo")*.[1]

Napoleon III was pressed by the necessity of providing glory and excitement, prosperity, and the sense of a fresh start. So Persigny, the Minister of the Interior, had reproduced past Napoleonic splendors with meticulous care. Esprit Auber wrote the special ceremonial music. Eugène Viollet-le-Duc and Jean Baptiste Antoine Lassus,

the architects who restored Notre-Dame, fitted out the interior of
the cathedral. The state coach was regilded. Makers of artificial
flowers attached thousands of white satin roses to the laurel bushes
in the gardens of the Tuileries, and a suave new perfume, Bouquet
Eugénie, was created for the young Empress by Guerlain. Bells
pealed. Silver trumpets sounded the flourish. Cannon roared for the
fair lady and her bridegroom.

Eugénie wore the same diadem of sapphires and diamonds that
Marie Louise had worn for her wedding with Napoleon I, and
rode across Paris in the same coach of glass and gold with a gilt
crown on top that had first carried Josephine and later Marie Louise.
Eugénie looked radiantly beautiful, seated beside Napoleon in a white
satin dress and her jewels; the Emperor, benign and joyous. Even
Eugénie's dentist, accustomed, as one biographer slyly noted, "to
a more prosaic view," was deeply moved as he caught — the words
are the doctor's — "through the windows of the coach . . . a glimpse
of the divinely beautiful bride who sat beside the Emperor . . . her
hair trimmed with orange blossoms, a diadem on her head, her
corsage brilliant with gems, wearing a necklace of pearls, and en-
veloped in a cloud of lace." As the procession left the Tuileries for
Notre-Dame, passing through the great archway of the Pavillon de
l'Horloge, the imperial crown broke loose from its pediment and
fell to the ground, as it had done in 1810. Many in the dense crowd
who watched hurriedly made the sign of the cross.[2]

The interior of the cathedral was hung with velvet and ermine,
gold and silver, flags of all colors, and banked with flowers in a
blaze of candle-lit glory, and an orchestra of five hundred musicians
played the Coronation March from Meyerbeer's *Le Prophète*. The
marriage was performed, in short, with every possible elaboration
of the Catholic ritual and every kind of pomp and circumstance that
the florid taste of the 1850s could devise.

Returning to the Tuileries, the couple entered in triumph the
famous château, which recalled memories of Catherine de Médicis,
of Marguerite of Navarre, of Marie Antoinette, and unhappy Marie
Louise. Eugénie was the last of the royal women whose names and
lives were intertwined with the palace. The imperial pair appeared
on the balcony of the Salle des Maréchaux, covered with petals from
the bouquets brought to them from every village in France. They
saluted the throng, then withdrew to begin their honeymoon.

In celebration of the nuptials, three thousand persons who had resisted the coup d'état, or had been denounced and punished for dissidence, were granted amnesty. The Municipal Council of Paris voted six hundred thousand francs for a wedding present for the new Empress. The Comte de Morny thought that it would be prudent to lay the money out in diamonds. The suggestion shows the classical reaction of one who lives dangerously, since the easy portability and stable value of diamonds have always appealed strongly to all who might have, in a useful old phrase, suddenly to "go to Texas." Eugénie vetoed the idea and instead distributed the money to charity, an act of generosity that was well received. Yet there was little enthusiasm shown for the new bride on the boulevards. Winning the affection of the French remained Eugénie's problem throughout the days of the Second Empire.

Many believed, as did Lord Cowley, that she had captured Napoleon III through the systematic scheming of an *intrigante*. Cowley reported to the Foreign Office that in France there was "universal disappointment" in Louis Napoleon's choice of a consort, but added that she was "very handsome, very coquette, very clever as her success shows." Lord John Russell, the British Foreign Secretary, concluded that the marriage was "a very false step," and there were cries of indignation from the Bonaparte family but unrestrained and malicious joy in Legitimist and Orléanist circles. A friendlier and an American view, though lightly expressed, came from New York, where George Templeton Strong wrote in his diary, "I maintain the cause of the French Empress sturdily . . . with no very tangible reason except that she has auburn hair and Eugénie is a very pretty name." Strong, who disliked Napoleon III intensely, hooted at the idea of the Emperor's friends calling the marriage "a *mésalliance* with the beautiful representative of one of the first among the haughtiest nobility in Europe . . . It will be a curious chapter for readers of history in 1953 . . . *Vivat* Donna Eugénie . . ."[3]

Another American with unusual opportunities to observe the Empress, and who gave her higher marks than did the representatives of the old royal houses of Europe, was Elihu Benjamin Washburne, American minister to France from 1869 to 1877. After paying homage to her manners and person, Washburne added that she was "intelligent, bright," and had "captivated the Court and the aristocratic society of Paris."[4]

Napoleon III settled a handsome dowry on the Empress and gave her a pearl and sapphire pendant that enclosed a fragment of the True Cross. It had been sent to Charlemagne by Harun al-Rashid, the Caliph of Bagdad, who also presented the great Emperor of the West with a splendid elephant. Charlemagne had turned the talisman into a clasp for his cloak. The sacred relic was removed from his tomb in the twelfth century. In 1804 the see of Aix-la-Chapelle had presented it to Josephine. Her daughter, Hortense, had inherited it and bequeathed it to Louis. Eugénie, being something of a mystic, paid the reliquary a kind of superstitious awe and vowed never to part with it.

For a few months the imperial couple were very much in love. Later Eugénie continued to respect and defer to the Emperor if not to the wayward husband. But in the longer perspective, what both loved was his career. Increasingly, with the passage of time, the Empress became the less than ardent but still loyal consort, actively promoting the Emperor's interests as she saw them, determined to play out the political drama to its conclusion, which for her, she thought, might well end in the same fate as overtook Marie Antoinette. Her grace and charm were beyond dispute. Her education and preparation were scarcely solid enough for the occupant of the throne of a great power, and her proper place in history still divides historians of the Second Empire.[5]

Because of her commitment to a personal religious life, Eugénie was often accused of leading a clerical camarilla when the question of the Pope's temporal power became a pressing issue in France. Dr. Evans came warmly to the Empress's defense. He declared, on the contrary, that Eugénie, though faithful to the Church, was "free from any suspicion of sacerdotalism . . . How could she ever have been bigoted with Henri Beyle as the mentor of her youth, and Mérimée the friend of her later years . . . materialists both, and each capable . . . of eating a priest for breakfast?"[6]

A celebrated anecdote, told by Dr. Evans, provides an example of Eugénie's ability to respond to a situation with a quick wit. When, on January 22, 1853, Napoleon announced the coming marriage in a speech from the throne to the Senate, the Assembly, and high government officials, a distinguished senator remarked: "A fine speech — excellent; but I prefer the sauce to the fish." The quip circulated, of course, and reached the ears of the new Empress. At a dinner a few weeks later at the Tuileries, the senator was seated next to Eugénie. She observed that after he had been helped to the turbot, he declined the sauce. So she turned to him, smiling, and said: "Monsieur, I thought it was the sauce you liked, and not the fish."[7]

Louis Philippe, too much the good bourgeois to please his subjects, made the mistake of living at the Tuileries like a middle-class paterfamilias. Napoleon III, who had a better grasp of the French character, was alert to the error. His subjects liked their sovereigns to live in style, and fashion and the display of wealth pleased the tradespeople of Paris. For the crinolines and gorgeous liveries, the glitter and gold braid, the seasonal movement of the court from town to country and back again, the receptions for eight hundred guests, all "fell back," the *Moniteur* pointed out, "in a rain of gold on the various industries."

So Napoleon III modeled his court on "the Other's," with an endless parade of high offices, such as Lord High Steward of the Palace, Master of the Horse, Great Almoner, Master of the Hounds. The Duc de Bassano was the Great Chamberlain, tall, slim, erect, a striking figure in richly embroidered scarlet coat, plumed cocked hat, the gold key of office hanging from a chain of gold and green acorns. There were squadrons of equerries, assistant chamberlains, postilions and outriders in green and gold liveries, secretaries, aides-de-camp, maids of honor, palace ushers in chocolate coats, short breeches, black stockings, with silver chains around their necks. According to their titles and functions, these members of the imperial household looked after the linen, silver, horses and carriages, balls and receptions, chapel and chamber music, and the medical attendance. A few who threw in their fortunes with the Second Empire were members of the old nobility, disdained as turncoats by the true keepers of the flame for the Legitimist monarchy.

Festivals, balls, and banquets followed one another in the social season, with dances at the Luxembourg and Palais Bourbon. Gentlemen wore knee breeches again — shades of the sans culottes! — and hunted the stag in the costumes of Louis XV, with plumes in their hats. Ladies curtsied before the canopied dais of the sovereigns in dresses with trains so long that little pages had to carry them. Etiquette was all the more strict and intricate because it, too, was, as Louis Napoleon described himself, a new arrival. No one wished to be caught, so to speak, using the wrong fork.[8]

Evans memorabilia that are still preserved show that the doctor and his wife were frequent guests at the dinners and balls during the winter season and spent weekends at Saint-Cloud or Compiègne in the spring and fall, which offered a relaxed version of town and country life. Special invitations were extended to men in the liberal professions, such as Louis Pasteur, the chemist and biologist; Urbain Leverrier, the astronomer; Ernest Legouvé, the dramatist; Charles Gounod, the composer; Jean Léon Gérôme, the painter and sculptor.

ᑫᔭ

As the curtain went up on the Second Empire — the theatrical metaphor has occurred to a number of writers on the period — Dr. Evans adapted easily to the elaborate etiquette of the court, the formal receptions, the way of life of a wealthy social milieu. The Evanses made an attractive couple, Agnes delicate, pretty, and well bred; the doctor handsome, well knit, with features neatly cut. His professional reputation grew with his social progress. Patients occupying high places in Empire society and government, as well as the bearers of ancient *lettres de noblesse,* filled the engagement book at the dental office or requested personal visits at their hôtels.

Among Dr. Evans's highly placed patients drawn from the cosmopolitan society of the period were the Princess Clothilde, daughter of King Victor Emmanuel II of Sardinia and wife of Prince Napoleon; the Princess Mathilde, whom we have now met a number of times; the Duchesse de Mouchy, née Anna Murat, granddaughter of Joachim Murat, daring cavalry leader of the First Empire who became King of Naples; and members of the diplomatic corps, notably Lord and Lady Cowley. Evans offered all these high personages expert care and preservation of their teeth, orthodontia when needed (a pioneering procedure then), genial conversation, including the latest stories from the capitals of Europe. He could drop a word to a patient if the imperial court was about to move to Biarritz, and, on his frequent travels, would deliver a message or package to a Swiss resort or German thermal bath.

But the most distinguished of Dr. Evans's patients, aside from the Emperor himself, was the Empress.

> A few days after Eugénie de Montijo — or, as I had always been accustomed to call her, the Countess of Teba — had been installed as Empress . . . [the doctor wrote] she sent word to me . . . that, having need of my professional services, she wished me to come and see her at the Tuileries . . . As Countess of Teba [she] had always been accustomed to come to my office and to take her turn with the others, and it was an innovation to ask me to go to her; so she was careful . . . to have it appear that she considered she was asking a favour, or at least was paying me a special compliment.[9]

Eugénie received the dentist most cordially, and he interrupts his somewhat solemn account of the incident with a light moment. The Empress's faithful Spanish maid, Pepa, who had been with her since her childhood, a somewhat rough specimen with the bark still on, entered the room and tried to address her mistress as "Your Majesty," but choked as she collapsed into laughter. Obviously, she was a privileged character. Since Eugénie was engaged to attend a reception that evening, Dr. Evans remained with her for several hours to be sure that she was well enough to appear. There was much time for conversation, and she talked to him about the great ladies of the past, once favored by fortune, later the victims of popular fury, and she showed him her souvenirs of Marie Antoinette.[10]

In the doctor's successful management of such intimate contacts with those on the highest social levels, all traces of the Philadelphia goldsmith's apprentice had been sublimated. The dentist-diplomat now moved confidently among the rich and powerful, just as he had expected to do. He, too, had a destiny to fulfill.

6

Years of Splendor

IN THE DECADES from 1850 to 1870 France returned to the rank of a great power, from which she had been excluded by the Congress of Vienna in 1815, and Dr. Evans's fortunes rose, too, as the Second Empire reached for *la gloire*. On the international scene his career was intertwined with the royal family of England, especially with the Prince of Wales. A chair and dental equipment were kept for him at Windsor Castle. Evans's personal friendship with the Prince is attested by an invitation to his marriage to the Princess Alexandra of Denmark. There were contacts with King Otho I of Greece, with Victor Emmanuel II, King of Sardinia, later of a united Italy, and frequent visits to the imperial court of Russia.

Even royalty, Dr. Evans said, needed orthodontia, and often "had their front teeth filled with an inferior amalgam which . . . made their teeth black . . . a disfigurement to the face." He replaced the offending fillings with malleable, polishable, everlasting gold; "always gold."[1] Other eminent patients, not to extend the list unduly, included Abd-el-Kader, the Emir of Algiers, defeated by an expansionist France. He was both patient and house guest of Dr. Evans, and the dentist worked on him for two solid weeks without, he said with satisfaction, hurting him. Others were Abdul Medjid, Sultan of Turkey; the Grand Duchess of Baden, only daughter of King William of Prussia; and King Leopold II of Belgium.

In a single week, Dr. Evans might travel from Sandringham to St. Petersburg with all his instruments, including a hand-operated dental drill. Various forms of crude cutting instruments for cleaning out a cavity existed in the period from 1840 to 1860 — the simple bow-drill of the jewelers; drills twirled by the operator's dextrous fingers; a ratchet drill with a grooved spindle that rotated when the ratchet was pushed toward the burr. One drill looked something like an egg beater. The hand drills were superseded after the development, in the 1870s, of a dental engine operated by foot power.[2]

At Stockholm Evans would check the teeth of King Oscar's sons, with a final stop at Berlin to visit his special friend, Queen Augusta. Overworked in the office and by continuous travel, in 1854 Dr. Evans made a three months' visit to the United States, leaving his office in charge of his older brother, Theodore Sewell Evans, who became in his own right a prosperous, if not famous, practitioner in Paris. During this decade Dr. Thomas also trained two nephews in his profession, John Henry and Theodore Wiltberger, sons of an older brother, Rudulph Henry Evans. The Thomas Evanses had no children of their own.

At the time of the 1854 trip to America, Napoleon III, hearing of the American dentist's imminent departure, invited him to come to Saint-Cloud. The Emperor received Evans in the Empress's antechamber, opened a small jewel case, took out the five-pointed star of the Legion of Honor, and pinned it on the jacket of the surprised doctor.

"We want you to go home a knight," the Emperor said. At that point Eugénie, obviously by prearrangement, entered the room to say "I want to be the first to congratulate the Chevalier."

"I hope," Napoleon III concluded, "your friends in America will understand how much you are appreciated by us."[3]

Louis Napoleon's especial grace in paying a compliment was frequently mentioned by contemporaries who admired him and grudgingly acknowledged by those who wished him ill. Thus it happened that Dr. Thomas Evans became the first dentist and one of the first Americans entitled to wear the medal or the little red ribbon of France's most famous decoration.

Souvenirs of the widening contacts of Dr. and Mrs. Evans still exist — a *carte de visite* from Prince Alexander Mikhailovich Gorchakov, Russian Minister of Foreign Affairs; a photograph sent by the colorful American minister at St. Petersburg, Cassius M. Clay, President Lincoln's friend; also one from Mrs. Clay to Mrs. Evans. Queen Sophie of the Netherlands was a luncheon guest at the Evans

residence, along with Henry (Labby) Labouchere, the British journalist whom Queen Victoria called "that viper" because he had
republican leanings. Labby found Sophie "very dropsical and wearing her everlasting crimson dress."[4] A detailed recollection of Dr.
Evans in his professional life comes from the Baroness Agnes de
Stoeckl:

How well I remember Dr. Evans, who was our family
dentist. He had a black beard. Many tales of his "successes" were whispered, perhaps fostered by himself —
be that as it may, he was certainly attracted by beauty.

My sister, Fanita, once had toothache . . . word was
sent to Dr. Evans and in a short time he drove up to the
door in his magnificent carriage.

He brought with him cogs and wheels and cases of instruments with which to stop the aching molar.

It was a profound honour, as he was considered to be
the first dentist in Paris and he chose his patients as a
King chooses his Ministers; and this deigning to disturb
himself created a veritable furor in the household . . .

Much was made of this visit, the servants were almost
in a state of collapse from excitement, the whole family
were overcome with awe, Fanita's tooth ceased aching,
whether from emotion or from being drilled I don't
know.

Dr. Evans had amassed a considerable fortune by arranging and repairing the teeth of half the crowned heads
of Europe.

His house in the Avenue de l'Impératrice looked pala-
tial, his stables contained a number of horses reputed to
be thoroughbreds. His fees were very high, hence his
money, but although he only attended the élite of the
grand monde, he kept one day a week for the *demi-
monde.*

My mother, accompanied by all us children, would
often pay a visit to the torture chamber of this famous
dentist.

We all liked him in the intervals between pulling out
my first teeth and straightening the scarcely visible new

ones, [when] he would first offer us delicious Boissier
petit fours. [Boissier was a well-known confectioner.]
    It seemed somehow symbolic of the fashionable Second
Empire that for the first time in history a dentist had
succeeded in achieving an establishment comparable only
to [that of] a prince.[5]

Dr. Evans was the first dentist in Europe to develop the use of
vulcanite rubber as a base for dentures. He experimented constantly
with new techniques, appliances, amalgams, and introduced nitrous
oxide gas as a general anaesthetic to his colleagues in London after
using it himself in some thousand surgical operations. Meanwhile,
his American contacts continued. He corresponded regularly with
his old Philadelphia friend S. S. White, the manufacturer of dental
supplies, and served as Paris correspondent for the American professional journal *Dental News Letter,* known after 1859 as the *Dental Cosmos*. The doctor also wrote frequently on orthodontics and
operative dentistry for *The Lancet* in England, and translated monographs of scientific interest from English into French and from
French into English.
    Perhaps his most important contribution was his steadfast support
of the principle of unrestricted diffusion of dental knowledge. The
doctrine of sharing openly one's discoveries with others, today a
moral norm in the scientific world, seemed almost quixotic to Eu-
ropeans with a long tradition of professional and trade mysteries,
closely guarded. Dr. Evans also pursued an investigative interest
in pathology and collected many pathological specimens.
    The decades under review brought France three risky and costly
thrusts for military glory. Napoleon's sympathy with the national
aspirations of Poland and his commitment to the integrity of Turkey
brought a collision with Russia in the Crimea. His dream of a unified
Italy led to war with Austria, the leading antinationalist power,
which controlled northern Italy. Colonial wars of limited scale were
also waged in Algeria, Cochin-China, Cambodia, and Senegal. An
effort to impose on Mexico a clerical, authoritarian empire, which
would be a counterweight to the world position of the United
States, turned out to be a disaster, a self-inflicted wound from which
the Second Empire never fully recovered.
    The Crimean War ostensibly grew out of an irrational dispute
between Catholic France and Mohammedan Turkey on one side,

and Orthodox Russia on the other, over the protection of the holy places in Palestine. For Napoleon III, protecting the holy places was a pretext. He was looking for an opportunity to strengthen his position at home by cutting a great figure abroad in support of the Roman Church. And it was a pivot of his policy to draw closer to England, which would not tolerate Russia in the Mediterranean Sea. An alliance, plus cordial personal relations with the British royal family, would raise his Empire to the same plane as that of the ancient monarchies. So in 1854 France, joined by England, declared war on Russia and went to the aid of the Turks. It was a bloody, wasting, pointless struggle; "a Quixotic war," René Arnaud wrote.[6]

Stalemate. Followed by peace in 1856. The tangible results were that Russia agreed to the neutralization of the Black Sea, France lost nearly a hundred thousand men, three fourths of them victims of exposure and disease, but gained in military prestige. Paris acquired a few place names with an exotic, foreign flavor — the Alma Bridge and Square, the Sebastopol Boulevard, and Malakoff Avenue — and at the peace conference held at Paris, one could say, as at Vienna in 1815, *"le Congrès s'amuse!"*[7]

There was a marked increase in the wearing of mourning, but in compensation elegant women were able to buy silks and brocades in two fashionable new colors, christened by an imaginative dressmaking industry as Crimean green and Sebastopol blue. Peace was signed on March 30, 1856, just after an event of great happiness. For on the sixteenth of the month occurred the birth of a son to the French sovereigns; he was christened Prince Eugène Louis Jean Joseph Bonaparte, known as the Prince Impérial, or by the affectionate family name of Lou-Lou. Lou-Lou gave the régime solid hopes for a long and brilliant future.[8]

Prince Napoleon was furious, since the boy cost him the succession to the Empire and made it quite irrelevant that he strikingly resembled his illustrious uncle, the man of St. Helena. The baby, laid in a rosewood cradle formed like a ship, dressed in robes of Alençon lace, did more to rally France to the Second Empire than the victories in the Crimea or the peace concluded at the Congress of Paris. The Pope telegraphed within the hour of the birth of the Prince, and his legate presented to the "Child of France," according to Dr. Evans, "a sumptuously enameled and jeweled reliquary containing a piece of the cradle in which Jesus Christ had laid [*sic*]";[9]

and a hundred and one cannon were fired off in celebration of the glad news. Eugénie dreamed of a son with a tall figure able to carry off a coat of ermine and a crown. She measured him constantly, gave him philters, and watched closely whenever Prince Napoleon took Lou-Lou on his knee. "She thinks that I have arsenic in my pocket," the Prince said with an affected gaiety that concealed but poorly his bad humor. It was a virtuoso act of social gymnastics on the part of Tom Evans that he enjoyed the confidence of both the Empress and her husband's ill-disposed cousin.[10]

In 1855 Napoleon III and the Empress Eugénie made a state visit to England, and the Evanses were present, taking rooms at Fenton's Hotel, St. James's Street. There was a ball held at the Waterloo Gallery, tactfully renamed for the occasion the Picture Gallery. Queen Victoria invested Napoleon III with the Order of the Garter and, somewhat in a flutter, paid him the supreme compliment of saying, "The Emperor is as *unlike a Frenchman* as possible."[11] In August the visit was returned. Paris was *en fête* for Victoria and Albert. There were balls, marching bands, arches of flowers, the waving of flags, and discharge of celebratory cannon. History took a queer turn indeed when Queen Victoria, granddaughter of George III, visited the tomb of the Great Napoleon on the arm of his nephew, and had the Prince of Wales kneel before England's implacable enemy while the great organ of the Invalides thundered out "God Save the Queen."[12]

Early in 1858, on the evening of January 14, the Emperor and Empress drove to the Opéra, which then stood in the narrow Rue Lepelletier, to attend a benefit performance. They were to hear an act from Rossini's *Guillaume Tell* and Schiller's *Marie Stuart,* with Adelaide Ristori, the tragedienne who had challenged Rachel's supremacy. Just as the imperial carriage, escorted by a troop of lancers, drew up at the private entrance, three explosions were heard above the music. Several persons were killed, many wounded. Napoleon and Eugénie were slightly cut by flying glass, shaken but essentially unharmed. The Empress especially distinguished herself by her steady nerves and the calm remark "Such things are our profession."[13] Whatever Eugénie's deficiencies may have been, a lack of physical courage was not one of them. Both rulers stayed for the performance, the audience cheered wildly, and the orchestra played the march from which there was no escape, "Partant pour la Syrie."

Shortly after, Felice Orsini, the chief conspirator, paid the ultimate price for his attack, for he was indeed dispatched by Monsieur de Paris on the guillotine in the long, white shirt of a regicide.[14]

Dr. Evans had been invited that evening by Lady Cowley to attend a reception at the British Embassy. His carriage was at the door when he heard of the attempt by Italian revolutionaries against the régime. "I drove at once to the palace," he remembered. It was his intention to take the Prince Impérial and his nurse over to the British Embassy for protection, but it was soon evident that the danger had passed. He did, however, go on to the embassy. Lord Cowley, in his book on his mission to France, wrote that "at about 11 o'clock Dr. Evans arrived . . . to report the tragedy," adding in a footnote that Dr. Evans "held a very peculiar position in the French capital."[15]

Louis Napoleon had dreamed since young manhood of going down in history as the liberator of Italy. Furthermore, he sensed that the volatile French nation needed something to celebrate. The stage had to be set, the country aroused, and his wife placated, for the Empress Eugénie would not tolerate any threat against the sovereignty of the Papal States. The plan was to liberate Lombardy and Venetia, which had been incorporated into the Austrian Empire. As an ally, France had the astute Cavour, Prime Minister of Sardinia and Piedmont, acting for King Victor Emmanuel II, who had put Napoleon under some obligation by sending a contingent of troops to the Crimea.

Napoleon got his war and took the field himself in 1859, leaving the Empress behind as Regent. His army was poorly prepared and led, with French élan expected to provide the margin of victory. The Austrians performed even more ineptly. The fumbling war lasted from April to July, with two big battles, Magenta and Solferino, and many murderous mêlées. The French were ahead when urgent messages arrived from the Empress-Regent, warning Napoleon III that the Prussians were massing on France's undefended eastern frontier. The Emperor hastily abandoned his idea of "redeeming" Venetia, broke off the campaign, and made the best peace that could be obtained under the circumstances. King Victor Emmanuel received Lombardy, Austria kept Venetia, France was rewarded by the annexation of Nice and Savoy, and Napoleon's cousin Prince Napoleon, a "sexually lurid" man of thirty-six years, married the sixteen-year-old Princess Clothilde, daughter of Victor Emmanuel. A Second Empire Bonaparte was linked at last with an ancient European royal house.[16]

Victory had been a very near thing. But the French army returned in an atmosphere of triumph. Incomes rose, the acquisition of the new territories flattered the national self-esteem, and there was a splendid march-past of the veterans in the Place Vendôme on the eve of the birthday of Napoleon I. Napoleon III rode alone, as was his custom, on a magnificent charger. In a symbolic act, the infant Prince Impérial, dressed in the red and blue uniform of the Grenadiers of the Guard, was placed on the pommel of his saddle. Captured weapons and tattered banners were paraded as the regiments marched past, their ranks thinned, to be sure, by frightful casualties. Paris got a new bridge, the Pont Solferino; fashion a new color, a pinkish mauve called Magenta, and France was esteemed as the strongest military power in Europe.

As a great body of cavalry poured along the Rue de la Paix toward the Place Vendôme, Dr. Evans described the scene:

> I remember, as if it were yesterday, the 14th of August, 1859 . . . the flags and banners in the Rue de la Paix . . . the triumphal arches; the immense ornamental columns surmounted by colossal Victories holding in their outstretched hands golden wreaths or crowns of laurel; the rich draperies spread from balcony to balcony across the façades of the buildings that front upon the Place Vendôme; the great tribunes to the right and the left, rising tier upon tier, and filled with thousands of people; and the gallery built over the entrance of the Ministry of Justice where, under a magnificent canopy of crimson velvet, studded with golden bees and fringed with gold, the Empress sat.[17]

This passage suggests that Dr. Evans saw only the surface of life, the confetti of history, reacting to the hypnotic effect of raw power. Yet there was another side to his character, a strong feeling of compassion for human suffering, especially evident in connection with the hardships, diseases, hygienic problems, and mutilation of war. This concern led Evans to pay personal visits to the battlefields of the Crimean campaign and, with Napoleon III's approval, the hospitals in Italy after Magenta and Solferino. The doctor's pre-occupation and personal involvement showed again in his study of the medical and sanitary lessons of the American Civil War, and in his leadership of the American Ambulance (a hospital) when the French fought the Prussians in 1870. Residual Quaker conscience in a polished man of the world? Perhaps . . .

After the Prince Impérial was born, with great difficulty, the doctors told Eugénie that a second pregnancy would be fatal. The medical prognosis and Napoleon's notorious liaisons caused the Empress to close her bedroom door to her husband. About this time, Napoleon entered into a sensational affair with the Countess of Castiglione, née Virginia Oldoni, a precocious Italian social butterfly reputed to be the most beautiful girl of the season. The countess has been credited with influencing Napoleon III's Italian policy, which grants too much to her intelligence and too little to his. Her presence at court, however, during 1856 and 1857, until Napoleon turned his attentions elsewhere, was painful and humiliating to the Empress. "There is no longer any Ugénie," she wrote to her faithful old friend Prosper Mérimée, imitating her husband's pronunciation of her name. "There is only the Empress." The two rulers still had in common the Empire, an overflowing love for the young prince, and the determination to see him succeed them on the throne.[18]

As Napoleon III gave his wife less than her due as a wife, he compensated her from a sense of guilt by granting her increased scope in the conduct of public affairs. Napoleon was experiencing a physical decline due to a stone in the bladder and an anaemia remaining from his years of imprisonment at Ham. The true nature of his ailments was kept from Eugénie as she began to pay particular attention to Italy, German unification and its immense possibilities for future trouble, and the improvement of relations with Austria as a counterpoise. Napoleon III, meanwhile, became an author.

It was the fashion for nineteenth-century French political figures to write history. The names of François Guizot, Louis Blanc, Alphonse de Lamartine, and Adolphe Thiers come to mind. In 1860 it was learned with some surprise that Napoleon III was engaged in writing a book about Julius Caesar. Though the research was the work of many savants whose services the Emperor could command, the writing was his own, as well as the point of view that rested on the "great man" interpretation of history. Napoleon was writing history with a key. The theme was nineteenth-century Caesarism, represented by a national leader who ruled by the will of the people as measured by the device of the plebiscite, a perennial favorite of dictators. The grand objective was to legitimate the First and Second Empires.

Despite the solid scholarship that went into the book, its chief interest was the fact that Napoleon III wrote it. Since the work was judged to be propaganda, it did not gain entry for its author into the French Academy, as he had hoped, but it did have a stimulating effect on archaeological excavation. At court, chamberlains and ladies-in-waiting developed opinions on Caesar, Cicero, and Cataline, and at the house party at Compiègne in 1865 the autumn theatrical performance was entitled *Les Commentaires de César*. In the following year Tom Evans received further recognition when he was promoted to the class of Officer in the Legion of Honor, along with Alfred Maury, a scholar who had helped Napoleon III with his book. Maury, in addition, was rewarded with the appointment of librarian at the Tuileries, a highly desirable post, since there was no library.[19]

In 1867 Napoleon III and France felt the consequences of a grave error the Emperor had made six years earlier. The Empress, too, must bear responsibility for what happened. A civil war in Mexico between conservative forces and a reformist government led by President Benito Pablo Juárez resulted in disrupted finances and suspension of service on foreign debts. Great Britain, Spain, and France as creditors occupied Vera Cruz to enforce their claims. Spain and Great Britain withdrew when it became clear that Napoleon had something much more grandiose in mind, nothing less than the notion of founding a Latin, Catholic empire as a rival to the Protestant United States, which at the moment could not assert itself because of its own Civil War. France sent in the flower of her army. A junta called to the throne Archduke Maximilian and his consort, Carlotta. They entered Mexico City supported by French bayonets and little else. Eugénie approached the enterprise with a zeal worthy of a better cause. She saw in the scheme the return of the conquistadores, Count Joseph Hübner reported to the Foreign Office at Vienna. Maximilian in Eugénie's active imagination was another Cortez, she another Isabella the Catholic, though she was warned that the United States was a great nation and would speak loudly and firmly when the secession was put down. But the prospect was too beguiling to give up, and clever Mexican émigrés encouraged her in her dreaming.

To the American minister to France, William L. Dayton, Eugénie explained that if Mexico weren't so far away and her son so young, she would wish to see him at the head of a French army to write with his sword one of the most beautiful pages in the history of the century.

"Madame," replied Dayton, "thank God that Mexico is so far and your son so young."[20]

The Empress was furious. The American minister and his daughters were no longer invited to the Tuileries. Count Otto von Bismarck, Minister-President of Prussia, said from the beginning that the Mexican venture was foolish, therefore probable. The war was extremely unpopular in France. No one understood why French money and French blood should be sacrificed to place an Austrian on the throne of a fiercely resisting nation in another hemisphere. By the end of 1865 the United States, now a land swarming with war-hardened veterans, stepped up the pressure. The project was doomed. Napoleon III, embarrassed, fearful of the United States as the champion of the Juárez government, withdrew the French troops in the spring of 1867, leaving Maximilian Emperor of a nation that did not want him. Napoleon III was looking at the western hemisphere when he should have been watching Prussia's expansion at the expense of Denmark, Austria, and, ultimately, France.

Strangely enough, Dr. Evans, who exerted himself with great energy and patriotic fervor to convince Napoleon that it would be a mistake for France to recognize the Richmond government during the Civil War, did not employ his influence in the Mexican affair or grasp the American point of view on the ill-advised Mexican Empire. Disconcerted, perhaps, Evans had little to say on the topic, excusing French adventuring by remarking, "The Emperor's motives were good and his action was well meant."[21]

If one spoke, in the decades under review, of the Boulevard, the reference was to the Boulevard des Italiens. It was the center of the universe, the end of all, the last word, but notably on the north side only, the side of the Opéra and of the Maison Dorée, where the *grande monde* gathered to inspect the parade and review the reviews. Here, Dr. Véron had a special table. Here once the philandering Prince of Wales was caned by an angry husband. The Café Anglais, with letters of gold on a white façade, illuminated at night, and gorgeous red curtains, enjoyed a similar clientele, presided over by handsome, inimitably discreet Ernest. One saved one's best witticisms for the audience at the Anglais, delivered over the sound of popping champagne corks and tinkling pianos. There, nightly reputations were made and lost while high-rollers dined with ladies of the evening in private chambers. The most famous room was No. 16, *Le Grand Seize*.

Present on the scene were grand dukes and speculators, toying over their ices on the terrace at Tortoni's, where Félix Nadar, caricaturist and famous photographer of celebrities, exchanged paradoxes with Nestor Roqueplan, wit, dandy, and part owner of *Le Figaro*.[22] Joining in the perpetual holiday were honest bourgeois folk and a sprinkling of rogues, bizarre strangers, and pretty demoiselles in regional costumes who spoke in the accents of the Midi, herded along by their curé in his black cassock and shovel hat. The Comte d'Orsay, who had returned from his London sojourn to escape his creditors, gave tone to the tailors. A Turk and a Pole dominated the whist tables. An Austrian woman decreed hat shapes. A Russian designed the ballets. Offenbach provided the music, and Rothschild lent the money.

Offenbach: a short man with a big head and long, drooping whiskers, gold pince-nez, sparkling eyes, and dramatic gestures, who had come out of a synagogue choir at Cologne; the acknowledged master of opéra bouffe. He wrote derisive operettas vaguely subversive in tone and filled with hilarious confusion about imaginary minor royalties. But his pieces were modeled squarely on the court of the Tuileries, where in real life the players were not secure in their roles and so copied Napoleon III's mustache, his sidling gait, his impenetrable gaze, and where, as in *La Belle Hélène,* the composer's triumph of 1864, they played charades featuring wayward Greek gods.

The pattern for the life of pleasure was the court, where a generous imperial civil list provided the wherewithal for gaiety, glamour, and conspicuous consumption. Eugénie adored the fêtes, the masked balls, the magnificence, and surrounded herself with cosmopolitan beauties, knowing well that she outshone them all. Her authoritarian views on princes and polity are revealed in a light remark she made

regarding the Prince of Wales: *"Oh, c'est un de ces rois constitu-
tionnels!"* ("Oh, he is one of those constitutional kings!")[23]

The Empress strove to create for France a court of elegance and
distinction. She was the world's authority, Dr. Evans said, "in all
matters pertaining to the graces and elegancies of life."[24] Her beauty,
vivacity, and feeling for fashion gave the Empire a brilliance lacking
during the stodgy reigns of Louis Philippe and the Restoration
Bourbons. These gifts were intermittently appreciated by the Parisians when they could forget that she was Spanish, extravagant,
and thought to be more Catholic than the Pope. Despite the frivolity and a certain coarseness of court life, gossip about the
Empress's personal virtue was totally false and had a mean, political
basis.

The hats, parasols, jewels, gowns, the fabrics of Lyon, the crinolines of satin and faille, the frills, flounces, wreaths of flowers, the
passementeries and laces, were simply, Eugénie insisted, her political
toilette. They carried out the Emperor's economic doctrine that the
luxurious consumption of the fortunate brought a shared prosperity
to the artistic trades and gave needed employment to the *midinettes*.
The Empress's tiny white slippers were worn only once, then sent
to the asylum Eugène-Napoléon, where Eugénie supported three
hundred orphan girls. They wore the slippers to their first communion and did their patriotic duty for France in sewing bags for
building earthworks when the Prussians besieged Paris. Their re-
ward during the Commune was to be raped.[25]

The palmary dressmaker of the period was the Englishman
Charles Frederick Worth, who arrived in France in 1846 with no
capital or friends and became, under the patronage of Her Majesty
the Empress, the leading couturier for the fashionables of Paris.
Worth's clients included Princess Mathilde, the Comtesse de Morny,
wife of Napoleon III's half-brother, and Princess Pauline de Metternich, wife of the Austrian ambassador. Pauline was a *grande
dame* in her own right and an original character who showed her
legs, made outrageous remarks, and once offered Lord Cowley a
cigar before lighting up her own.

It was Pauline de Metternich who first brought Charles Worth
to Eugénie's attention. Outside his establishment at Number 7 Rue
de la Paix, just a few steps from Dr. Evans's office, satin-lined
daumonts and barouches stood in line while ladies who were noble,

wealthy, or ambitious lingered in salons lined with mirrors so that they could see exactly how their *toilette de bal* would look at the next gala event. Daylight was excluded, but the premises were brilliantly lighted with gas jets, which gave off a loud and rather melancholy sputtering sound.

A particular occasion may be cited that reveals the scale of expenditures undertaken by those who had prospered since the seizure of power in 1851. In 1863, according to a British journalist accredited to Paris, the carnival that year netted Worth and his rival, Bobergh, the equivalent of $200 million. This figure does not include the cost of costumes designed in the ateliers of Laferrières, Félix, and other eminent dressmakers.[26]

Among those present at a ball in 1863 were "Mrs. T. W. Evans of Paris" and "Miss Willing, of Philadelphia," which may well be the first time that the West Philadelphia Evanses mingled with an old Philadelphian in whose aristocratic veins ran the blue blood of Thomas Willing the banker and of highly placed Carrolls, McCalls, Chews, and Shippens. But Napoleon III elevated men of talent rather than family, which helps to explain Dr. Evans's unwavering loyalty. On another occasion the same journalist wrote, "The Empress smiled on all with sweet and exquisite friendliness, but reserved her speech for Dr. Evans, who was fortunate enough to monopolize her attention."[27]

The Empress Eugénie's taste in the arts was conventional for the time and place. She tried her hand at water colors and entered a design for the new opera house. It won an honorable mention, according to Dr. Evans, though that may have been a complimentary gesture from a gallant committee. However, Eugénie faithfully performed her ceremonial duties and attached with her own hands the Cross of the Legion of Honor to the jacket lapel of Rosa Bonheur, she the first woman to receive it.[28]

The sovereigns attended the first nights of Offenbach's comic operas at the Bouffes-Parisiennes on the Champs-Elysées. They could scarcely avoid the duty, since his foot-tapping tunes were being danced to at the embassies, in the great houses in the Faubourg St.-Germain, and at the Tuileries itself. Napoleon III's limited response to music has already been noted. His consort was equally deficient in this area. Once, after a first night when the Emperor and Empress went backstage, Eugénie hesitantly asked the composer, whom Rossini called "the Mozart of the Champs-Elysées," whether he was born in Bonn. Offenbach replied that he was born not in Bonn but in Cologne. The composer she was thinking of was — "let me see . . . ah yes! — he was called Beethoven."[29]

When the social season was centered on town life, the gilded phaetons streamed down the Champs-Elysées after an obligatory promenade in the shady, winding alleys of the Bois and a slow drive around the lakes to show off the carriage dresses. The Empress Eugénie was accompanied on her daily drive in her green daumont by postilions and outriders, a lady-in-waiting sitting beside her. She traversed the Avenue de l'Impératrice and drove around the lakes. This route makes it understandable that she would know the home address of Dr. Evans, a crucial piece of information when the Empire was overthrown. In the Tuileries gardens a colorful crowd strolled under the plane trees, discussed the latest elections to the French Academy, a new treatment for freckles, or newspaper strictures on the outrageous crinoline, the wicked fashion "which spreads terror among husbands."[30]

The greatest pageant of the Empire was a world's fair, the glittering Exposition Universelle held in 1867, which outshone all previous similar efforts. Dr. Evans saw it as "the apogee of the Imperial Power." Opening in April on the Champ-de-Mars, the elliptical glass and cast-iron galleries, concentric ring on ring, were arranged like a monster wheel and were filled with the newest wonders of the industrial world, from a great Krupp cannon to the latest steam-powered threshing machines. Everywhere those who came to "see the elephant" marveled at the blue of cold steel, plunging pistons, whirling wheels, rocketing levers. Six million visitors inspected the exhibits and enjoyed the amenities of the city during the long, sunny summer afternoons. Among the rulers and potentates who appeared were Sultan Abdul Aziz of Turkey, Ismail Pasha of Egypt, Francis Joseph of Austria, and from England the Prince of Wales. King William I of Prussia and Count von Bismarck were received with suitable honors, and Emperor Alexander II of Russia was shot at by a Pole. Altogether, there were between fifty and sixty royals who visited the exposition, Dr. Evans told an American friend, Edward Matthews, who also saw the sights himself and visited the dentist professionally, according to the recollection of his son Brander, later the Columbia University professor of dramatic literature. Evans was himself an exhibitor, having prepared at his own expense an exhibit demonstrating medical and sanitary advances made by the U.S. Army Medical Corps during the Civil War. The exhibit won a gold medal, and the Emperor Napoleon III came to see it, asking in English, "Is this the collection of Dr. Evans?"[31]

But behind the gloss of surface appearances there were weaknesses and deep shadows and intimations of events yet to come as time ran out for the Second Empire. This was the year the first volume of *Das Kapital* appeared. Napoleon's health was deteriorating. The harvest was bad. France's best troops were in Mexico. The bourgeois class was leaning toward parliamentarism. *L'Avenir national* reproached Eugénie for wearing a crown of diamonds. Students rioted. Artisans broke windows along the boulevards. Ominously, the Prussians had already dismembered Denmark, annihilated Austria in five weeks ending in the crushing Austrian defeat at Sadowa, and brought together the North German Confederation and the German states south of the Main. All Germany had become a training school for war. Denmark — Mexico — Sadowa — how could Napoleon have so miscalculated? France was isolated. Yet Paris waltzed and showed the world "its Offenbach side." On the day the little Prince Impérial distributed the prizes for the great exhibition, the news came that the Emperor Maximilian had been shot by a Mexican firing squad at Querétaro.

The last lingering rays of Napoleonic glory came late in 1869, when the Empress Eugénie inaugurated the Suez Ship Canal. The planning and engineering were the work of her cousin Ferdinand de Lesseps, and the canal was paid for with substantial infusions of French capital. The Empress was the leading figure in the ceremonies, surrounded by her suite, which included Dr. Evans. Many observers thought Napoleon III had made a mistake in sending a woman to a Mohammedan country on such a mission, but Eugénie carried off the affair with great tact and spirit. The Empress left Paris on September 30, 1869, with thirty-seven ladies and gentlemen. On the way to Egypt she visited the Sultan of Turkey. Dr. Evans tells the story as an eyewitness. "I had watched from the villa of Sefer Pacha the *Aigle* as she rounded the Seraglio Point and entered the waters of the Golden Horn, bringing the Empress as the guest of the Sultan, and had witnessed the unparalleled magnificence and splendour of the ceremony with which she was received." The doctor continues in rather lush prose to describe the superb October day, the opalescent sky, and how just before sundown the Sultan's barge of polished cedar, ornamented with gold, silver, and velvet, with forty oarsmen as motive power, conducted Eugénie to the palace on the Asiatic shore. The Empress was seated alone on a dais of crimson silk, in evening dress, with jewels and diadem, supremely happy over "this magnificent tribute paid to the glory of France."[32]

Then came the rendezvous at Port Said. There was a grand ball for the squadron. The flotilla, carrying the rulers of Western Europe, steamed down to Ismailia, the French yacht leading the way. "I can never forget," wrote Dr. Evans, "her radiant figure as she stood on the bridge of the *Aigle,* while the Imperial yacht steamed slowly past the immense throng that had assembled on the banks . . . with cannon firing, and a thousand flags and banners waving." And he saw her cover her eyes with her handkerchief to suppress her tears.[33] The *New York Herald,* which provided coverage of the events by Henry M. Stanley, who was on his way to find Dr. Livingstone, predicted a new importance for the Mediterranean Sea, a new era for France and the dynasty. The prominence of the Empress at the opening of the canal, the *Herald* continued, "will make her a power in Europe" and speculated that if Napoleon died before the Prince Impérial reached maturity, she would be the Regent of France.[34] Within months, although Napoleon had not died, she *was* Regent.

In January 1870, responding to the revival of republicanism in France, and threatened by the persistent pounding of the opposition, Napoleon III instituted a parliamentary system of government but with himself still exercising the powers of the executive under a new constitution that had the appearance of and, to a limited degree, the realities of democracy. Thus the Emperor hoped to arrest his declining popularity and secure the succession of his son as Napoleon IV, perhaps in 1874, when the Prince Impérial would come of age. A plebiscite held in May confirmed the liberal Empire. But it blurred over those elements in society which opposed the Empire totally or the heavy pressure from the government apparatus that had produced the wanted result. It was not the 7.3 million ayes that were significant, but the 1.57 million noes. Liberty, it was demonstrated, cannot be administered in carefully measured doses. The permanent savior "condemns himself to infallibility," wrote

Maurice Paléologue, French diplomat and Academician, "for nothing will be forgiven him."[35]

Louis Napoleon was skillful and often lucky, but he was not infallible. And there was no margin for error. Dr. Evans, whose personal horizon extended far beyond Paris, sensed the danger to the regime in the late sixties, and even friendly Prosper Mérimée said of the Empire, "It will last as long as it can." When someone remarked at a dinner in London that the career of Napoleon III had been even more successful than that of Napoleon I, Garibaldi, the Italian patriot and guerrilla leader, replied, "We must wait for the end of the story."[36]

7

Rebuilding Paris

THE MOST ENDURING and beneficial accomplishment of Louis Napoleon in the field of public works was the rebuilding of Paris, and it made Dr. Thomas Evans a rich man. Thus it was Paris real estate, not dentistry, that accounted for the doctor's becoming a millionaire several times over and provided the means for his generous support of the various philanthropic enterprises that engaged his interest.

"From his illustrious patients," wrote a British journalist, "Dr. Evans learnt many a secret which he was able to turn to account in the advancement of his private fortunes, though," the writer emphasized, "in no corrupt way." The plan for a more beautiful, more functional, and more livable city, a monument to the Second Empire, had been germinating in the mind of the Emperor for a long time. The authoritarian regime gave him the power to proceed. His choice of the bold and aggressive Baron Georges Eugène Haussmann as prefect of the Seine and chief collaborator in the great project of renewal proved to be decisive to the success of the program.[1]

Paris in 1850 was not substantially different from the medieval city of filthy, crooked, dark, and chaotic streets and dangerous alleys, all wretchedly lighted. Gutters still ran through the middle of the streets, carrying a noisome burden. At every corner there was a rubbish heap. Water was polluted, sanitation rudimentary. Poverty, crowding, and cholera were endemic. Armed with an expropriation law and a law against unsanitary housing, Napoleon III cleared the approaches to the railroad stations and opened up the slum districts with broad, new streets ending in long, classical vistas. Handsome new bridges and broad avenues connected the city's districts for the first time from north to south and east to west. A good deal has been made of the facts that the new squares and tree-lined boulevards surfaced with asphalt instead of paving stones made it more difficult for rioters to build barricades and that straight streets were well adapted for cavalry charges and artillery fire for the control of revolutionary mobs. But these were more likely attendant circumstances than major objectives. At any rate, the ideas became clichés of the republican opposition and were enshrined in the polemical writings of the Third Republic. Napoleon III, with all his faults, deserves better from posterity than this cynical view suggests, omitting as it does credit due for new systems of water supply and sewers, the building of the Opéra, the Polytechnic, and the great produce market, Les Halles, and the reconstruction of the National Library.[2]

In 1852 Napoleon III decided that the Bois, the Boulogne woodland west of Paris, should be developed into a great pleasure ground on the order of Hyde Park, in London, with broad lawns, flowers, villas, chalets, cascades, winding driveways, and lakes where everybody could skate in the winter season along with the Emperor himself. There may have been an element of nostalgia for "the years . . . the locust hath eaten" in Louis Napoleon's plans for the Bois. It held sweet memories for him. After Napoleon I's return from Elba, during the short interval of the Hundred Days before the final disaster at Waterloo, Hortense often took Louis and his older brother in her carriage to the woodland, where they walked and played.

What was needed was a broad thoroughfare connecting the park-to-be with the gilded gates of the Porte Dauphine. Dr. Evans watched with a lively interest as real estate values increased and observed the generosity of the courts in fixing indemnities for condemned property. The doctor was intimately familiar with the low-roofed, overheated apartments between the Pavillon de l'Horloge and the Pavillon de Flore, which the Emperor occupied, and especially the gilded chamber where he sat in informal dress and skullcap, among his portraits, books, papers, historical relics, and industrial models. There, dribbling cigarette ashes on his maps,

Napoleon lined out new plans for the city with red, blue, yellow, and green pencils.

"How often," Dr. Evans exclaimed, "have I not been with him in this room." He also accompanied the Emperor in the field, for Napoleon III had a taste for landscaping. When the Bois was being developed, Evans once saw him take a hammer from a workman and plant stakes to mark the line that was to be followed.[3]

So the work advanced during the 1850s. Paris glowed with the illumination of the new gas lighting, which shone forth from great white globes mounted on branching candelabra. The horses went *clip-clop* on the smooth new asphalt surfaces of the grand boulevards, and Dr. Evans was drawn into the planning for the finest avenue of all, to be located in the old commune of Passy. One evening when the doctor was at the Tuileries, taking tea with the Empress and Napoleon, Baron Haussmann came to request a conference with the Emperor. When Napoleon returned to the room he announced the plan to open a magnificent boulevard leading to the woods of Boulogne, a broad avenue four hundred and sixty feet wide with tree-planted grass verges from the Place de l'Etoile to enter the Bois at the Porte Dauphine. Dr. Evans made a felicitous suggestion for naming the new street Avenue de l'Impératrice (now the Avenue Foch), in compliment to Eugénie. The next morning Evans made a cash offer to a gardener who owned one of the fields the street would cross.[4]

"You can imagine the surprise," Dr. Evans told his nephew Theodore, "when news became known that an Avenue was to be opened through the fields."[5] And he hastened to make other investments in the vicinity. One can scarcely call them speculations, since they were based on accurate knowledge of the government's plans, the power of the state to expropriate, and the liberal compensation allowed by juries, which Haussmann said was always "in excess of our estimate."[6]

"It is curious," Dr. Evans once said, "each time I buy property, a street is cut through!"[7]

On one occasion the tall, imperious Baron Haussmann took a charming American lady, Mrs. Charles Moulton, in to lunch and asked her how she liked the new boulevard that was just completed and was named after him. She said she liked it, though it had deprived the Moultons of a good part of their garden. Haussmann replied, "It brings you nearer the Bois . . . I hope the Government paid you well for it."[8] The baron had good reason to think that it did. But there were side effects. Many poor families were forced out of the center city by the rise in rents. This was accepted as a regrettable part of the price of progress, but it added to social unrest.

The "haussmannization" of Paris eventually raised the price of land some twelve times. Dr. Evans did even better. The land he bought in the fashionable Sixteenth Arrondissement for thirty francs the square meter rose in his lifetime to a value of one thousand francs, or thirty-three and a third times the original cost. Yet even with the special advantages he enjoyed, Dr. Evans required courage and faith in the future of Paris to commit his funds so deeply, for beyond the Rond Point of the Champs-Elysées and the Place de la Borde there were only a few scattered structures, some ugly wine shops in wretched buildings near the Arc de Triomphe, and after that, open fields and wild woodland.[9] Evans had the prudence to diversify. From his profits he made substantial investments in Philadelphia, in Lancaster, Pennsylvania, and on New York's Broadway. He had a "feel" for real estate, and these American ventures, too, were successful, doubling and tripling in value, for he knew how to buy, how to wait, when to sell and repeat the process.

The splendid Avenue de l'Impératrice, begun in 1854 and completed in 1856, quickly became a show place for the fashion parade, with traffic jams every pleasant afternoon. Carriages and horsemen filled the new roadway on their passage to the boating on the lakes, the Pré Catalan with its gardens and huge copper beech tree, the Longchamps racecourse, or such other amenities as the children's amusement park, a miniature railroad, the zoo, a brasserie, and elegant café-restaurants. In 1857 and 1858 on a plot halfway down the slope between the Etoile and the gates of the Porte Dauphine, then known as the Porte de l'Impératrice, Dr. Evans erected a luxurious mansion, really a small palace, in the architectural style favored by the Second Empire. The land had but lately been devoted to the growing of cabbages.

The residence was called an *hôtel*, which in nineteenth-century French nomenclature meant a home with aristocratic pretensions. It was located at Number 41, surrounded by the greenery of a pretty park facing the new avenue on the corner of the Avenue St.-Denis, which became the Avenue Malakoff after 1864, and near a footpath through Dr. Evans's property used by gardeners who drew their water from a pump called La Croix Blanche. The doctor gave the city the ground for transforming the path into the Rue de la Pompe. This left him room for his new house in the shape of an irregular lozenge, bounded by the Avenue de l'Impératrice, the Avenue St.-Denis, and the Rue de la Pompe, and a larger parcel on the far side of the Rue de la Pompe upon which he later built an apartment house. Adjacent to Evans's property was a hippodrome, a vast riding school open to the sky with covered galleries for spectators. There, balloon ascensions and reenactments of military triumphs drew large crowds during the summer season. Fortunately, the hippodrome burned down in 1869.[10]

There was a carriage entrance to the property, extensive stables with stalls for twenty horses, a greenhouse, a fountain and jet, a heated, rat-proof aviary (the doctor was an enthusiastic collector of exotic birds), and beds of roses everywhere, which gave the estate its name, Bella Rosa. Elihu B. Washburne describes in his *Recollections* "the elegant grounds of Doctor Evans." A touch of home was provided by hickory and walnut trees brought over from America. Later a weeping willow, imported from Philadelphia in the Centennial year, 1876, was installed in the center of the lawn.[11]

Bella Rosa comprised six rooms on each floor, including a grand stairway of Pyrenees marble from plans by Charles Garnier, the architect whose masterpiece was the Paris Opéra. There was a library where Dr. Evans took his "cat naps," a gallery for his paintings, and a white and gold ballroom. Stained-glass windows cast a jeweled light on Sèvres vases, rare tapestries and carpets, on gifts from Europe's nobility, and a display of decorations and bibelots received from royal patients. Dr. Evans as an art collector began with representations of Niagara Falls, cows, and sunrises, including a portrait of his dog, Mitzy, a gift from the Queen of Belgium, which gave him a point in common with his imperial patron, who had had his dogs sculpted by Jean Baptiste Carpeaux. Evans's collection of paintings improved in quality with the passing years as his taste became more cultivated.

Mrs. Evans received from two to five o'clock on Tuesdays and Sundays, the latter time known as "the Doctor's day." Her salon was very feminine, done in soft colors, white, blues, and rose, Louis XV style. There were easy chairs, including as a homely touch an American rocking chair. Dr. Evans entertained extensively for French friends and leading personalities in the American colony, political figures from the United States, and representatives of the arts, such as the portrait painter G. P. A. Healy, a close friend. Celebrities from the entertainment world included Adelaide Ristori, the tragedienne who was playing in *Marie Stuart* at the Opéra the night of the Orsini bomb attempt, and who later achieved lasting fame for her interpretation of Lady Macbeth. Jenny Lind and Adelina Patti dined and sang at Bella Rosa. Other dinner guests were Rossini, Anton Rubenstein and Stephen Heller, who often entertained at the Evans's Pleyel piano, Christine Nilsson, and Mme. Emma Albani, the Canadian operatic star who derived her stage name — surely a curious caprice — from Albany, New York.

As to comfort, the Evans residence has been described by a French scholar as the best conceived in all Paris, being the first to utilize central heating in Europe. The system included the aviary, the greenhouse, and an invention of the doctor's own fertile mind that brought warmth to his lawn and flowers through a complex of pipes. The doctor maintained a numerous domestic staff, from whom he demanded the same kind of disciplined service he required in his dental office. Though he himself drank only a glass of table wine at dinner, Evans possessed a choice cellar and offered male guests the best Havanas when they adjourned to the library after dinner.

Secure in his snug fortune, acquired through arduous professional labors and his gift for capitalizing his connections in high places, Evans knew how to enjoy the position he had reached. It was a source of deep satisfaction to him that he lived on the most fashionable street in Paris and had in fact given it its name. It was a street of notables. Among the doctor's neighbors were such figures as the Comte Boniface de Castellane; Auguste Joseph Delaunay, doctor of medicine and surgeon, who owned a choice library and once wrote an epic poem in 1106 verses; Jean Hippolyte Cartier de Villemessant, founder of *Le Figaro;* Octave Mirbeau, playwright, art critic, novelist, and biographer of Balzac; and Michel Chevalier, the free-trade economist with links to William Cobden in England, a friend of Evans's and an eminence listened to by the Emperor. The United States Legation, too, was on the avenue, at Number 75, when Washburne was Minister; and William L. Dayton, the American envoy during the Civil War years, and later General John A. Dix, lived nearby at 6 Rue de Pressbourg. Add François Ponsard, a dramatist successful in both tragedy and comedy, and Jules Janin, critic and noted personality in the literary life of the period. All contributed in one way or another to the excitements and satisfactions of the Paris scene, where Dr. Evans, too, the Happy Expatriate, found his very heaven in living out the youthful dream of West Philadelphia days, mingling by right of talent with men of power, position, and attainment, and he himself able to sustain the style of a grand bourgeois.[12]

But now we turn to another nuance of the doctor's character, his sturdy attachment to his own country in its time of greatest trial.

8

The American Civil War — As Fought in Paris

By the 1860s a large and growing American colony found Paris a splendid world capital in which to live comfortably, even sumptuously, without paying personal taxes. The gold dollar, bless it, could be exchanged for $1.35 in francs, and rents remained low, luxuries cheap, and domestic service — the phrase is Dr. Evans's — "nearly perfect." Along the Champs-Elysées, up to the Arc de Triomphe, in the Bois, throughout the quarter of Saint-Honoré, one met richly dressed blond women, so wrote a French social historian, the same type as the English but with "nothing of English coarseness." This was his description, spiced with traditional Anglophobia, of the American women he saw living in Paris.[1]

A people without ancestry, the same author continued, naturally hold distinction of family in high regard and "find that even a ducal coronet suits marvellously well their blonde hair and 'Madame la Comtesse' is a most charming complement to their elegant toilettes. Some who ornament the Rue de Pressbourg or even the Tuileries are said to 'come from the oil regions. What of it? In . . . Paris . . . such oil does not spot.'"[2]

According to the historian: "These republicans are very fond of worldly pomp, and have not the prejudice against monarchies that we have. Does this astonish you? Consider a moment . . . Monarchs belonging to others do not alarm them. They . . . wish *to see everything* and . . . upon their return home to say that they have been presented . . . Having come to see curiosities, why neglect the greatest?" Each month the United States minister was obliged to present some hundred of his countrymen who were "neither serfs nor seigneurs" but all certified Americans who had made successful speculations in pork, sewing machines, or California.[3]

Often the Emperor asked Dr. Evans for the names and addresses of presentable Americans sojourning in Paris who might like to receive invitations to reviews, festivals and spectacles, to gala days and Venetian nights at Saint-Cloud, Fontainebleau, or the skating on the lakes at the Bois de Boulogne. Ladies planning to take in the Opéra or whose names were down for presentation at court rushed to order elaborate dresses at once from Worth, Alexandrine, Lucy Hoquet, or Wolff, eager to join the pageant when the elegant and celebrated guests mounted the grand stairway to the great salons of the Tuileries château. Thus the pretty Americans shared the glories of a thronging scene, of brilliant uniforms and noble decorations, of tiaras and couturier fashions, of lilting music, flowers and candlelight, the intoxicating excitement of hearts beating in three-four time in a Winterhalter setting.

These polite Americans brought to the Paris scene, the sly chronicler of American social aspirations concluded, low corsages, the Bible, and "shoulders far more beautiful than those of the British Channel."[4] Like Dr. Evans himself, who wrote that he had introduced more than three hundred Americans to the privileges of the court, they were staunch democrats at home but loved the pomp and ceremonies of an aristocratic, hierarchical society. Dr. Evans, while on a visit to America, once explained how the system worked for Americans. "An American on the Continent," he said, "has a social position gloriously indefinite, untrammeled by distinctions fixed upon this side of the water or recognized on the other side."[5] Small wonder, then, that Thomas Gold Appleton, the Sydney Smith of nineteenth-century Boston society, encouraged Bostonians to live virtuously, assuring them, in an oft-quoted remark, "Good Americans, when they die, go to Paris." Evans agreed: "It used to be said, 'Paris is the Heaven of Americans.'"[6]

Apart from cultivated or wealthy Americans who joined the Paris colony to marry off a daughter or to enjoy the art life and social amenities, there were, of course, on another level, idlers, students living on short commons, social exiles seeking oblivion, the fugitives from bankruptcy proceedings, and, after the fall of Tammany Hall, a pride of New York politicians. There were class distinctions, the old resident versus the new arrival, the unacceptable man who had made his pile in war contracts from "shoddy" during the Civil War, the proper American eligible for the clubs, the American who spoke French and the one who didn't, and in a special class the American entitled to wear the red ribbon of the Legion of Honor and who was invited to enter *"la bonne Société du faubourg Saint-Germain."*[7]

Typical of the attractive Américaine who moved into the highest social circles of the Second Empire was the former Lily Greenough of Cambridge, Massachusetts, who learned her German and French in the select school conducted by young Mr. Agassiz, her manners from Mrs. Agassiz, and who cultivated a remarkable singing voice in London. In 1859, at age seventeen, she married Charles Moulton, son of a rich, Europeanized American banker. Her father-in-law was a dear, quixotic old gentleman who had lived in Paris for forty years without conquering the language, had seen two revolutions and a coup d'état, and had calmly laid down his casks of the best Château Lafitte during the Revolution of 1848.

As the charming wife of a millionaire and mistress of three residences, a handsome hôtel in the Rue de Courcelles, a country château some twelve miles from Paris, and a villa at Dinard, Lily (who later became Lillie) was ready for the social fray, and skated easily, and literally, into the coterie that surrounded the sovereigns. It was in January 1863, on the coldest day Paris could remember, that she drove out to the Bois, put on her skates, and astonished Tout-Paris with her proficiency upon the ice. Not for nothing had she learned to skim like a bird on Cambridge's Fresh Pond. Soon she was skating with the Emperor, he in a tall hat, and Eugénie left the protection of two trembling chamberlains to make a few turns with the incomparable Lily. Shortly afterward, she became an appreciated and regular guest at the Tuileries and the livelier embassies.[8]

The agreeable Mrs. Moulton became the diva of the Tuileries, singing at Eugénie's "little Mondays." Sometimes she danced a spirited Virginia reel with old General Nicolas Changarnier, Prince Richard Metternich at the piano; and when the Moultons provided from their estate some authentic American sweet corn, Lily showed how to eat corn on the cob. The amazement of the guests knew no bounds, and Baron Haussmann asked her if she was playing the A-flat flute. (There is no A-flat flute. A flute is a flute is a flute.) At a charity performance in the theater of the Conservatoire, Lily took the part of a Greek slave in Molière's *L'Esclave,* although she made it clear she "did not copy [Hiram] Powers's Greek slave in the way of dress."[9] But she did introduce a song by Alexander Nicho-laevich Alabieff, gifted amateur composer of Russian music, and a cadenza especially written for her by the imperial *maître de chapelle,* Esprit Auber. Her triumph was complete. The Empress Eugénie sent her a bouquet of violets taken from her corsage. Another bouquet bore the card of Dr. Evans.

"It was very nice of him to . . . send me such beautiful flowers," Mrs. Moulton recalled in a private letter. "Dr. Evans is so clever and entertaining. Every one likes him, and every door . . . is open to him. At the Tuileries they look on him not only as a good dentist but as a good friend."[10]

Here in translation is the form followed for an invitation to the palace of Compiègne, which the Moultons, the Evanses, and others in the charmed circle received.

Palace of the Tuileries
10 November, 1866

Vicomte de Laferrière
First Chamberlain to the Emperor's Household.

Sir,

By order of the Emperor I have the honour to inform you that you and Mrs. Charles Moulton are invited to spend a week at the Palace of Compiègne, from the 22nd to the 29th of November.

The train for Compiègne leaves Paris at 2:30 on the

22nd, and carriages will meet you and bring you to the Palace.

I have the honour to remain, Sir, your obedient servant,

Laferrière

MONSIEUR
MADAME CHARLES MOULTON

So the Moultons boarded the special train with valet and maid and eleven trunks that held a different evening dress for every night's festivities, with the big letters WORTH in the waistband. Landaus and wagonettes, the horses' tails neatly plaited, harness gleaming, rolled briskly as postilions in gold-embroidered jackets and powdered wigs cracked their whips and sounded their horns. The Moultons' quarters consisted of a salon, anteroom, two bedrooms, and two servants' rooms. A log fire was blazing. Tea was served at once while soldiers brought up the trunks.[11] It was *la dolce vita* in the gayest capital in the world.

There was also a floating, ever-changing population of tourists with hatbox, valise, cane and shawl, umbrella and soft hat, who favored the Grand Hôtel, Boulevard des Italiens. Their numbers included the alert dowager with three daughters to marry off, the Yankee tinkerer with an invention he would like to have boomed by the Paris press, the preacher with a cough, traveling on a purse made up by his congregation, who intended to go on to Rome to dispute points of theology with the Pope. All, all came to stroll in the gardens of the Tuileries among the ordered flower beds, the rows of chestnut and lime trees, and appraise the statuary inspired by classical themes — Prometheus, Diana, Flora, and Venus. For two sous they sat on iron chairs to watch the sauntering Parisiennes — "the women of the Empire had chic," Dr. Evans said[12] — and their escorts in black frock coats, top hats, and large mustaches. They roamed the Opéra quarter, climbed up to the Rond Point of the Champs-Elysées to look toward Neuilly, turned around to view Notre-Dame, shopped in the smart avenues of the First Arrondissement, where the tradesmen charged twenty-five percent more than the prices prevailing on the Left Bank. And sometimes they had the happiness to catch a glimpse of the imperial family driving to the Bois.[13]

Once safely back at their hotel, the gentlemen, over wine and cigars, noted with regret the absence in Paris of such features of their accustomed cuisine as fishballs and buckwheat cakes. They counted their money, deplored the ruinous rate of exchange, and denounced the languid treatment they received at the American consulate when they reported lost luggage or being overcharged for candles.[14]

The agreeable state of affairs that has just been roughly sketched was rudely interrupted by the outbreak of the American Civil War. The Paris colony was split into a Southern and a Northern wing, with the Southern sympathizers dominant. The latter found that French feeling leaned in their direction, and Napoleon III, smiling his inscrutable smile, led them to believe he was with them. The supposition was that the Emperor's sympathies were naturally with the rural aristocracy of the South, based on land as against the manufacturing democracy of the North, and that at just the right time he would come out for recognition of the Confederate states and a denial of the validity of the Northern naval blockade.

There were other cogent reasons for a French tilt toward the Confederacy. The Southerners resident in Paris were members of a plantation class accustomed to spending money graciously and freely. Overlooked for the nonce was the fact that the funds of the charming Southerners were derived from the profits of slave-grown cotton, tobacco, and rice. Furthermore, the American ministers for more than a decade had been Southern men: William C. Rives, John Y. Mason, and Charles J. Faulkner, who was recalled on May 12, 1861; all were Virginians.

Economic factors reinforced social attitudes. Trade and revenues were falling. And France needed cotton. There were riots among the unemployed in Lyon and the suburbs of Paris. Napoleon III liked Southern low-tariff ideas, and the existence of two nations in America would smooth the way for his grandiose Mexican plans. The Emperor's ministers, including the Foreign Minister, Edouard Antoine Thouvenel, state officials, the imperial press, the banking circles, most army officers, strict Roman Catholics, and possibly Napoleon himself, took as an accepted fact the opinion that the Union could not be put together again. French high society and supporters of the Empire believed that a Northern defeat would strengthen the monarchical principle and discourage radicalism; besides, the Northern statesmen were really demagogues and not, well, gentlemen.

Among those highly placed in French life, only Prince Jérôme Napoleon, who conspicuously espoused liberal principles, stood firm for the North, and — perhaps it was a calculated indiscretion — quoted his imperial cousin as saying, "If the North is victorious I should be happy. If the South is victorious I should be delighted."[15]

Thomas Evans stood staunchly with the minority in the American colony who supported the Union cause. "I, excepting perhaps Prince Napoleon," Dr. Evans said, "was the only person with pronounced Northern views having frequent access to the Emperor. I firmly believed in the eventual success of the Federal Government . . . being almost alone in that belief." But, he added, Napoleon III "was never unwilling to hear 'the other side.' "[16]

Therefore Evans had unusual opportunities for defending the national government. He tried to convey to the Emperor the determination, courage, and devotion of the men of the North; showed documents, newspapers, maps, delineating the progress being made; and watched Napoleon III in his chart room mark on his maps the movements of the armies with pins and little flags. Dr. Evans had Southern patients who knew his loyalty to the North and were suspicious of his easy relationship with Napoleon III and the Empress, but he accepted the risks to his dental practice and persevered in placing before the Emperor information that would offset the Confederate influences.

Beckles Willson, biographer of John Slidell, the Southern envoy who arrived in Paris in February 1862, paid a kind of grudging compliment to the doctor's influence in building confidence in a Northern victory: "To do that supremely one must be a dentist, and, of course, an American dentist. The Court dentist of Napoleon III then, astute, receptive of impressions, manifestly had the root of the matter in him . . . His name was Thomas W. Evans." Willson provides a description of Evans in 1862. He was "a plump and competent Pennsylvanian in his early forties, whose fluent side-whiskers were in the most approved style of the period." Willson adds, "The Doctor's services, though dental, were not accidental. He was known in the most exalted circles to be well-informed, discreet and trustworthy."[17]

Slidell came from Louisiana, once French territory, which got him off to a good start. He was a man of breeding, with a dignified presence, a bowing figure in an enormous felt hat, and with a gift for political intrigue. On his arrival in Paris he was driven to the Hôtel du Rhin in the Place Vendôme. It was in the Place, at Number 12, that Eugénie's mother, Doña Manuela, had received Louis Napoleon's formal proposal of marriage. Students from New Orleans gave Slidell a vociferous welcome. Before the gendarmes could intervene they got off one verse of a song:

Bienvenu, notr' grand Slidell
Au coeur loyale et l'âme fidèle.

The commissioner established the Confederate mission at 25 Avenue d'Antin and an office in the Rue Marignan. The socially imposing and politically skillful Southerner put the U.S. Legation at a disadvantage. His assets included his Creole wife, the former Mlle. Mathilde Deslonde, two pretty daughters, and a son who became a cadet at the military school at Saint-Cyr. When Slidell was elected to membership in the exclusive Jockey Club, it was clear evidence of the links between the Southerners and the social establishment in Paris.[18]

Energetic Southern ladies formed the Confederate Woman's Aid Society for the collection of drugs, clothing, comforts for the soldiers, and organized bazaars and concerts. A vivacious soubrette from New Orleans, Miss Sophie Bricard, who had had a professional singing engagement at the Bouffes-Parisiennes, and draped her piano with the rebel flag, sang with passionate feeling "La Bannière Bleue," which included the appeal *"Aide-nous, O France aimée."* And on the birthday of Jefferson Davis, June 3, 1863, the societies of the Sons of the South and the Daughters of the South gathered at an hôtel in the Avenue de Wagram to honor the Southern President's birthday, with one of the Misses Slidell at the piano.[19]

"The loyal men of our country," Elihu B. Washburne remarked gloomily, "were everywhere in the background."[20]

To counter the Southern propaganda, Secretary William H. Seward had sent an unofficial mission to Paris in 1861. It was led by his political ally Thurlow Weed, who was accompanied by two clerics with a national reputation, the Protestant Episcopal Bishop Charles Pettit McIlvaine of Ohio, and John Joseph Hughes, Roman

Catholic Bishop of the Diocese of New York. Early in 1862 France was excited over the sinking of twenty old whaling ships, loaded with stones, to block the channel in Charleston harbor just as Napoleon III was preparing his annual speech from the throne on January 27. His position might have been hostile, denying the legitimacy of the Union blockade, possibly even calling for the recognition of the Confederate government. Weed briefed Dr. Evans on the Stone Fleet question, and the Emperor himself brought the matter up with Evans, enabling him to present the Northern point of view. At the end of the conversation the doctor felt reassured and hurried to inform Weed, who was thus able to write to Seward, "This morning [January 22] Dr. Evans, on his return from the Tuileries, stopped to say that he did not believe the Emperor would harm us in his speech of the 27th. The Doctor threw out some suggestions I made to him yesterday; in reply to which the Emperor induced a belief that he would not do what we fear."[21] Napoleon, in fact, made only a brief reference to the American war, and what he said was mild enough — that as long as the rights of neutrals were respected, France would limit herself to prayer.

What came to be known as the "Roebuck affair," in late spring 1863, gave Dr. Evans another opportunity to be of service. John A. Roebuck, a member of the British Parliament who wished to bring about full diplomatic recognition of the South, represented Napoleon III as having said in a confidential talk that he was ready to act if England would do the same. "Napoleon's American dentist, Dr. Thomas W. Evans, ever a watchdog for Union interests," wrote two American historians, ". . . heard that Roebuck planned to speak in Parliament about his conversation with the Emperor; he went immediately to Fontainebleau." Both Napoleon and the British government denied the whole business, so "Roebuck was made to look a fool."[22]

Because of staff weakness at the Paris legation, Secretary Seward in 1861 appointed John Bigelow, co-owner and managing editor of the *New York Post,* as consul general at Paris. Bigelow's task was what we would now call public relations, to mold public opinion and promote sympathy for the Union cause. William L. Dayton, a successful politician from New Jersey and a Lincoln appointee, in May 1861 became the American minister and therefore Bigelow's superior. Dayton was courtly, well meaning, patriotic, but unversed in French politics or history, unable to speak or write French, and so at a disadvantage in making useful social contacts with Frenchmen of importance. Yet he was a deeply loyal American, kindly and upright, a good liver who on his death left a stock of over two thousand cigars. It is to his credit that he suggested the need for stronger staffing. "I had personally the greatest respect for the American Minister," Dr. Evans said of Dayton, which was an unusual accolade, because there was often an acerbic difference of opinion between the occupants of the legation and the dentist as to who represented the United States most effectively in Paris.

Dr. Evans kept in close contact with Dayton throughout his mission. "I always let Mr. Dayton know that I was keeping the Emperor informed of what was passing," Dr. Evans wrote, "and he rendered me all the assistance he could, never feeling that I was in any way interfering with his duties or prerogatives."[23]

Consul Bigelow, at his level, was even more useful. He was studying the language, made friends easily, got on well with Evans, and had a good understanding of European politics. He stirred up support among liberals, republicans, and monarchists alike, and acquired articulate friends among intellectuals and journalists. Yet Bigelow worked under a handicap, because he was not at the ministerial level in rank and could not mingle with the official society of the government. It was at this point that Bigelow explicitly brings Dr. Evans into the mainstream of history. He explained about Evans to the Secretary of State: "It sometimes happens when the crowned heads of Europe wish to communicate with one another without any responsibility they send for Evans to fix their teeth . . . the messages of this sort, which he bears, are always communicated to him by word of mouth and in the presence of no witnesses."

The two Americans had become personal friends during a visit Bigelow had made to France in 1859, and throughout the Civil War period they met at dinners and included each other in their private entertainments. Evans had regular Monday morning meetings with Napoleon III in which he passed on to the Emperor news and opinion favorable to the United States. When Dayton died suddenly on December 1, 1864, Bigelow was commissioned minister, a post he held until December 23, 1866.

So Bigelow worked with and through the dentist, benefiting from the circumstance that the doctor knew everyone in the French power structure, was well versed in the subtleties of French politics, and had had most of the diplomats accredited to the imperial government in his dental chair, his home, or both. During the period of their association Dr. Evans at one time contributed to the costs of printing Union literature when government funds for that purpose had been exhausted; and he noted in his writings that in the early days of the war he had as a private citizen obtained arms and military stores in Europe for the United States.[24]

Bigelow maintained an independent mind in assessing the reports that the doctor passed on to him. In commenting on one interview between Dr. Evans and the Emperor, Bigelow wrote to Seward in Washington, "You will observe that the Doctor did most of the talking." He thought on that occasion Napoleon was using Evans to give the impression that his government "does not wish to be *suspected* of entertaining unfriendly feelings against the U.S. at present."[25]

Sometimes the flow of information was in the opposite direction; that is, Bigelow counted on Dr. Evans to carry to the right person ideas not ready for formal utterance. An instance of this occurred one night when the dentist called just as Bigelow was going to bed. The Emperor wanted to see Evans at nine o'clock in the morning, shortly before a council meeting on American affairs. The doctor had to be ready for the questions. So the two Americans talked fully about the state of the Union armies, the Confederate raiders known to be under construction in French shipyards, and French military adventurism in Mexico.

A selection from the Seward-Evans correspondence begins, in Seward's words:

> I have long known very well your professional and your social position at Paris . . . and the good esteem in which you are held by all true Americans who sojourn in Paris . . . Your letter is very welcome. I have submitted it as you authorized me to do to the President. It will be known to no other person . . . You did not interpret too strongly the feeling of our country on the subject of Mr. Drouyn de L'Huys' [then the French Foreign Minister] unfortunate overture to Great Britain and Russia.[26]

The reference was to a proposed tripartite initiative for concerted intervention as mediators between the North and the South. It ended in a diplomatic defeat for Napoleon III. In his letter to Dr. Evans, the Secretary of State characterized the scheme as "hostile to the U.S. and an aggression upon our country," since it implied the existence already of two separate sovereignties.[27]

There has been some skepticism expressed by later writers as to whether Dr. Evans's diplomatic efforts were all that he said they were; they cite his well-developed sense of self-esteem and the absence of supporting evidence. After the end of the Civil War Seward had something to say that explains and confirms the doctor's influence. Following an introductory discussion, based on broad historical grounds, of the need on the part of those who wield absolute power to relieve their sense of isolation through adopting unofficial persons as friends, Seward wrote:

> Dr. Evans . . . was early accepted in that character by Napoleon soon after the *coup d'état* . . . If it had been doubted whether he did not exaggerate the measure of imperial favor he enjoyed, those doubts were entirely removed during our civil war, when . . . Dr. Evans came to the Department of State at Washington, with confidential messages and inquiries from the Emperor of France . . . these messages were . . . of course, fully made known to the president, and responded to by his authority. At the same time, the execution of the trust by the doctor was in all respects moderate and becoming.[28]

Always quick to defend and explain Napoleon III's policy toward the United States, and to reject any suggestion of duplicity, Dr. Evans called to mind a particular day in the summer of 1864 when the Emperor sent for him to come to Compiègne. It was just after the great battle of the Wilderness and the failure of Grant's first movement against Richmond. On July 11, General Early's army was in sight of the Capitol. The capture of Washington appeared imminent. "You see," Napoleon III said, "how hard I am pressed."[29] Dr. Evans assembled his arguments. The South was near the end of its resources. The North could field nearly a million men, battle-tested soldiers all. Foreign intervention would never be tolerated by the Unionists, no matter what further sacrifices it might call for.

"I became warm," the doctor recalled, "and was quite carried away by my subject." At that moment the eight-year-old Prince Impérial entered the room, thinking it unoccupied. The doctor had an inspiration. "For this boy's sake," he declared earnestly, "you cannot act." For if France recognized the Southern government, "the people of my country would visit it upon his head . . . I will go to the United States. I will leave by the very first steamer and learn for myself what the situation is . . . the feeling of the people . . . the power of the Government. I will . . . see Mr. Lincoln and Mr. Seward, and I will report to you the exact truth . . . and I entreated His Majesty to suspend all action until I could report to him."

The Emperor listened without saying a word. When the doctor had finished, he said, "Well, Evans, go! I shall be pleased . . . to get your impressions and opinions." He ended, with a smile, "I don't think I shall recognize the Southern Confederacy until you have an opportunity of communicating to me the results of your visit."[30]

With Mrs. Evans, the doctor left Paris on August 11 for Liverpool, sailing from there on the *China* for New York. After visiting his family briefly on the way to Washington, and having his portrait taken by Frederick Gutekunst, Philadelphia's leading photographer, Evans went on to the capital and put up at Willard's Hotel.[31] He was received by Secretary Seward and met other members of the Cabinet. Atlanta had just been captured, yet the government seemed gloomy and anxious, chiefly perhaps because of the presidential election coming in November and because a spirit of defeatism in midsummer made victory appear by no means certain. Then came a more cheerful interview with the President. Evans had met Lincoln at his home in Springfield, Illinois, in 1860, following his nomination but before his election as President. After some general conversation referring back to that meeting and to "persons both of us knew . . . I told him what I had come to America for," and Lincoln "seemed much pleased" and promised full cooperation.[32]

> I had a long conversation with Mr. Lincoln . . . but before the interview ended Mr. Seward joined us, and I was furnished . . . with information that gave me a very clear insight into the situation from the official or govern-

mental point of view. Mr. Lincoln was in much better spirits . . . summing up his forecast of coming events in his homely way as follows: "Well, I guess we shall be able to pull through; it may take some time. But we shall succeed, *I think,*" with an emphasis on the last words that was significant.[33]

Arrangements were made for Evans to go to City Point, Virginia, and see General Grant at the headquarters of the Army of the Potomac in front of Petersburg and Richmond. He arrived on September 4, dined with the general, and had a number of evening talks with him, sitting in front of Grant's tent beside a fire that kept off the damps of the evening and the mosquitoes, the general in a relaxed mood, throwing his leg over the arm of his chair and lighting a cigar. The *New York Herald* mentioned among others present "the world renowned surgeon dentist, Dr. Evans. The latter, it will be remembered, has exacted tributes to his skill from the Emperors of France and Russia, and has probably received more foreign decorations of honor than any half score of American citizens living."[34]

Dr. Evans spent five days at Grant's headquarters. During this time there were visits to Generals Meade, Hancock, and Butler, and occasionally the party was under fire from Confederate pickets. Another visitor at the time was Washburne, then a U.S. senator from Illinois, who had pushed hard for Grant's promotion and was later in Paris, as has already been noticed, as U.S. minister during Grant's administration. Dr. Evans learned, among many other aspects of the war effort, of the plan for General Sherman's famous march to the sea, which Sherman said would "make Georgia howl."[35]

General Grant and the doctor got on well. After the visit Grant wrote to his wife, "Have you thought any more about letting one of the boys go to Paris to receive an education? Since I have learned more about Dr. Evans I am more in favor of having one of them go. If Buck [nickname for Ulysses S. Grant, Jr., because he was born in Ohio, the Buckeye State] would be contented I would prefer sending him." He added assurance that such an arrangement would be under Evans's auspices. He also mentioned General Sheridan's "brilliant victories" and the prospect that "in a few days more I shall make another stir." When Dr. Evans returned to Washington he found everywhere a more hopeful feeling and "a confidence that was contagious."[36]

On returning to Paris, Dr. Evans told Napoleon III that he was "entirely convinced that the end of the war was not far distant," and the Emperor replied, "'When the plan of campaign arranged between Grant and Sherman was reported to me, I saw by my maps that *it was the beginning of the end* [*ce fut le commencement de la fin*].'"[37] So the doctor was able to report to the Secretary of State, "I have continually conversed with the persons whom I know have his confidence & I am fully convinced that there is now no idea of recognition."[38] Evans gave the entire credit for French restraint to Napoleon III personally, not to his ministers or to French public opinion, and loyally contrasted Napoleon's conduct as he perceived it with English deviousness, saying, "No *Alabama*s were allowed to escape from French ports."[39]

Actually, Confederate prospects for foreign recognition had dropped disastrously months before the doctor undertook his journey. What we are more concerned with here is what Dr. Evans thought at the time, his own estimate of his diplomacy, and the fact that Napoleon III, for his own reasons, authorized the mission. The doctor should have been well aware that Napoleon was disingenuous, cautious, and had no particular love for the United States or republican institutions. From the events of these difficult Civil War years in Paris what we learn most about is Evans's remarkable fidelity to Louis Napoleon Bonaparte, uncritical if you like, but an attachment that remained unshaken, as we shall see, when the star-crossed Empire fell.

With a growing perception in Europe that recognition of the Confederacy meant acquiescence in human slavery, French public opinion gradually turned in favor of the North. The Richmond government, in a desperate throw, sent to England and France an unofficial emissary who could act more boldly than a regular diplomat.

The agent chosen was one of the most celebrated spies in American history, dynamic Rose O'Neal Greenhow, sometimes called "the wild Rose," a fascinating beauty, wit, temptress, and ardent pro-slavery expansionist. Mrs. Greenhow, who had been a political hostess in Washington and an accomplished intrigante, enjoyed close social relations with the French Legation in Washington. When she arrived in Paris, she had a private audience with the French Emperor in the Tuileries on a January day in 1864. Napoleon was courteous but careful. Mrs. Greenhow read the war news, which got no better, in the newspapers on file at the Grand Hôtel, drove in the Bois, was welcomed in the salons, and viewed "the gorgeous trappings of the Eugénie era." She attended a ball and was presented to the Empress. But it was too late. France had chilled, and the insistent demand of the United States for the removal of French troops from Mexico could not be resisted indefinitely.[40]

The military success of the North, Seward's wise diplomacy, the emancipation policy, and Dr. Evans's timely help had won the Civil War in Paris before success came at home.

9

Mercy on Europe's Battlefields

As a student of what had been accomplished in delivering health services in the American Civil War, Dr. Evans often talked with the Emperor Napoleon, and especially with the Empress Eugénie, about his theories and observations.

> As early as 1862 [the doctor said] . . . she asked me if I could furnish her with any information respecting the provisions that had been made by our Government for the care of the sick and wounded; and more particularly to what extent, if any, voluntary aid was supplementing the official service . . . I explained . . . how the medical service of the United States Army was organized; and informed her that a Sanitary Commission had been created, unofficial in character but recognized by the Government . . . The Empress asked me to write out what I had told her . . . which I did.[1]

Encouraged by Eugénie, who was little interested in battles and sieges but responsive to suffering, Dr. Evans worked feverishly outside his regular professional occupations on a book-length manuscript. It took shape during the autumn of 1864 and described in detail the organization and work of the United States Sanitary Commission as a voluntary citizens' association, supplementing the work of the Army Medical Bureau, but with no government aid. For the first time in history, Evans pointed out, the health and welfare of ordinary troops were a topic of concern. "It was my privilege," wrote the doctor, "to first repeat in Europe the eventful story of the United States Sanitary Commission." The lives of free men must be saved by a free society, Evans declared, no longer expendable as servants of a particular royal house.[2]

The book was a solid piece of work, though no stylistic triumph. It drew on such sources as Henri Dunant's writings, the *Documents of the U.S. Sanitary Commission,* medical monographs, the *United States Sanitary Commission Bulletin,* reports of the surgeon general and Secretary of War, and *Medical Statistics of the United States Army,* incorporating as well the history of mortality rates in wartime from the period of the Napoleonic wars down through the American experience.

The commission had addressed searching questions to the United States Army Medical Corps, whose chief replied with elaborate courtesy and flowery compliments, but gave assurance there was no need to get excited. All arrangements were in good hands. As a slight concession the army agreed that the Sanitary Commission might furnish a small quantity of articles of secondary importance, such as nightgowns, and women could perhaps be useful in sewing and in picking lint. It was the typical response of a functionary devoted to precedents. The medical chief stoutly resisted any change. Only after the leaders of the Sanitary Commission got a new chief appointed did real cooperation come into play. At every level the established governmental agencies fought the volunteer effort to save lives. It was "one of the unhappiest pages of Civil War history," wrote Professor Allan Nevins, that "the War Department under [Edwin M.] Stanton continually impeded" the functioning of the Sanitary Commission, which was "the forerunner, and to some extent the parent, of the American Red Cross."[3]

Dr. Evans's book was published in French in 1865 under a title of inordinate length but one that said with exactness what he wished to say: *La commission sanitaire des Etats-Unis: son origine, son organization et ses résultats: avec une notice sur les hôpitaux militaires aux Etats-Unis et sur la réforme sanitaire dans les armées européennes.* On the title page the doctor placed an impressive list of his titles and connections to lend the work authority.

The reaction to the book by the French Service de Santé was predictable — a mixture of hostility, contempt, and the chilling fear that the authority of the bureaucratic system might be diminished. But the impact of *La commission sanitaire* on the general public was such that six editions were published between 1865 and 1867. The book, Evans declared, "exerted a powerful influence upon the organization and growth of kindred institutions. Old prejudices have been corrected, the practicable and the possible demonstrated."[4] Congratulatory messages on the publication of the volume flowed in from rulers and highly placed persons, among them the Empress Eugénie and Marshal Certain Canrobert, who had commanded the expeditionary corps in the Crimea; Sophie, Queen of Holland; Prince Metternich, on behalf of the Emperor Francis Joseph of Austria; and Queen Augusta of Prussia, whose husband, King William I, conferred a decoration on the American for his humanitarian work.

At a time early in his career, Dr. Evans had offered to finance a prize of twenty-five thousand francs for the best essay by a young medical student on dental problems, but there were no entries. Medical students were not interested in teeth. So the doctor turned his philanthropic energies to the field of practical humanitarian usefulness — military hygiene and sanitary reform in the management of armies and the care of wounded soldiers. It was a compassionate response to grim realities and served to strengthen further the esteem in which Dr. Evans's royal and imperial patients held him.

When Evans went to the Crimea to study the care of wounded soldiers and sanitary conditions in camps and hospitals, the misery and suffering he saw moved him profoundly to try to arouse the interest of the civilized world in urgently needed reforms. Professionally, the experience was rewarding. His attention was naturally drawn to cases of lower or upper jawbones broken by firearms or other weapons. He mentions in his writings attending several French and Russian officers wounded at the siege of Sebastopol. In one case there was a fracture of the left part of the lower jaw, and a large portion of the maxillary bone was lost. Dr. Evans used vulcanized rubber, a novel operative procedure at the time in buccal surgery, to repair the damage and make the face as it was before.

Early in June 1859, the French and Piedmontese allies and the Austrian armies clashed five miles west of the river Mincio, neither expecting the other. The result was the bloody slaughter of the battle of Solferino. It was a day-long struggle in oppressive heat followed by a torrential thunderstorm in the afternoon. The Austrians retreated; the French, too exhausted to pursue, held the field. Peace came quickly in the Treaty of Villafranca, and the reason for this, the Prussian threat to France, has already been discussed. But forty thousand men were killed outright or died of wounds and neglect.

Napoleon III watched the battle from the tower of the Chiesa Maggiore in Castiglione, shaken and sickened by what he saw — bayonets thrust home between the ribs of desperate men, sword slashes in hand-to-hand fighting, the bodies of the wounded mangled by the hoofs of horses and the wheels of gun carriages. When ammunition was exhausted, the men fought on with fists, stones, knives. Every farmyard became a fort; every sand heap was fertilized with blood. At Castiglione six thousand wounded were concentrated, attended by only two doctors and the compassionate women of Lombardy, bringing water, crying out *"Tutti fratelli"* (All are brothers), while long caravans of ox- and mule carts carried in more groaning loads. Five hundred men were deposited in the church; others lay on the stone steps or straw pallets, remaining sometimes one, two, or three days without care or help, food or drink, many naked or half-clad, with terrible wounds never bandaged or with original bandages never changed. Priests walked among them with the viaticum, kneeling beside those with working eyes or convulsive twist of arm or leg.

The doctors labored to the point of exhaustion with knife and saw. It was often a race between gangrene and the saw: "Only one minute more!" Then the grinding sound of the steel teeth penetrating the living bone. Mercifully, the amputees usually lost consciousness. Often the physicians whispered, "There is nothing more to be done." Often the dying man, crusted with dirt and his own dried blood, saw ghouls rifle his knapsack, knowing he could not oppose them.[5]

The scene was worthy of the nightmarish paintings of Hieronymous Bosch dealing with evil triumphant. Louis Napoleon, his long, pale face paler than usual, his nerves shaken, smoked more than fifty cigarettes that day as he watched the blood bath and later readily agreed when Dr. Evans asked for a pass to visit the military hospitals at Turin, Milan, Brescia, Desenzano, Castiglione, and other locations, where he studied surgical procedures, especially those involving the head and face, and pondered again what he could do to awaken the conscience of the nations of Europe to the inhumanities he had seen.

There was an incident similar to the one that occurred near Sebastopol. Dr. Evans wrote, "While I was visiting the hospital upon the field of operations, my attention was called by the minister of war to an officer whose maxillary bone of the upper jaw had been completely carried away by a ball."[6] The man could not speak. But Dr. Evans was able through an apparatus of molded rubber to give the face its natural form again and restore the man's ability to speak. Evans's confidence in the potentialities of rubber in dental surgery was further reinforced when President Lincoln was assassinated and Secretary Seward's jaw was broken in a simultaneous attack but, the doctor noted, was restored by "processes caoutchouc."

Evans felt a deep commitment to bring together in usable form the lessons of sanitation and hygiene he had drawn from his personal experience and observation, and to publicize again the contribution that a private, volunteer organization could make in reducing the horrors of war. The project seemed all the more urgent when an international European conference was held in Geneva in February 1863 to study the means of preventing such scenes as the battle of Solferino produced. Yet, strangely, so new were the progressive ideas of the time that even the delegates at the Geneva meeting, all men of compassion, nevertheless faltered and described as "dark riddles" the problems that had already been met with marked success in America by a well-organized private society.[7]

In the following year, however, there came better news from another conference, which drafted the Treaty of Geneva. The document was officially known as the Geneva Convention. It was signed by sixteen countries and within two years joined by eight more. Though the U.S. Sanitary Commission provided the pattern for the relief societies, later known as the International Red Cross, the United States did not participate in the Geneva Convention at the time, because noninvolvement in European affairs was viewed at the State Department as a corollary to European noninterference in the western hemisphere. The treaty stipulated that the wounded should be cared for regardless of nationality, that all nurses and medical workers should no longer be treated as prisoners if they were taken but as neutrals, and that all enemy wounded should be delivered to their authorities without exchange as soon as their condition permitted the return. These provisions, as a matter of fact, had been decreed unilaterally by Napoleon III after the victory of Montebello and promulgated on May 29, 1859. There was no question of his genuine sympathy with suffering, provided he saw it.

The first opportunity for the new European volunteer societies, serving under the white flag bearing a red cross, to get into active work occurred during the short but sanguinary Austro-Prussian War of 1866, sometimes called the Seven Weeks' War, and especially in the violent shock of the battle of Königgrätz, or Sadowa. Dr. Evans surveyed the whole experience and presented the practical results in a sequel to his earlier volume on the history of the United States Sanitary Commission. The work was entitled *Sanitary Institutions During the Austro-Prussian-Italian Conflict*. One catches a glimpse of the affectionate relationship between Tom and his wife in the dedication to Agnes Josephine Doyle Evans. She is his "dear Agnes," who enjoys his "unalterable affection," deserves public recognition, and who even before their marriage had given him "the example of an indefatigable charity" that inspired him to search for the means "to render less terrible the sufferings which are caused by war among the human family."[8]

The book was first written in French. The doctor apologized to readers of the English version, which was often a literal and hurried translation of French idioms and syntax, and came off rather oddly at times, but Evans explained that he could not rewrite the volume, because of his pressing engagements. During the war the doctor visited Berlin, where he found a confusion reminiscent of Washington at the opening of the Civil War. He reached the scene of the battle of Sadowa while the wounded were still lying where they fell. He visited the extemporized hospitals and noted with satisfaction that the obligations of the Geneva Convention were being scrupulously observed, and that for the first time associations of women were prominent in the relief work, such as, for Baden, the Badischer Frauenverein, and on the Austrian side by the Patriotischer Damenverein.[9]

Evans moved on to Vienna. There he inspected the Holtzhospital, a wooden, single-story building in the Prater, well lighted and aired, which, he said, "reminded me forcibly of the wooden hospitals such as were constructed in the United States," and where the mortality record was very good.[10] But in general he thought the Austrian societies lacked the vigor of those in Prussia, Bavaria, Saxony, and Hanover, or in Italy, which had been an ally of Prussia but was quickly taken out of the war by the Austrians before Austria in turn was crushed.

In his critique of European practices, Dr. Evans focused particularly on the field ambulances of the various countries, which he found to be unnecessarily heavy and clumsy. The French four-wheeled wagon weighed 1860 pounds, the Italian even more. The wheels of the English vehicles were solid enough to support gun carriages. Evans characterized all as "omnibuses." He advocated lightness of construction, a four-wheeled vehicle that could be drawn by two horses over fields and rough ground as well as roads, weighing ideally about 1250 pounds. It should be able to make a tight turn, and be well ventilated, the interior open to light and air. He went into detail about the arrangement of the equipment, the kind of mattresses, the placing of the water tank, stretchers, and medical stores, his idea being that the advances and inventions which had proved themselves in America could be applied in Europe.[11]

"As early as the year 1865 I decided to assemble in a collection and at my own expense," Evans said, "the inventions which had enabled the Sanitary Commission to obtain its wonderful results."[12] His calculation was that the progress made by the United States sanitarians during the Civil War had saved the lives of a hundred thousand men. Dr. Evans approached inventors and manufacturers in the United States and sent his friend Dr. Crane to America to select and supervise. The result was an important collection of medical books, documents, photographs, apparatus, and equipment illustrating the work of the Sanitary Commission.

The commission had planned to send an exhibit to Napoleon III's great Paris fair of 1867. But the American government refused to cooperate. Dr. Evans, with his own collection as the nucleus, now came forward to fill the vacuum. France gave him space on the fairground, and Evans paid the cost of transporting exhibits from the United States and constructing a building on the grounds of the Champs-de-Mars.

Relations had never been especially cordial between Evans and the Reverend Dr. Henry W. Bellows, of New York, a Unitarian minister conspicuous in the civic, social, and religious life of the city, and president of the Sanitary Commission. Bellows charged Dr. Evans with being presumptuous in writing a history of the commission, and one of his associates, Charles Bowles, referred to Evans loftily as the "Foreign Historian of the Commission."[13] We hear again the voice of George Templeton Strong, the New York diarist whom we met earlier, and an active participant in the affairs of the Sanitary Commission, saying that "Dr. Evans of Paris . . . reports himself the originator and father of the Sanitary Commission . . . whereas we never heard of his existence till long afterward. This disgusts the Reverend Bellows."[14] There was not, it appears, glory and honor enough to go around.

The pebble in the shoe for the Bellows-Strong faction was that Dr. Evans received the appointment of United States commissioner in charge of medical and surgical instruments and apparatus. He was an exhibitor and a member of the international jury for dental apparatus and material and wrote the report on dental exhibitions, ambulance wagons, and hospital tents. Excessive modesty was not a prominent characteristic of Tom Evans, but there is no evidence to support the claim, or rather suspicion fostered by his critics, that Evans had ever represented himself as founder of the commission, though the canard has survived in some modern writings.

The varied exhibits included a railroad hospital car, horse- and hand litters, hospital furniture, surgical instruments, apparatus for producing the anaesthetic nitrous oxide, pictures of war scenes, comfort kits with letter-writing materials, medicine wagons, buttons, sewing kits, soap and combs, clothing, bandages, crutches, lint and cotton batting, prepared foods such as Baker's Chocolate and Baker's Cocoa, Hecker's Farina and Gail Borden's condensed milk and coffee extract, for which Borden received a silver medal, cotton duck material that shed water better, and at less cost, than the linen used in Europe. Outside in the park regulation U.S. Army hospital tents were set up, provided by Joseph K. Barnes, surgeon general of the United States, and also a Philadelphian. Evans himself designed a light, inexpensive, four-wheeled wagon to be drawn by two horses, open to the air and deserving the adjective *volante* — flying — for its ability to traverse rough ground. He received a special prize for his design.[15]

Perhaps the exhibit with the broadest popular appeal was a coffee wagon, or *cuisine ambulante,* designed by J. Dunton of Philadelphia, which was in service on the day General Robert E. Lee surrendered at Appomattox Court House. Dr. Crane had assembled the scattered components of the wagon. After searching in several states, he found the front wheels in one New Jersey village, the rear wheels in another, the coffee pot in a third, the fireplace in a fourth, and the boilers in a Pennsylvania soap factory. A carriage builder put the wagon together again. Taken as a whole, nothing like the American exhibit had ever been seen in Europe.[16] Certainly Dr. Evans believed that the American department surpassed all other collections and demonstrated the American commitment to supplementing army medical service with volunteer battlefield aid.

Evans's opinion was confirmed when the imperial commission conferred the gold medal, or Grand Prix d'Honneur, on his exhibit. The doctor's response was wise and graceful: "We may *sometimes* teach; it is always possible to learn."[17] The medal was delivered to Dr. Evans by the Emperor personally in solemn assembly and was duly turned over to the Reverend Dr. Bellows. The old coffee wagon, ancestor of the modern field kitchen, saw service once more, in 1870, when it came to a spectacular end amidst the shell bursts, dust, confusion, and flying fragments of steel in yet another war.

It is to this war, its improbabilities, its follies, its unimaginable consequences for France and for Tom Evans, that the next chapter is addressed.

10

To Berlin!

NEVER WAS SPRINGTIME in Paris more enchanting than in the year 1870. The sun sparkled on the breastplates of the cuirassiers, the scarlet of the Imperial Guard, the green uniforms of the hussars as they paraded along the boulevards. There were glittering balls at the Tuileries. Tourists thronged the Champs-Elysées. Emile Ollivier formed a ministry to govern the Empire, just become parliamentary under Napoleon III, who chose to be no longer Caesar but a constitutional ruler. A plebiscite confirmed that France approved the new, more open system of government. The Emperor could look forward to a graceful retirement. True, he was ill, largely a spent force, but the state of his health was a well-kept secret still, even from the Empress Eugénie.

Then, like a thunderclap, came the word that a Hohenzollern prince was the candidate for the throne of Spain. There had been a generals' revolution in Spain in 1868, when Queen Isabella II (an Evans patient, incidentally, since 1850) fled to France and the new regime was hard-pressed to find a king. Several dukes and princes were approached but declined the offer. Prince Leopold of Hohenzollern-Sigmaringen, a distant cousin of King William I of Prussia, accepted. His candidacy was galling to the French, who were struck with consternation at the possibility of having Prussians behind them as well as in front. On the surface, the acceptance was a private family matter. Actually, as the French suspected, the offer was planned and promoted by the Prussian statesman Prince Otto von Bismarck. From the early days in July, when the whole affair came into the open, France was swept by war fever, an outlet for old feelings of frustration and apprehension dating back to the military pre-eminence Prussia gained through the victory at Sadowa. Prussia must back down and be humiliated before the world, French opinion said, or fight France.

This is how matters stood when Dr. Evans gave his July Fourth garden party, an annual reception at Bella Rosa for some hundred and twenty-five guests drawn from the American colony and the Evanses' French friends to celebrate the fête day of American independence. Through the spacious entrance hall, with its statues, paintings, and rare vases, through the central salon, decorated with flowers and beflagged pictures of Washington and La Fayette, through a shaded alley to a clipped lawn, the guests moved into a large tent with the Stars and Stripes and the Tricolor floating above it in the sun. Inside they found a portrait of President U. S. Grant prominently displayed, with Napoleon III and Daniel Webster on either flank, and a sit-down repast with champagne to wash it down, followed by cigars, coffee, and liqueurs.

The Evans celebration was the principal social event of Independence Day in Paris. There was some speaking. Patriotic sentiments were expressed. Dr. Evans remarked "that the flag of our Union is never so beautiful or so glorious as when raised on foreign soil."[1] Later the guests visited a wooden chalet, where Dr. Evans housed his collection of articles relating to military medicine and hospitals — the instruments, litters and stretchers, layouts for hospitals, and the coffee wagon that had attracted so much attention at the exhibition in 1867. But the mood of the occasion could not be entirely one of gaiety and congratulation. News of the Hohenzollern-Spanish question had just been received, and the doctor gravely told his guests, "Within a few days this country may be at war."[2] Henry Labouchere, the British newspaper correspondent, recalled hearing Dr. Evans speaking of the possibility of war as far back as 1867 and 1868. Even before the Hohenzollern incident, when Dr. Evans saw his friend Queen Augusta of Prussia in May, his forebodings were reinforced by hers.

"I see in the *Figaro* which I have received this morning from Paris," the Queen told him, "that the Emperor has named the Duc de Gramont minister of foreign affairs in the new government . . . It is unfortunate . . . he dislikes Prussia and you will see this man bring war."[3] Augusta, who had liberal tendencies, was hostile to Bismarck. "She comprehended," Dr. Evans said, "that Bismarck was anxious to have war."[4] The diplomatic game was to bring on a war but to shift to France the blame for breaking the peace.

The Emperor Napoleon had asked Dr. Evans to let him know how the garden party went off. The next day the doctor, pleased and proud of its success, was up early and off to Saint-Cloud. He looked up at the balcony, where he expected to see the Emperor taking the morning air and smoking his usual cigarette. But it was empty. Napoleon was occupied with an ominous dispatch from Gramont and was convinced that France had really been insulted. Evans, who was sure the issue could be solved and very nearly quarreled with his friend and patron over the drift of events, departed with the feeling that the Emperor was getting bad advice. During the next ten days he saw Napoleon III frequently. The French Foreign Minister continued to threaten dire action if the Prussians didn't withdraw the candidacy, and the ladies in the visitors' gallery enthusiastically gave the handkerchief salute when demagogues in the Chamber rattled the saber. The press called almost unanimously for war, and Marshal Edmond Leboeuf, Minister of War, made a foolish remark, which circulated all over Europe, on the extraordinary readiness of the French army. "Not even a gaiter-button," Leboeuf declared, "is wanting."[5]

Disappointment. King William quietly saw to it that Leopold withdrew his name. But the French court and public wanted more than the substantial diplomatic victory they already had in hand. Prussia must be made to squirm. The French government instructed its ambassador to Prussia, Comte Vincente Benedetti, to follow King William to the rather sleepy, solemn little spa of Bad Ems, where he was taking the cure, and demand an apology in writing with a categorical guarantee that Leopold's candidacy would never be renewed. These were proposals that it could be foreseen the King would not accept; they were sheer folly propelled by the engine of Gallic pride. William indicated politely to Benedetti that there would be no further discussion and telegraphed a report to Bismarck in Berlin. This was the famous Ems telegram.

Bismarck published a summary of the message in the *North German Gazette*, containing a paragraph designed, as he told General Helmuth von Moltke and other dinner companions, to "be like a red rag to the Gallic bull."[6] The substance was not changed, but the tone of voice became curt, defiant, challenging. The response that was wanted, and expected, came. The French reacted with fury and ordered a general mobilization. War sentiment became irresistible. Napoleon knew that King William could lose a war and keep his crown, but defeat for the Second Empire would mean its end. Yet Napoleon III, with his streak of fatalism, his belief in his star, his willingness to let events lead him, or perhaps reacting with an inertia created by the calculus in his bladder, made no serious attempt to prevent the French declaration of war, which followed on July 19. Strangely enough, the *North German Gazette* was not an official journal. Stranger still, the French government never saw nor cared to see the actual text of the King's telegram. The Chamber of Deputies voted for war without even examining Benedetti's account of the Ems interview.

The Empress's busy enemies — republicans, radical pamphleteers, monarchists, and anticlericals, with the malicious assistance of Prince Napoleon and M. Adolphe Thiers, each for his own reasons charged Eugénie with promoting the war to save the throne for her son. It was pure fiction, Dr. Evans insisted, that she had said, as was often claimed, *"C'est ma guerre"* ("This is my war"), and he had a denial directly in her own handwriting.[7] Evans returned to the subject again and again, and since he was at Saint-Cloud frequently during the last fatal days, his view is entitled to consideration. Modern historiography generally supports the view that Eugénie went along, somewhat reluctantly, like the Emperor himself, because opposition to the régime was gaining rapidly. In any event, there is no clear evidence that she could have taken any decisive step. So the position was that the French nation insisted on fighting because of the candidature for the throne of Spain by a German prince who had already renounced the idea. And to compound the tragedy of errors, the Hohenzollern aspirant had not even been accepted by the Spanish people.

Paris omnibuses could not follow normal routes for the surging crowds that shouted, "Down with Prussia!" and "Long live war!"

and "To Berlin in eight days!" For the first time in years the police permitted the singing of the "Marseillaise" at the Opéra and under the gaslights of the open-air concert gardens. People shook hands over the war prospects and hummed Hortense Schneider's show-stopping song from *The Grand Duchess of Gerolstein,* "Que j'aime les militaires." Maps of Prussia enjoyed a brisk sale to a public eager to follow the promenade of the victorious army as it gave the Prussians a lesson they would not soon forget.[8]

Outside a bookseller's shop a placard announced the sale of French-German dictionaries for the use of the French when they got to Berlin. The people of Paris made impromptu jokes, and placed their confidence in the battle-tested generals who had campaigned so successfully in Africa. What they did not know was that the generals were experienced in fighting only small wars, in handling only small units of troops; did not know the geography of their native country; or that confusion and indiscipline were endemic in the army. There were no allies and no maps. But knowledgeable peasants would show the way, and French élan plus the new breech-loading rifle, invented by Antoine Alphonse Chassepot, would be too much for the Germans. Dr. Evans, who was grateful for the hospitality and career opportunities he had received from France, also knew Germany far better than General Leboeuf: "I was perfectly prepared to hear of a defeat of the French arms."[9]

Napoleon III left for the front on July 28, after appointing Eugénie Regent on July 26, and Evans went to say farewell to him. The imperial train left from the Emperor's private railway station at Saint-Cloud under a cloudy sky with the light fading, autumn in the air. Perhaps it is invoking the pathetic fallacy, but the falling leaves seemed to establish a spirit of foreboding, of melancholy, of something finished. Napoleon III wore the uniform of a general; the Prince Impérial, then a boy of fourteen, was dressed as a sub-lieutenant of grenadiers, a sword at his side and the military medal shining on his chest. Eugénie made the sign of the cross on the forehead of the little Prince and told him to do his duty. A handkerchief fluttered from the window of the green and gold car that took Louis Napoleon to his destiny. The train steamed out, the track curved, and the farewells were over. Paris was avoided because Napoleon III was too ill to ride on horseback through the city, as the ritual of the occasion required. Dr. Evans, leaving the park after the goodbys, reflected that "the future of France could look but dark and uncertain."[10]

The first war news was sketchy but encouraging. The superiority of the chassepot and the new French machine guns was evident. But at dinner at Saint-Cloud, the Abbé Poyol wrote in his journal, Eugénie often leaned on her hand for support. The atmosphere was tense. This much was known: on August 4, the fête day of St. Dominique, the armies were maneuvering, and old General Mollard, filling in for the lack of hard news, obliged the company at dinner once more with a richly detailed account of his experiences in the Crimean War, and the Empress in an aside begged the abbé to pray for her and for France at the basilica of Notre-Dame-des-Victoires.[11]

Word came soon enough. It was of one bloody defeat after another, at Wissembourg, at Wörth, Forbach, Reichshoffen, and Gravelotte. The gallant charge of the cuirassiers at Reichshoffen is still remembered. There, on August 6, the French cavalry dashed headlong into a ditch five meters deep that did not appear on the maps used by the general staff. Thirty-eight thousand men were annihilated, and Prince Bismarck said, half-smiling, half in pity, "Ah! Those brave men . . ." These battles became names of infamy to a proud nation constrained to discard its expectations and its maps showing the road to Berlin. Then came the death stroke, the disaster of September 1 and 2 at Sedan. There the main French army was mousetrapped, captured, and destroyed. Another under Marshal Achille Bazaine was shut up in Metz. Alsace was lost, Lorraine invaded. The road to Châlons was open and Paris threatened. Napoleon III was on his way to Wilhelmstrasse, near Cassel, as a prisoner of war, escorted by the Death's Head Hussars. The Prince Impérial escaped across the Belgian frontier dressed in the smock of a peasant lad, then crossed the Channel to England.

Eugénie, heading the government, hardly eating or sleeping during those terrible days of August, no longer elegant arbitress of fashion but the leader of a defeated nation, wearing day after day the same black cashmere dress with white linen collar and cuffs, kept going somehow on black coffee and chloral. The news from Sedan filtered into the capital on the afternoon of September 3, confirmed by a tragic telegram from Napoleon III. Already two

Prussian armies were reaching toward Paris like the claws of some giant crustacean.[12]

The prefect of police warned Eugénie that there was great agitation in Paris. Bands from the radical left ranged the boulevards, challenging the Empire. Several hundred attacked the police post in the Boulevard Bonne-Nouvelle but were for the moment driven back. One rioter was killed and the leaders arrested. Eugénie labored with the energy of desperation. She brought in naval guns to strengthen the ramparts. France's art treasures were sent away to safety, official papers destroyed; imperial jewels, wrapped in old newspapers, were spirited off to Princess Metternich. The Regent's courage never faltered, though she could reflect bitterly that the same Chamber of Deputies which had voted so enthusiastically for the war had also blocked all efforts to prepare for it.

Although Dr. Evans had been treated brusquely by the French army medical service, he showed no rancor because of their chilly reception of his proposals for reform. The doctor moved quickly to render assistance to the sufferers of both armies. His Quaker background stood him in good stead. He kept his head. Even before the formal declaration of war Evans saw the grief and pain that lay ahead, recognized "how deplorable, from a humane point of view, such an event would be . . . I determined . . . to embrace the opportunity . . . thus offered to me both by means of my position and of my professional calling, to render assistance to the casualties of both armies, although my heart leaned naturally towards the French." His plan: to establish an American ambulance (*ambulance* in French meaning both a wheeled vehicle and a hospital), in conformity with the Geneva Convention and organized along the lines of the United States Sanitary Commission.[13]

The day before the declaration of war Dr. Evans called a meeting of representative men of the American colony in Paris. Twenty-five gathered at his office and established a committee called the American International Sanitary Committee. Dr. Evans was named president, with his faithful colleague, Dr. Crane, as secretary. The doctor at once ordered ten U.S. Army regulation tents through his friend and New York lawyer, Horace Ely. What Evans had in mind was to set up a field hospital under canvas, instead of crowding the sick and wounded into churches and public buildings, as was customarily done in Europe. It was decided that the best place to establish the ambulance was at Paris, since the Germans might advance rapidly, as indeed they did.[14]

A plot of ground, about an acre and a half in extent, covered with weeds and poorly drained, was obtained from the Prince de Bauffremont, one of Dr. Evans's patients and a friend of the Empress. The site was across the street from Bella Rosa, with its entrance on the Avenue de l'Impératrice, where the great avenue sloped gently down toward the fortifications. The first tents went up on September 1. A big American flag was borrowed from Bowles Brothers & Company, an American banking house, and in the bright sunlit days of early September the volunteers drove tent pegs and greased the ambulance wagon wheels. American ladies, wearing the brassard of Geneva strapped on an arm, ranged the principal streets, carrying sticks with a sack attached at the end to receive contributions for the wounded: napoleons worth about twenty francs from persons in easy circumstances, sous from working men and *grisettes*. But most of the money was provided by Dr. Evans himself. He estimated that during the period of the operation of the ambulance he drew on his personal account with the Rothschilds for approximately 1.25 million francs, or $250,000 as he calculated his expenditures in 1873.[15]

Looking toward America, Dr. Evans turned for help to the Reverend Dr. Bellows of New York, who, it will be recalled, had been founder of the United States Sanitary Commission. The results of the contact were disappointing. Bellows was unhappy about the name of the Paris effort, though it was carefully described as a committee, not a commission. He responded with objections, equivocations, regrets that he could not send the condensed milk, Borden's beef extract, and dried eggs as requested, though payment was guaranteed. "Not one particle of assistance, either in money, kind or counsel," Dr. Evans wrote indignantly, "was ever received by the Paris Committee . . . during the entire duration of the Franco-Prussian war."[16] However, the American government did provide the tents asked for, through the interposition of General Montgomery C. Meigs, quartermaster general; and a generous English gentleman, Richard Wallace, gave an unsolicited five thousand francs. Wallace was an enthusiastic Francophile who also equipped and financed a field ambulance attached to the French army's Thirteenth Corps, and two sedentary hospitals in Paris. This was at a time when the French felt especially hostile toward England for having done nothing to rescue their country from its diplomatic isolation. The French people were grateful to Wallace as an individual, but made the nice distinction that since he was either the illegitimate son of the late Lord Hertford by an actress, or perhaps the son of the Marchioness of Hertford by an unidentified father, Wallace was not a typical British milord.[17]

The committee laid in a large supply of ether, preserved beef, biscuits, wine, candles, bedding, and clothing, and Dr. Evans turned over to the project the sanitary collection in his possession. The borders of the encampment were set with young spruce and fir trees for "purifying the air," with a grove of evergreens also in the central portion of the grounds. A bright and cheerful atmosphere was created with the white tents, bright-colored awnings, graveled walks, flower beds, orange and pomegranate bushes set in green tubs. There were two tall flagstaffs. One carried the Red Cross flag, the other the American flag. The amenities included a piano, several singing birds, a tortoiseshell cat, a yellow dog, and four cows.

Supporting facilities included a barracks, kitchen, washhouse, storehouse, offices for the surgeon, the committee, the volunteer aides, and the ladies who did the nursing and cooking, read to the patients, wrote letters for them, entertained them with a game of checkers or backgammon. The ambulance wagons were manned by high-spirited young Americans who formed, Evans noted, "a sort of connecting wire between it [the field hospital] and the whole of the American colony in Paris."[18] Sometimes they accompanied their work with songs, including a lusty rendition of "Marching Through Georgia" in times of greatest danger. This caused a considerable degree of astonishment among the French and German soldiers, whose immediate task was to disembowel each other.

There was an ingenious system of drainage, and the tents were heated by pipes connected to a large coal-burning stove located in a central cellar. The tents were floored, lighted by oil lamps; some were carpeted. Beds were equipped with linen sheets and plenty of blankets. The chief medical officer was Dr. John Swinburne, of New York, "a beaming, grizzle-bearded, sure-handed master surgeon working," a correspondent for the *London Morning Post* wrote, "for pure philanthropy." His aides called Dr. Swinburne, with affection and respect, "Old Compound Fracture," because of his advocacy of conservative surgery, meaning conservation rather than amputation.[19]

Other miscellaneous helpers included a spruce Quakeress, easily scandalized; two ladies of the Opéra; an extremely evangelical parson; bankers; young men free of the need for gainful employment; a stray Englishman or two; and a rich woman of color who left a life of luxury to perform the most menial tasks, and to be snubbed. All Paris came to see and appraise the American hospital, to marvel at its cheerful atmosphere and aesthetic appeal, its efficient arrangements for heating, and its daring reliance on fresh air, since the French were normally paralyzed by the fear of air currents. Visitors were captivated by the reconstituted coffee wagon, with its enormous pots for tea, coffee, and soup and large boilers for heating water, the whole drawn by two horses and belching clouds of black smoke.

Among the visitors were Washburne, the American minister, two Civil War generals, Burnside and Sheridan, the French Generals Ducrot, Thomas, and Trochu with their staffs, and Georges Darboy, Archbishop of Paris. The medical regimen was simple. Only four remedies were used, fresh air, hot and cold water, opium, and quinine.

As a result, *La Patrie* was able to report: "The Ambulance where the fewest wounded die was founded by Dr. Thomas W. Evans." A French journalist who surveyed thirty-three hospitals in the city agreed that the American tent system succeeded marvelously well. Four out of five patients, Labouchere wrote, recovered. Press coverage was extensive. *L'Illustration* published a large engraving of the buildings, tents, and grounds. The *Journal Officiel* praised the innovations. *Le Rappel* was especially intrigued by the portable tents, and *Le National* credited the benevolent work to Dr. Evans. *La Liberté* noticed that some of the American ladies serving at the Ambulance were young and pretty, which "can do no harm, and may even singularly assist the cure," and called the Ambulance a generous return for the hospitality that France had always exhibited to the world "and especially, in these later years, to the American people, who, it may be said, have made Paris their veritable capital."[20]

There were several kinds of emergency hospitals in Paris: the inefficient military facilities; those connected with the Société Inter-

This home, purchased by Dr. Evans for his parents' old
age, stood on the northwest corner of Spruce and Fortieth
streets in Philadelphia. The site is now occupied by the
University of Pennsylvania Dental School.

The Tuileries palace, royal residence of the sovereigns of
France in Paris, commenced in 1564 by Catherine de Médicis,
enlarged by Henri IV and Louis XIV, abandoned in 1870
by the Empress Eugénie, and burned by the Commune in
1871.

III. Le grand escalier des Tuileries, élevé par Louis-Philippe. Entrée à un bal sous Napoléon III. Dessin de Thorigny.

Guests of Napoleon III entering the Tuileries by the grand staircase. Notice the crinolines of the women, the gas globes, and the Guards (minimum height five feet, eleven inches), standing at attention with drawn swords.

Dr. Evans, addressed as "Surgeon Dentist to the Emperor," is invited to an entertainment at the Tuileries château, wearing his court dress as a member of Napoleon III's medical staff.

A hitherto unpublished photograph of Dr. Evans taken during his 1864 trip to America by Frederick Gutekunst at his studio, 704 and 706 Arch Street, Philadelphia. Other prominent sitters included Mrs. Lucretia Mott; Rachel, the French tragedienne; General George B. McClellan; Rembrandt Peale; and Thomas Sully.

Agnes Evans, from a painting by the American portrait painter G. P. A. Healy, a resident of Paris for many years and a close friend of Dr. Evans's.

Dr. Evans's residence, Bella Rosa, combined the
characteristics of a French *hôtel* with such interior novelties
as American plumbing and central heating.

Eugénie-Marie de Montijo de Guzman, Countess of Teba, wife of Napoleon III, and Empress of the French, celebrated for her courage and beauty.

Charles Louis Napoleon Bonaparte, nephew of Napoleon I. As Napoleon III he became Emperor of the French, husband of Eugénie de Montijo, and the great and good friend of Dr. Thomas W. Evans, whose life became intertwined with that of the imperial couple.

A traveling dentist in France whose office is his carriage triumphantly holds up his dental "key" after an extraction. Dentistry as a form of entertainment, and the outlandish costume of the practitioner, are in the classic tradition of charlatanism.

Note from Secretary of State Seward to Dr. Evans about arrangements for his visit to General Grant's headquarters.

Rear view of Dr. Evans's own design for a light ambulance
wagon, "decidedly American in type," which was exhibited
at the 1867 Exposition Universelle in Paris.

General view of the American Ambulance, or hospital.
Dr. Evans was its moving spirit at the beginning of the
Franco-Prussian War and its principal source of
financial support.

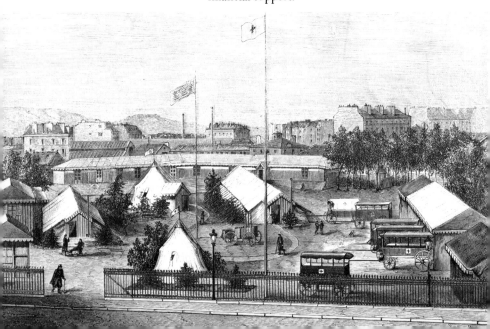

A tense moment: the Empress Eugénie, fleeing from the
mob, exits to the street from the Louvre and is recognized
by a hostile street boy.

The departure from Dr. Evans's house: the doctor hands
the Empress into his carriage, with Mme. Lebreton and
Dr. Crane waiting to follow.

At Mantes Dr. Evans's horses were used up. As his coachman turned them back toward Paris, the resourceful doctor was able to hire a landau and team. The artist, Dupray, erred in depicting only one horse.

At midnight in threatening weather, Eugénie and her lady companion boarded the British yacht that took her through squalls and surging seas to England and safety.

The Empress Eugénie and her son are united at a hotel
in Hastings. Dr. Evans described the meeting, which he had
brought about, as the climactic moment in his life.

Paris besieged: the cat hunts the
rat, the man stalks the cat, which
may appear upon the menu of the
restaurant in the background under
some coy disguise.

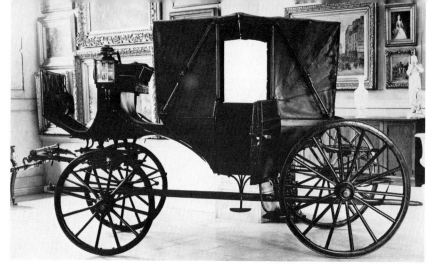

The carriage in which the Empress Eugénie escaped from
Paris, still in existence, now owned by the University of
Pennsylvania Dental School. In the background is part
of the Evans art collection.

After the Tuileries was burned by the Communards the
gutted home of the most famous kings of France stood until
1883, when every trace was removed. During the 1878
World's Fair the courtyard was used for balloon ascensions.

Camden Place, Chislehurst, the Empress Eugénie's first
residence in England. There the imperial couple were united
and surrounded by a court in miniature, and there
Napoleon III died.

Theatrical publicity shot of Méry Laurent, *circa* 1872, about the time Dr. Evans made her acquaintance.

Dr. Evans posed with Méry Laurent's pet dog during a holiday that the doctor and Méry shared with the poet Mallarmé, in August 1888, at Royat, a spa in the Auvergne.

The Prince Impérial in
artillery uniform.

Trained by Dr. Evans and the
University of Pennsylvania, Arthur
C. Hugenschmidt, Class of 1885,
succeeded to the Evans practice, and
like Evans had influence with men
of power and enjoyed Eugénie's
friendship.

The Empress Eugénie dressed in mourning after the loss of her husband, her son, and all political hopes for the restoration of the Empire. But she firmly believed that time would do justice to the Emperor "and perhaps to me."

nationale de Genève, which included Dr. Evans's; and others sponsored by individuals or organizations, some of which actually touted for patients in the early days of the siege, before wounded men were in plentiful supply, because under the fifth article of the Geneva Convention the presence of a wounded soldier protected a building against incendarism, pillage, or the quartering of troops. According to one story that was circulating in November, a lady went to the *mairie* of her arrondissement and asked for a wounded soldier. She was offered a swarthy Zouave. "No," she said, "I wish for a blond, being a brunette myself."

"Nothing like a contrast," Labouchere commented drily.[21]

It was the devout wish of every French soldier to be taken, if wounded or ill, to the American hospital, because of its known low mortality rate. The wounded often even clung to the superstitious belief that the Aesculapii from the United States could make arms and legs grow again.

But this is getting ahead of the shape of events on September 3, 1870, when the Ambulance was barely in place, and the German armies had not yet encircled Paris. On the fourth, suddenly, without a word of explanation, Thomas W. Evans disappeared.[22] The next chapter explains the reason why.

11

The Dentist
and the Empress

IT WAS A SUNDAY of early autumn radiance in Paris. Watering carts traversed the Champs-Elysées and damped down the Rue de Rivoli. There was birdsong in the chestnut trees and a joyful tintinnabulation of church bells. The temperature was a delightful 58 to 59 Fahrenheit under a true sun of Austerlitz. Tom Evans long remembered the cloudless sky, the special quality of the light over the Ile-de-France, the broad thoroughfares, the noble trees, the crowded sidewalks, the play of fountains in the gardens. All was tranquil in the Passy quarter, where the doctor lived, but the newspapers and placards confirmed the rumors of disaster at Sedan.

Those who rose early, the concierges, house servants, *colporteurs,* people on the way to Mass, grabbed the newspapers or saw on the thresholds of houses and the façades of the wineshops the terrifying words: "Napoleon III prisoner." Many men were now on the streets in the uniform of the National Guard and carrying arms or at least wearing the képi, but whether they intended to maintain order or start a riot was not yet clear. From the chimneys of the Tuileries and the prefectures of police curls of smoke rose as the sun mounted. Connoisseurs of revolutions could have speculated that official papers were being burned.

That morning Dr. Evans visited the work of the American Ambulance and arranged to meet Dr. Crane at four in the afternoon at his office. About three o'clock he ordered his horses to be attached to his light American trap, since he wished to drive himself. He followed the Avenue de l'Impératrice to the Etoile, turned down the Champs, finding no sign of popular excitement as far as he could see in the direction of the Palais de l'Industrie. Jets of water rose gracefully and fell from the monumental fountains. Monsieur and Madame strolled under the trees, sipped at the cafés, or listened under glass at the Winter Garden to Adolphe Sax play the new instrument he had invented, called the saxophone. Children romped in the shaded alleys, rode on the merry-go-rounds or in little wagons drawn by goats, while their *bonnes* flirted with soldiers.

But as he approached the Place de la Concorde, where historic events happened, Dr. Evans saw little groups coalescing into bands, bands forming into crowds, as workers, the petit bourgeoisie, and the white blouses descended from the Batignolles and Montmartre, from Menilmontant and Belleville, expressing surprise mingled with curiosity, then breaking out in anger over the defeat and surrender. The cry "Resign! Resign!" began to be heard. A detachment of the National Guard, affectionately known to the populace as *moblots,* sang the "Marseillaise" with gun butts turned up, some with flowers in the barrels. Workmen in their Sunday best mingled with agitators, descendants of the revolutionaries of '48, and pushed on toward the Palais Bourbon, where the Legislative Corps was sitting. Already leaders were parleying with the officer in command of the guard stationed at the Tuileries.

In the Rue Castiglione the doctor saw a man wearing a tall silk hat standing on a ladder, striking furiously with a hammer in an effort to smash a large shield on the front of a shop bearing the imperial arms and, in letters of gold, the words "Fournisseur de Sa Majesté l'Empereur." As he passed on into the Place Vendôme and the Rue de la Paix, other shopkeepers were destroying the insignia of imperial patronage but lately so proudly displayed.

From the balcony of Dr. Evans's office, he and Dr. Crane watched for some time as the crowd grew and its mood turned definitely against the régime. The populace cut red strips from the Tricolor and attached them to sticks and umbrellas as a sign that they adhered to the Red Republic. The mob milled about restlessly, many drunk, and danced the carmagnole, the round dance of the Revolution that became popular in 1793, under their improvised banners.

Edmond de Goncourt called these manifestations "the carnival masks of revolutions," and the doctors reflected on the inconstancy of the French, who yesterday roared their approval of the Empire, and today were crying for a republic. In fact, Dr. Evans's judgment was that he was seeing not so much opposition to the dynasty as "a protest of the proletariat against every form of orderly government."[1]

After the doctors had watched the scene for a while, they drove past the Madeleine, up the Boulevard Malesherbes, through the Parc Monceau, and reached Bella Rosa about six o'clock. Dr. Evans intended to stop only briefly, then continue with Dr. Crane for a turn in the Bois de Boulogne. Crane stayed in the carriage while Evans went into the house to check on arrangements he had made for "a gentlemen's dinner party" to discuss the affairs of the Ambulance. "On entering my house," Dr. Evans wrote in his *Memoirs,* "a servant said to me: 'There are two ladies in the library who wish to see you. They have not given their names, and decline to state why they have come here; but they seem to be very anxious to see you, and have been waiting for you more than an hour.' "[2]

Tom Evans stepped into the room. It was the beginning of a totally unexpected and hazardous adventure, for he found himself standing in the presence of Eugénie, the Empress-Regent. "My astonishment," he said, "can hardly be imagined."[3]

ᘯ

During the last day of the dying Second Empire, the Empress had turned for protection to General Louis Trochu, military governor of Paris, who had made a creditable record as a division commander in the Crimea and also at Magenta and Solferino. Trochu was a bombastic and ambitious officer who coquetted with the radical republicans but pledged his loyalty to Eugénie in ringing phrases. He would defend her to the death. His body would be found on the steps of the palace. "Madame," he concluded, "I am a soldier, a Catholic, and a Breton." Maxime Du Camp, who chronicled contemporary history in his *Souvenirs d'un demi-siècle,* said of Trochu that he had a maniacal loquacity and was drunk with *"l'alcoolisme de la gloriole."*[4] On his personal road to Damascus, the soldier, the Catholic, and the Breton saw an opening to the left and took it.

Thus Trochu. A grumbler with a popular following. He chose to guard neither Eugénie nor the Corps Législatif, which was evicted from its Chamber that very afternoon by the rabble. All legitimate authority vanished. The Third Republic was proclaimed, according to a historic ritual, at the City Hall, symbol since 1789 of opposition to whoever ruled France. Who then should turn up as President of the Provisional Government of National Defense? Trochu! An armed multitude, wearing improvised red caps and carrying the red flag, streamed along the Rue de Rivoli — factory workers, small-shop keepers, members of the Garde Nationale, rioters out of St. Antoine who could be counted on to emerge from the old streets, alleys, and passages of Paris whenever there was an opportunity to threaten public order. The throng crossed the Concorde, pressed on to the Tuileries, shouting for abdication, pushing against the gates, shaking the gilded spikes of the fence, ripping down the imperial eagles. When Henri Chevreau, Minister of the Interior, cried, "All is lost, Madame!" Eugénie had a moment for a bit of gallows humor. "Has poor General Trochu been killed, then?"[5] she asked. Since in political matters Paris spoke for France in 1870, the Empire was overturned by a handful of seditious republicans, an ambitious general, and a new urban proletariat, to whom the Empress-Regent was simply "Madame Bonaparte," and her government "valets of Bonaparte."

Friends and court functionaries quietly disappeared. Servants became thieves before the Regent's eyes. The curtain was falling on the gay scenes celebrated by Winterhalter and Lami and set to music by Offenbach, and on Eugénie herself as a political figure and the arbiter of cosmopolitan elegance. But all who did remain near the Empress agreed that in these last hours of crumbling authority she was firm, courageous, tenacious, and steadfast to her post, maintaining the dignity of a monarch, rising to the disaster in a kind of exaltation consistent with her lineage and steadfast character. There had been a touch of the theatrical at times in her persona, but in the moment of crisis her conduct was fully equal to her gestures. Up to the very last possible moment, the Empress Eugénie believed in the chivalry of the Parisians, believed that they would respect her as a woman, a mother, and a sovereign. But when the Chamber of Deputies was overrun by the revolutionaries and they menaced her palace, she acknowledged sadly, "In France, one must not be ill-starred; it is a crime."[6] Like a gladiator of old, when she fell, it would be with grace.

One must think first of the country, she said. *("Il s'agit du pays; sauvons — sauvons la France!")*[7] If her presence was a danger to the country, she was ready to leave. Still at her side were Conti, the Emperor's secretary, Admiral Jean Pierre Jurien de la Gravière, naval equerry to the Emperor, her chamberlains and dames of honor, Marshal Certain Canrobert, Constantino Nigra, the Italian ambassador, and Prince Richard von Metternich, the Austrian ambassador, both platonic lovers who had been devoted knights in her train and sometime flatterers; Metternich with blond whiskers and sweet, reassuring eyes; Nigra an accomplished gallant, who canoed with the Empress on the pond at Fontainebleau and read poems of his own composition in a Piedmontese lisp at Eugénie's teas. Swiss guards, halberds in hand, still stood impassively on the grand staircase, but the antechambers of the fading régime were deserted.

Menacing reports came in rapid succession from Emile de Kératry, the prefect of police. The rabble were at the Place du Carrousel. They had breached the light railing between the public and private gardens in some twenty places. They were charging pell-mell over the flower beds, crying "Down with the Spaniard! To the guillotine! Death to Badinguet!" By way of parenthesis, the Empress was, remember, of Spanish birth. "Badinguet" was a derisive nickname for Napoleon III, an epithet used by Paris workmen to describe a gold-bricker. Pouring past the basin of the great fountain, shouting "To the Tuileries!" the crowd in minutes would be in the palace unless the Imperial Guard went into action. They unstacked their arms. But Eugénie barred a military defense of her person as the beginning of an unthinkable civil war, added to the existing catastrophe of a foreign invasion. All present urged Eugénie to depart at once. "Had the Empress been found there and then," Lord Ronald Gower, the art critic and biographer, wrote in his *Reminiscences,* "her life would not have been worth a moment's purchase."[8] The Empress hesitated. Chevreau whispered, "Remember the Princess de Lamballe."[9] The princess had been the devoted friend of Queen Marie Antoinette and victim of the massacre of September 1792, subjected to the grossest indecencies both before and after she was butchered. The expectation of similar popular rage remained terrifying.

"Quick, Madame, quick. You must hurry," Chevalier Nigra urged.

Richard Metternich cut in, "Don't you hear the cries, Madame? They are coming!"[10]

The last scene. Eugénie: "I yield to force. The Tuileries are violated."[11] She leaned upon a mantel, then made the sign of the cross, as Nigra, interrupting the adieux, the clasping of hands, the tears and kisses, handed the sovereign a hat, veil, and light waterproof cloak. She must leave as she was, without money, jewels, souvenirs, even toilet articles. In minutes *les blouses* would be in the palace of the kings of France, as in a replay of 1792. Haste, haste. By delaying, Eugénie's Italian adviser argued, the Empress would only destroy her friends, and both ambassadors pointed out that if she escaped now, she would carry the authority of the Regency *de jure* with her wherever she went.[12]

The Empress Eugénie "bowed as only she could bow as at some great state function," put on a black straw Derby bonnet, the cloak, and the veil. She picked up a reticule with two handkerchiefs in it, forgetting a black leather bag that had been got ready for her. There were embraces; then at three-thirty Eugénie made a sign to a small group to follow her. M. de Cossé-Brissac announced to the rest, as in times of solemn ceremonies, that the Regent was no longer in the palace. The three chamberlains lighted cigarettes, descended the grand staircase, and told the Swiss in their tricorne hats to ground their arms: all is finished. The imperial flag that floated over the Pavillon de l'Horloge when the sovereign was in residence was lowered, never to be raised over the château again. Eugénie saw this happen as she passed a window.[13]

The Empress-Regent was accompanied in her escape by her "reader," Madame Lebreton, whose post at court was somewhat of a sinecure, since she was not a very good reader and in any event Eugénie preferred to do her own reading. But the lady reader's loyalty was unshakable. Others in the group were the admiral, the two ambassadors, Lieutenant Louis Conneau, son of Napoleon III's court physician, and a few *dames d'honneur*. The fallen ruler, passing through her private rooms, whispered to herself, "Is this the last time?" She descended to the courtyard of the palace, intending to take her coupé, which stood as usual, the coachman on the box, awaiting orders. The Place de Carrousel was filled now with rioters. Metternich pointed out the livery of the driver, the crown embossed on the door of the carriage, the imprudence of using it. The group retraced their steps to Eugénie's private apartments and entered the long suite of rooms that led to the galleries of the Louvre. They tried the door that gave access to the Grande Galerie. Locked. No answer to knocking. The shouts of the mob could be heard distinctly, despite the thick walls. Providentially, the Emperor's treasurer, Charles Thélin, appeared with a master key. Eugénie and her little company traversed the great gallery, crossing the Salon Carré, the Galerie d'Apollon, and came out into the Salle des Sept Cheminées.

There the Empress turned, gave the men her hand, told them to seek their own safety, not forgetting to instruct young Conneau to take off his showy uniform before leaving the Tuileries, then embraced the women once more. She looked up. On the wall she saw Théodore Géricault's famous picture of ill omen, *The Wreck of the Medusa,* a large painting of a shipwreck that had occurred off the coast of Africa, realistically depicting the suffering and terror of the survivors on a raft. "How strange," she later told Dr. Evans, "that this picture should be the last one I should ever look at in the galleries of the Louvre."[14]

Now, with only Mme. Lebreton and with Metternich and Nigra, who had nothing to fear, being diplomats, the Empress passed through the Egyptian Gallery. Then, descending the three broad flights of stone steps that led to the ground floor, the Empress and her friends threaded their way past colossal god images, sarcophagi, and funeral monuments of dead kings, to reach at last the door that opened on Claude Perrault's arched colonnade leading to the little, tree-planted square in front of the church of St.-Germain-l'Auxerrois, itself a monument to much French history. Here, a first aid station had been established during the heaviest fighting in July 1830, when Charles X lost his throne. Here on Shrove Tuesday the following year, when a service was being held in memory of Charles's ultra-royalist son, the Duc de Berri, who had been assassinated earlier, an angry mob stormed the church, tore down the altar, threw the sacred vessels at the stained-glass windows, and left nothing of the interior but bare walls. And in still earlier times, it was the pealing of the bells of the church on the night of August 23–24, 1572, that signaled the massacre of the Huguenots on St. Bartholomew's Day.[15]

Eugénie accepted Nigra's arm. The demonstrators surged through the square, one stream coming from the Quai, joining another appearing from the Rue de Rivoli. There was singing, wild shouts of "Death to the Spanish woman! *Vive la République!*" As the group stood in the vestibule, hesitating, Chevalier Nigra asked Eugénie if she was afraid.

"Why do you ask me?" she replied. "My arm is resting on yours. Do you feel it tremble?" And she added, "Now let us go, boldly" (*"Il faut de l'audace"*). Just as they passed between two flower gardens known as les Jardins de l'Infante, a street gamin shouted, "There's the Empress!" Nigra caught hold of his arm and silenced him. One account says he boxed the youth's ears, another that he frightened him by accusing him of saying "Long live Prussia!"[16]

At that moment a large, closed cab with four places, such as was used at the railroad stations, jogged past, and Metternich (or, according to some chroniclers, the Italian ambassador) handed the ladies into the cab. At any rate, Eugénie compressed her skirts to make room for her escorts, when the door was brusquely slammed shut. Liberators? Gallants? Prince Charmings? They who had sighed after her and beguiled her now abandoned Eugénie to the hazards of the streets and the menace of popular resentment, fearing no doubt to compromise their governments with the rising sun of the new Republic. This is the view of staunch Bonapartists, including Dr. Evans, but Eugénie always expressed feelings of gratitude to her cautious admirers and saw nothing of a political nature in their actions. Imperialist writers, however, have never forgiven them.[17]

As the fiacre reached the corner of the Boulevard des Capucines, the brawlers were tearing from a shopfront a gold-lettered blazon indicating imperial patronage. "Already!" Eugénie said sadly. Her *dame de compagne* had two addresses. At the first, no one answered the door. At the second, a servant recognized the Empress, who was adjusting her veil, and slammed the door violently, saying angrily, "Thank me for not denouncing you!" The cab was dismissed. The two women wandered on foot, forlorn. Then Mme. Lebreton had an inspiration. She suggested going to the American Legation and Monsieur Washburne, who had made a very favorable impression during the year and a half he had been in France. "The revolutionists," Mme. Lebreton continued hopefully, "will respect the American flag."[18]

"But," objected Eugénie, "we don't know his address. I will go to Dr. Evans. He is an American also, and has no political responsibilities. Besides, he is an old friend."[19] It is a singular fact that the Empress of France knew Dr. Evans's address but not that of the envoy of the United States, who lived at Number 75, a short distance down the same street, near the entrance of the Avenue de l'Impératrice to the Bois de Boulogne. And so it was that the Regent and her lady-in-waiting arrived at the home of the dentist, with just enough money between them left to pay their fare, and found refuge, for the moment at least, in the doctor's library, with its walls done in brown leather paper, thick red carpet, sofas and chairs in red and brown leather, and oak bookcase. Time dragged. As the sun dropped toward the horizon, the Empress had good reason to review anxiously how she would be received by the doctor. He was, after all, a foreigner, with perhaps even less inclination to take grave personal risks in her behalf than many high personages who had already abandoned her.

At last, Dr. Evans entered the library. The Empress stood erect, her hands gripping the back of a chair. "Monsieur Evans," she said, "you know what has taken place today. I have no friends left but you. I come as a fugitive to beg your help. I am no longer fortunate. The evil days have come, and I am left alone."[20]

The Empress-Regent had made a fortunate choice in her moment of need. Dr. Evans was level-headed, devoted, resourceful, a citizen of the American Republic who acknowledged, however, that the Empire had done much for him. There was no hesitation. Evans made an instant decision to leave his practice, his property, his whole way of life. What of his stable of horses, the rare birds in his aviary, his collection of paintings, the royal gifts that he prized so highly? Such intimate details are lacking from the dentist's account of this day. There is always a certain reserve and sometimes imprecision in his recollections, as though nothing was important in his life except his relationship with Napoleon III and his family.

We do know that Dr. Evans was deeply touched that this sad, careworn, still beautiful woman, the pale light falling upon her still paler face, who had wielded the sovereign powers of the state, had now come to him seeking asylum. But he was human enough to savor the situation. It was romantic, historic, and possibly dangerous. The doctor was familiar, as Eugénie certainly was, with the fate of Louis XVI and Marie Antoinette, how they were discovered in their flight from the Tuileries at Varennes, just as it seemed they had made good their escape, and were ignominiously hauled back to Paris as prisoners of state and eventually sent to the guillotine.

Eugénie wished to leave Paris at once and go to England. Orders for her arrest might be issued at any moment, for the opinion was widely and resentfully held that she had instigated the disastrous war with Prussia. Dr. Evans hurried back to explain the situation to Dr. Crane. Indeed, as the two doctors conferred, the gate bell announced the arrival of the first dinner guests. While Crane received them and acted as host, Evans returned to the library to make plans for the escape. Dr. Crane joined the discussion as soon as the guests had departed. Eugénie first suggested that the doctor take her in his carriage to the railroad station at Poissy, some fifteen miles from Paris, to catch a night train arriving at Le Havre the next morning. There, she could board the Channel boat to Southampton.

The doctor reflected. The revolutionaries might well fear a reaction in favor of the Empire unless Eugénie were safely under lock and key. Yet it was worth a delay to see if the revolution was definitely master of the country. This possibility, added to the Empress's weariness and the risk of recognition of a famous face in a public conveyance, enabled Evans to persuade her to wait until the next morning to make the dash for the coast. The doctor, not trusting the servants, made up her bed himself in Agnes Evans's blue and white bedroom. He could not provide changes of linen or nightgowns, because Mrs. Evans's clothing was locked up in a wardrobe and she was away, spending the month at the seaside resort of Deauville, on the Normandy coast. Evans urged that the party travel by private carriage, aiming for Deauville. There he hoped to find some means of getting across the English Channel.

Passports. The prefect of police had provided a valid document, with visa, issued by the British Embassy and for some unknown reason never called for. It was issued to a "C. W. Campbell, M.D.," who was returning to England, and to his patient, "Mrs. Burslem." (This passport still exists in the archives of the University of Pennsylvania Dental School Library.) Dr. Evans recognized this document as the perfect way to explain the flight at various checkpoints. There would be some role-playing. Dr. Crane would be the British physician, the Empress the patient, Dr. Evans her brother, and Mme. Lebreton the nurse. During the evening Dr. Evans scouted in the direction of the Porte Maillot, where they would attempt to leave the city in the morning. He was encouraged when he noted that vehicles were passing through the gate without unusual inspection.

At five o'clock the next morning, after coffee and rolls, the party entered Dr. Evans's brown landau, a four-seated, enclosed carriage, marked with the initial *E*. Eugénie noticed the letter and remarked that *her* carriage had always had an *E*, but with a crown added. From now on there would be just the *E*. All present were in the clothes they had worn the night before, and carried nothing except Eugénie's little purse containing the two handkerchiefs. Eugénie wore the thin mackintosh over her cashmere dress and a little round hat belonging to Mrs. Evans, because it sheltered her face better than the modish bonnet she had worn the day before. The departure scene was later painted, in 1884, by the French Academician Henri Dupray, painter of battle scenes and portraits and one of the best *évocateurs* of memories of the "Terrible Year."

Mme. Lebreton took the back seat, right-hand side. The Empress was on the left. Crane sat opposite Mme. Lebreton, Dr. Evans opposite the Empress. This arrangement kept the Regent out of the line of vision of guards stationed on the left side of the gate. With Dr. Evans's faithful Célestin on the box, they were off a few minutes before sunrise. It was a lovely morning, the air cool and fresh. The city was just waking up. Street-cleaners wielded their brush brooms. Water carts were rolling, and the concierges came out to dip their cleaning rags in the flowing gutters. Three-wheeled push carts passed, filled with long, thin, fragrant loaves of bread stacked upright. Larger carts with milk cans slung underneath clanked along. An old woman arranged flowers in her tiny stand while the working people of Paris scurried to the omnibuses.

The guard at the Porte Maillot ordered a halt. Dr. Evans let down his window, leaned forward so as to fill the opening, and held a newspaper loosely in his left hand, concealing the face of the person sitting opposite him. The doctor explained that he was going into the country with friends, that he was an American, well known to everybody in the Sixteenth Arrondissement. The officer stepped back, looked up at Célestin, and ordered, *"Allez."* The clever coachman gave the horses the whip, and the carriage bounded past the barrier. With a rumble of wheels the vehicle crossed over the moat and passed the sentries, with the doctor's two good English horses moving at a brisk trot.

Spirits rose as the carriage followed the great highway, the *route impérial,* which led west to the Normandy coast and safety. They passed through Neuilly, crossed the Seine to the left bank, with Courbevoise off to the right, then through Puteaux and Saint-Cloud as the sun illuminated the hills, just beginning to be touched with autumn tints. A few kilometers farther on, the road descended gradually in a hollow, to the little village of Rueil, and the church where the ashes of the Empress Josephine and Queen Hortense rested beside the High Altar. The travelers skirted the park and château of Malmaison, with its pointed towers and tall roofs, where Josephine had lived gaily before and sadly after her divorce from the great Napoleon. There Bonaparte waited to be sent to prison on St. Helena; there Hortense and her young sons shared his last days in France; and there little Louis, the future Napoleon III, made his last farewell to his grandmother Josephine, who died after catching a chill. "Everything was suggestive," Dr. Evans reflected. "The very road we were travelling had been a *via dolorosa* in the history of the Bonaparte family."[21]

And so on through Bougival, Marly, and Le Pecq. Eugénie was calm, composed, wholly without self-pity, and even laughed as she remarked, "Only a few days ago I said I would never leave the Tuileries in a cab, like Louis Philippe — well, that is exactly what I have done."[22] But sometimes her mood changed and she cried when she looked at a locket containing a miniature of her son, Lou-Lou. Where was he? A prisoner of the Prussians? Dead? Safely over the frontier into Belgium? She did not know.

At St.-Germain-en-Laye, where Louis XIV was born, where Mary Queen of Scots once lived, and Alexandre Dumas wrote *The Three Musketeers,* there would be an unavoidable halt at a tollgate for an inspection to determine whether they carried articles subject to the *octroi,* or city tax. Dr. Evans was ready with an ingenious story, if questioned, but the officers decided the group did not look like peasants smuggling in hams, chickens, or cheese, and waved them on. At Poissy the road followed the right bank of the Seine, passing through Triel and Meulan toward Mantes-la-Jolie. The doctor had learned his French history, and knew the historical associations of the places along the way; how at Mantes, for instance, William the Conqueror received the injuries from which he died, how Henry IV played ball there with his lovely favorite, Gabrielle d'Estrées, and how at Mantes there once stood a statute of St. Yvo, with an inscription praising honest lawyers.

It became clear that the horses needed a rest. A stop was made at a little *cabaret,* where Mme. Fontaine, a stout, red-faced country woman, produced a liter of excellent wine, a loaf of bread a yard long, two or three kinds of cheeses, a big bologna sausage, and a knife. The repast was shared with the ladies, though they did not venture to leave the carriage. So on through fields of wheat, orchards, and vineyards, until the party reached Limay, a suburb of Mantes. Here Célestin turned back on the Paris road. From now on, without Evans's own horses and carriage, the journey would be completely in the hands of chance.

At Mantes Dr. Evans was able to get a landau, two fairly good horses, and a driver who agreed to travel as far as Pacy-sur-Eure. The women stepped from one carriage to the other, with the coachmen facing in opposite directions so that they did not see the passengers. Evans was able to buy copies of the *Journal Officiel,* under its new rubric *de la République Française,* and *Le Figaro.* With relief, he found no references to Eugénie. But General Trochu had been appointed President of the provisional government, bitter news to the Empress. She dropped the newspaper. Her voice trembled: "How was it possible for him so to betray me!" Later, when Trochu published a rather tendentious account of his performance on September 4, Eugénie remarked with heavy sarcasm, "But when I left the Tuileries there was no corpse of General Trochu there."[23]

The hamlet of Pacy proved to be a hard place to get out of. Finally the doctor, demonstrating impressive skills as an improviser, succeeded in negotiating for an old calash, an ancient chariot that had not been used since the advent of railways. It was pulled by a good gray mare and an unmatched plow horse, the harness pieced out by strings and ropes, but good enough, from the local point of view, for the Americans, or perhaps they were specimens of those eccentric English *milords;* both nations were regarded as quite *drôle.* As the coach traversed the chalky hills of Normandy, Dr. Evans made the professional observation to Dr. Crane that the stock of tooth powder in those hills remained prodigiously in excess of any probable demand.

Evreux, where Louis Philippe had passed through on *his* Calvary in turned-up coat collar and wig on the way to Honfleur, a sleepy provincial town except when there was a fair or a fire. At Cambolle there was a stop at a café to rest and water the horses. Suddenly, the sound of the "Marseillaise" was heard and the now familiar cries of *"Vive la République!"* The Empress turned white. Mme. Lebreton shuddered. But it was only a unit of the Gardes Mobiles returning from a review in Evreux, full of wine and Dutch courage.

At sunset the coach reached the small village of La Commanderie. There, it was possible to hire fresh horses because of Dr. Evans's well-filled purse and to push on in the same old rattletrap vehicle. It threatened to collapse, almost did, but after roadside repairs the party arrived at La Rivière de Thibouville in the valley of the Risle at about ten o'clock at night. They entered a primitive inn, Le Soleil d'Or. Madame, a rather overweight blonde, appeared. She declared with relish that no carriage could be hired and that both of her rooms were occupied. Once again Dr. Evans and his supply of francs prevailed. The rooms were had, with their hard beds and rough washstands. The Empress laughed nervously and exclaimed that it was "really too funny!" *("C'est vraiment trop drôle!")*[24] Then, in the middle of the night — men shouting, horses clattering. Perhaps the cavalry had arrived to make the arrest. Relief. It was a party of gamekeepers looking for poachers.

The next morning Dr. Evans found that the nearest horses were sixteen kilometers away. Why bother with horses, the proprietress pointed out, when La Rivière was on a branch rail line that connected with the Paris-Cherbourg express at Serquigny? An hour on the train had to be risked. Entering the compartment, Eugénie made a mistake and pulled back her veil. The stationmaster stared as the train moved off. The Empress was frightened and never forgot the incident, though it had no sequel. In a little more than an hour they were at Lisieux, chief town of the rich Pays d'Auge. Caution dictated a return to private transportation. Rain was falling. The Empress, while waiting, got wet and later came down with a cold. When the doctor arrived with a carriage he found her, soaked and mud-stained, in the doorway of a carpet factory. His mind traveled back. He saw her as he recalled her only a year before, gliding across the Golden Horn in a forty-oared barge, receiving in supreme happiness an international tribute paid to the glory of France.

At Lisieux another close call. Eugénie forgot herself when she saw a policeman abusing a man in the street. Rising in the carriage, she commanded, "I am the Empress, and I order you to let that man go." It was a sticky moment. But Dr. Evans was equal to it. He conveyed to the crowd that the poor lady was mad. One can imagine the gesture by which he did this — and it worked.[25]

The clouds lifted and the sun appeared fitfully as the hackney coach lumbered the last thirty kilometers through a rich land of yellow wheat, green belts of clover and sugar beets, apple orchards, and lush meadows with grazing cattle. Eugénie's spirits revived, and she recounted gaily how she had washed her two handkerchiefs and pressed them by pasting them on a windowpane. "When there is no necessity to move us," she said, "we little suspect our own cleverness or ability to do things." In narrating this small incident, an admiring biographer comments, "Luxury and power had not corrupted her."[26]

Threading the valleys of the Auge and Touques rivers, passing quickly through Pont-l'Evêque, of cheese fame, the landau entered Trouville and crossed the bridge to stop discreetly near the Deauville racecourse just as the bells of the Angelus called the faithful to their devotions. Dr. Evans walked into the town and located Mrs. Evans at the Hôtel Casino. She noticed that "he looked pale and trembling."[27]

"Tom entered my chamber saying 'I must save the Empress!' " Agnes Evans later wrote to her mother. "He appeared tired and pale. Large tears ran down his cheeks . . . I assure you, dear mama, that Tom is not wrong in devoting himself to her. He left all his papers, jewels, assets to save her, disappearing in a mysterious fashion, risking his reputation, and even his life for a time since rumor had it that he was a Prussian spy." And she noted, with what satisfaction one can imagine, that this was the only time in history that a dentist, her "dear Tom," proved to be the savior of an empress.[28]

The doctor was relieved to learn that no one knew where Eugénie was. It was officially reported to the British Embassy and the Belgian Legation, and passed on to the foreign offices of both countries, that the Empress Eugénie and an attendant took the train on Sunday,

September 4, at the Gare du Nord for Belgium via Maubeuge. This version of the escape appeared uncorrected in a standard French reference work, *Vapereau's Dictionnaire universel des contemporains,* as late as the 1890s.

Concealing Eugénie with an umbrella, Dr. Evans escorted her to Agnes's apartment. A touch of feminine vanity: Eugénie was astonished and somewhat piqued that during her flight no one had recognized her! The next step was to find a way to get to England. Evans and Crane sauntered along the Quai de la Marine. There they saw a pretty craft called the *Gazelle,* owned, they learned from a sailor, by Sir John Burgoyne, obviously British. Dr. Evans presented his card and asked if they could inspect the yacht. Sir John obligingly showed the doctors around the forty-two-ton cutter. Dr. Evans then revealed what he had on his mind — that he wanted the *Gazelle* to take the Empress to England — and appealed to Burgoyne as a chivalrous English gentleman.

Burgoyne threw up various objections but finally agreed to submit the question to Lady Burgoyne. She knew Paris well, had heard of Dr. Evans and his connection with the imperial court, and said, "Well, why not?" So the matter was decided. Preparations having been made for the departure, Sir John thought it wise for him to appear at the casino that evening, circulate a bit, and dance a set of lancers. Later a police agent appeared and searched the yacht. What information the detective acted on is not known, and this curious affair has never been satisfactorily explained. Fortunately, Eugénie was not yet on board.

Dr. Evans escorted the Empress to the cutter at midnight. He reflected again on the drama of her fall from a life of ladies-in-waiting, chamberlains in gorgeous uniforms, cheering crowds, sedulous journals reporting every detail of her charming hats, jewels, and crinolines, and her rôle in exercising the power of a monarch. Now, spattered with mud, she walked on the arm of a foreign escort, a man attached to a wholly different political system, past brilliantly lighted cafés where militia heroes shouted, sang, and clicked glasses, enjoying at once the heady levitation of Calvados, disorder, and war, uncaring that the Emperor of the French and some eighty thousand Frenchmen were prisoners of war and their country already defeated.

At six-thirty in the morning Dr. Crane departed for Paris to deliver confidential messages and to prepare the field hospital to receive the wounded from Sedan. Half an hour later the *Gazelle* sailed for Southampton. It was a rough day and wild night. The sturdy little craft rolled and pitched but reached Rye Roads, Isle of Wight, and let go her anchor about four o'clock in the morning. Lady Burgoyne proved to be a cheerful, nervy, accomplished hostess, and at the happy ending of the crossing Eugénie's health was drunk in champagne.

"They tell of Roman matrons," said Eugénie in recalling that roaring night at sea, "but nothing is more wonderful to me than the sight of an English lady moving about a yacht cabin in a storm."[29]

Dr. Evans quickly discovered that the Prince Impérial was safe in England, at the Marine Hotel in Hastings. Eugénie hurried to join him. Acting for the Empress with full authority, the doctor searched for a suitable residence. Napoleon III had written to his wife from Germany, "When I am free, it is in England that I would wish to go and live with you and Louis in a little cottage with bow windows and climbing plants."[30] In his survey, Dr. Evans came across Camden Place, a stately eighteenth-century mansion, French in feeling, set in its own secluded park at the village of Chislehurst. Only twenty minutes from Charing Cross station, Camden Place was convenient to London, furnished in the style of a French château, and on the direct route to France. It was far from being the little cottage by the side of the road that Louis Napoleon had dreamed of, but it did have bow windows. Just across the common stood conveniently the small, Gothic Catholic Church of St. Mary's.

The party arrived late on a Saturday afternoon, and at eleven o'clock the next morning Dr. Evans walked across the common with the Empress and the Prince Impérial to hear High Mass. The identity of the new tenant and her entourage was not known until some days later. Evans's discretion may be put in evidence at this point. He did not mention to Her Majesty that her husband had made frequent visits to Camden Place as a guest of the Rowles family when he was a young pretender; that he had once thought of Emily Rowles as a possible wife and made her many gifts; nor that the property was leased to Eugénie by Nathaniel William John Strode, who looked after the investments of the wealthy Miss Howard, the beautiful courtesan whom Louis Napoleon once thought he loved.

With the Empress and her son installed in their place of exile, the doctor settled in London for the next few months. Mrs. Evans had arrived with her Swiss maid. The doctor could not return to Paris, since the Prussians had completely cut off access to the city. Even if he had been able to pass through their siege lines, his background as a loyal supporter of the imperial family would have been highly distasteful to the provisional government, and possibly dangerous. Under these circumstances, Evans journeyed to Williamshöhe, the German château near Kassel where the French Emperor was held, to tell Napoleon III that his wife was safe and other details he could not know at the time. The dentist was able to accomplish this because of his old and warm friendship with Queen Augusta of Prussia, who made the visit possible and smoothed the way for him. "Handsome Tom" had put a fair distance between himself and the social position of the European tooth doctor who made his professional visits through the servants' entrance. Evans mentions this with considerable satisfaction in his reminiscences.

But this expression of vanity must be balanced against his compassion and his generosity. For on a return visit to the Continent in January 1871, he devoted himself to the needs of the French wounded and visited the prisoner-of-war camps, where he distributed shoes, food, underwear, money for postage; and later, when it was still unwise for him to risk going back to Paris, he continued his visits to Camden Place and organized in London a "Clothing Society" for the conduct of relief work among the ragged remnants of the French army.

Preliminary peace terms were concluded between France and a now united Germany on March 1, 1871, and a few weeks later Napoleon III was released and joined the Empress at Chislehurst. Surrounded now by a court in miniature, Napoleon and Eugénie lived, wrote Octave Aubry, the French historian, "in that atmosphere of respect which saddens and solaces the vanquished at the same time." At nine-thirty the Prince Impérial went to his room. Napoleon retired soon after, and at eleven Eugénie, too, the guests all bowing as she "made her long, her marvelous curtsy of the Tuileries," a poignant evocation of the graces and elegancies of happier times.[31]

Queen Victoria liked Eugénie and visited her early in her exile while the British Foreign Office, with eyes only for Paris, fidgeted nervously. The visit was returned at Windsor Castle in December.

The Queen received Eugénie with warmth and dignity so that all Europe might see that fallen sovereigns remained sovereigns still. It was a duty that she owed to the profession. Queen Victoria heard a "fearful" account of the Empress's escape and "pressed her poor little hand" — "poor" was her favorite adjective — and the imperial exile showed the most delicate tact in visiting the mausoleum at Frogmore Lodge, where she knelt before the tomb of Victoria's beloved Prince Albert, making her reverence to "the dear reclining statue."[32]

Despite the fact that the Empress of the French was not a member of old royalty, Dr. Evans found himself more than ever persona grata with his noble patients after his rescue of Eugénie, for he was deemed to have shown himself a trustworthy friend of the royal caste. The Prussian Queen, who became Empress of Germany, expressed such sentiments. King Leopold II of Belgium wanted to hear the story of the adventure directly from Evans, and Eugénie herself did not forget. A letter written by her to Dr. Evans on the first anniversary of the escape has survived. With the letter she sent a handsome gold bracelet encrusted with two diamonds and two emeralds as a gift for Mrs. Evans, a little *"souvenir"* she called it, inscribed with the date of the episode, as a reminder of "the support I found during the days of grievous trials in the *sangfroid* and courage of her husband. The date which she will find engraved upon it [September 4, 1870] can never, alas! be effaced from my heart, for it is . . . the day I bade adieu to France!"[33]

While there was some feeling in England that it was, after all, an Englishman who got the Empress safely into their country, Henry Labouchere, who was British but no chauvinist, wrote that in view of the great risks Dr. Evans ran and of his known disapproval of the French war policy, "it was highly honorable to have stood by the Empress as he did on the Fourth of September and the following days."[34] The exploit made the name of Thomas W. Evans internationally known, and he considered his service to Eugénie the most important and satisfying experience of his long career. When William H. Seward was in Paris in late August and early September 1871, on his travels around the world, he enjoyed "a pleasant renewal of acquaintance with Dr. Evans . . . It was interesting," he said, "to hear Dr. Evans's account of the Empress's escape . . . The doctor could scarcely suppress his emotion when he concluded his narrative by saying: 'I conducted the Empress to him [her son, Louis] and, when I witnessed their embrace and heard their exclamations . . . I felt that my mission, not only for this emergency, but for life, was accomplished.' "[35]

But when he was ready to go back to France, France was not ready to receive him.

12

The "Terrible Year" and the Third Republic

WHILE THE PRUSSIANS deployed two armies around Paris — their strategic plan being simple: that it would be cheaper to starve the city than take it by military assault — the Tuileries was looted by its guardians. One Dardelle, a chasseur of Africa, was in command, but having no horses, he spent his time playing polkas and waltzes on the chapel organ. The new government searched the palace thoroughly for compromising documents, turning up such items as a portfolio of music, a prayer book that had belonged to Mme. Mère, mother of Napoleon I, a bill for the darning of the Emperor's socks, and one of Goethe's visiting cards. The results of their scholarly investigations were published under the title *Papiers et correspondence secrets de la famille impériale*. To their regret the material turned out to be pretty tame stuff. Dr. Evans continued to send remittances from London to the American Ambulance as long as the mails could get through, and later heard occasionally from Dr. Crane by balloon post.[1]

During various bloody sorties attempted by the defenders, the drivers and stretcher bearers of the Ambulance performed gallantly and continued to function until peace came. To the end, the Americans were always first on the field of battle. "It rejoices one," wrote a British journalist, Thomas Gibson Bowles, "to see the workmanlike and yet tender care they give to the unhappy victims." A greatly regretted casualty was the coffee wagon, which was destroyed by German artillery fire during a battle at Montretout. Dr. Evans speculated that perhaps its large black smokestack, with clouds of heavy smoke boiling up, and its strange appearance had made the enemy fear it as "some monstrous machine of destruction."[2]

The defenses of Paris were formidable: a garrison of roughly two hundred thousand troops, consisting of regulars and contingents of sailors and marines, plus three hundred thousand reservists, called Mobile Guards, and National Guardsmen, the latter untrained, part-time soldiers, but full of spirit and, often, spirits. Ramparts averaging thirty feet in height were surrounded by a ditch eighteen feet in depth, with a glacis in front. The fortifications enclosed a circle of nearly twenty-one miles, with a belt railroad running around the inside. Seventeen detached forts defended the approaches to the city.[3]

An odd euphoria seized Paris. Amidst general rejoicing over the end of the Bonapartist Second Empire, the foreign invader was for the moment strangely ignored. Uncomplimentary stereotypes about Napoleon's big nose and the Empress's morals provided the radical opposition with material for acerbic and often scurrilous commentary. Inside the city, the theaters, cafés, and boulevards were crowded. There were constant patriotic illuminations, the sound of bugles, a rolling of drums, and much marching to and fro. Meanwhile the Germans neither bombarded nor attacked.[4]

Wounded vanity and a sense of national humiliation were assuaged by the belief that St. Geneviève, patron saint of Paris, who had protected the city from Attila, would intervene yet again, and furthermore, the idea was strongly held that France had been defeated only because of treason. Spy hysteria erupted. An old professor was arrested for closely studying a post marking the number of kilometers to somewhere. An American clergyman, sitting under a tree on the Champs-Elysées, was seized by a policeman for making a plan of the city, though what he was actually doing was writing in his diary what he had had for breakfast. A Philadelphian and his daughter, sketching in the Bois, were captured by a *sergent de ville* who had a psychosis about people who made drawings. In a restaurant, a French patriot asserted loudly that the American Ambulance was in all probability a cover for spying. Turning to a stranger who didn't look French, he declared, "You may look at me, sir, but I assert before you that Dr. Evans, the ex-dentist of the Emperor, was a spy";[5] and an article in *Les Nouvelles* proposed that to simplify the question of whether the English were spies, "all English in Paris should at once be shot." A man with a German name, one Harth, was in fact tried, convicted, and executed.[6]

Semaphores signaled by day from the Arc de Triomphe, and at night giant electric searchlights on the hill of Montmartre, an innovation of the period, swept the northern approaches to the city. War industries hummed in factories and railroad stations and the Government of National Defense put out reassuring bulletins to the effect that there would be food enough for all. Thousands of meat animals milled in the Luxembourg Gardens, agitated cattle bawled and blocked the boulevards, pushed against the plane trees and urinals. The partially completed Opéra, the marble and gold masterpiece of Charles Garnier, was converted into a water reservoir below and a bakery, hospital, and clothing depot above.

Upper-class families departed for Brittany, Normandy, Tours, and Bordeaux, and food prices began to rise steeply. The theaters were closed by decree of the government, not for any good reason, but because that is the sort of thing governments think of. One asked for news, but there was no news. By mid-September, Paris saw its last train depart and received its last regular mail delivery. Meanwhile, carrier pigeons were tried in place of postmen, and Félix Tournachon, who, under the professional name Nadar, was photographer of the great and near-great, experimented enthusiastically with balloons, which sometimes worked, as a means of communication with the outside world. Louis Trochu, as military governor of Paris, was pessimistic, expected to do no more than put up a reasonable show of resistance, and considered capitulation inevitable. But he talked endlessly about his strategic plan, success guaranteed, which he said he had deposited with his notary, Maître Duclos. For Parisians, the plan of Trochu became a subject of raillery — "plan, plan, plan, plan, plan."[7]

Mid-October. Leaves scudding before chill winds along the boulevards. Cold rains turning to sleet. Gray skies instead of the cerulean blue of the Ile-de-France. There were heat, light, and food problems. All Paris was seized by a sudden and uncontrollable hunger. A laying hen was truly a bird that laid golden eggs. "Lamb" was still displayed in the shops and appeared on restaurant menus, but, curiously enough, at the same time the dog population dropped sharply. "Rabbit" became a euphemism for cat or kitten, often smothered in onions or served as a stew. Accomplished hosts offered without apology *le rat, sauce madère*.

Sorties were made but decisively repelled. November and December intensified the cold and the gloom. And it snowed. Transportation was almost nonexistent, since most of the omnibus company horses had been sacrificed. The theaters reopened briefly, only to close again for lack of fuel and light. Paris became Dullsville. Washburne, the only representative of a major power who remained in Paris during the siege, and who had been a congressman from Illinois, said that the Champs-Elysées in January made him think of Main Street in Galena, Illinois. And he noticed on the elegant street where he lived women and children hacking away at the trees, gleaning twigs and green wood, which produced much smoke and discomfort but little flame or heat.

The menagerie animals represented a last food resource. The order in which the animals were butchered is interesting. At first only those species of which the zoo possessed two or more specimens were sent to the abattoirs. Those considered most valuable were spared as long as possible. Last to be slaughtered were the monkeys. "These were kept alive," wrote an English correspondent, "from a vague and Darwinian notion that they are our relatives, or at least the relatives of some of the members of the Government."[8]

The bombardment. Often predicted, surely it would come — but when? A German newspaper explained that Bismarck was waiting for the psychological moment. French wit played over the *moment psychologique* as an example of heavy-handed Teutonic philosophy. On January 5, 1871, shells began to fall on the Left Bank with a hiss and an explosion. The French nodded and joked about the psychological moment for eating, shaving, or carrying on any daily activity. Shell fragments became souvenirs. A hot piece of metal was worth an extra fifty centimes. Casualties were light, and there was no panic. Trochu, generally regarded as a military imbecile, led a hundred thousand National Guardsmen in a desperate attack in the direction of Montretout and Buzenval, where the German positions were especially strong, and he did it without any effort to feint or confuse the enemy — surely a curious strategy. It was the day after William I of Prussia was proclaimed Emperor of a united Germany in the Hall of Mirrors at Versailles. A few days later, an angry, radicalized battalion of the National Guard tried unsuccessfully to overturn the government. For the first time during the Terrible Year, French troops fired on Frenchmen.

In the end, famine brought Paris down after a siege that lasted a hundred and thirty-five days. An armistice was followed by a peace treaty. Relief ships arrived from England and the United States, and order was restored at the food shops and Les Halles, the famous wholesale produce markets known as the stomach of Paris. Once more the fragrant, crusty wheaten French bread emerged from the ovens, every morsel tasting as though it had been blessed by the Church. The people of Paris quickly recovered their physical health. But the accumulation of frustration on the part of the bulk of the population, the feeling of having been betrayed by the responsible authorities, the political and psychological damage — all this was beyond repair. Resistance to the Prussians became transformed into a class struggle between the revolutionary Paris Commune and the forces of the national government, which had retired to regroup at Versailles, thus further alienating Paris. During April and May, when the government troops returned to capture the city, the French fought each other in a no-quarter civil war, street by street, barricade by barricade, with a kind of savage fury recalling the frenzies of the Middle Ages, while the sound of German accordions and military bands floated down from the outer forts into the burning city.[9]

The word "Commune" has had many meanings in French history. It can refer to self-government, especially in a town, or in a small administrative unit such as a borough, or to the militia. In 1793, during the Reign of Terror, it had meant social revolution, the upsetting of all traditional values. When the idea revived again in 1871, memories of Robespierre and Marat frightened the upper classes and inspired the proletariat of Paris to assume the power more or less legally belonging to the conservative republican government and to continue the war with Germany to the last extremity. Some of the insurgents were convinced collectivists; some acted dramatically in the name of all humanity; others were simply rioters. But unfortunately for Paris, under the terms of the armistice the radicalized, staunchly republican Guard, backbone of the Commune, with a revolutionary mentality, retained its arms. Adolphe Thiers, as Premier, and the National Assembly agreed that the Guard must be crushed before order could be restored. The civil war followed when General Joseph Vinoy tried to seize the communards' cannon on Montmartre.

There followed five weeks of chaos, fighting, and burning, and atrocities committed by both sides, as the government forces moved in successfully to retake Paris, and a new National Assembly sitting in Bordeaux formally dethroned Napoleon III, blamed him for the nation's disasters, and ratified the peace terms with the Germans. The treaty imposed on France was draconic. It provided for an indemnity of five billion francs, a German Army of Occupation, and the annexation by the German Empire of Alsace and part of Lorraine.

The physical damage to Paris from the fighting and from the torches of the retreating communards went far beyond what the Prussians had been able to do with their bombardment. The Left Bank suffered cruelly, with the palace of the Legion of Honor becoming a smoking mass of débris. "All is re-established," including orgies and brothels, wrote Arthur Rimbaud, the sixteen-year-old Symbolist poet, angry and despairing: "And maddened gas-light on blood-stained walls / Flames sinisterly upward to the dark blues of the sky." On the Right Bank the Palais de Justice burned, also the Prefecture of Police, the Hôtel de Ville, its ruins so graphically described by Edmond de Goncourt, and the Tuileries château.[10]

The Tuileries, a fateful edifice, palace of doom for both monarchy and empire, went up on May 23, just before the *fédérés* of the Commune made their last stand in the eastern quarters of the city against the Versailles forces. Furniture, papers, and barrels of gunpowder were piled in the ground-floor rooms; ammunition and barrels of tar were rolled up the well of the grand staircase into the Salle des Maréchaux. Tapestries and rare hangings, flooring, woodwork and doors, furniture and objects of art, were drenched with liquid tar, petroleum, and turpentine. About ten o'clock in the evening, after a good dinner, a certain Victor Benot, a butcher's assistant by trade, who had risen under the Commune to a colonelcy with the right to wear a red belt, high boots, and a long sword, fired a powder train, and the masterpiece of Philibert Delorme was a blaze of light for the last time. The great clock stopped at midnight. The central dome collapsed at about one in the morning. Still beautiful, the palace burned for three days, gutted inside, but with the massive outer walls standing, "mementoes," Ernest Alfred Vizetelly wrote, "of the madness of Paris in those terrible days of 1871."[11]

ᴄᴧᴈ

During the Commune, Dr. Evans was compelled to remain in London, making regular visits to Napoleon and Eugénie at Camden Place while waiting for the restoration of order in France, but "immediately after the collapse of the Commune," he wrote, "Mrs. Evans and I returned to Paris." He found his home and its contents safe and sound "due to the cleverness and faithfulness of my servants" and the respect accorded him because of his compassionate efforts on behalf of French soldiers.[12] But he was startled and astonished when he drove through the streets and saw for himself the destruction visited on the city, not by the Germans but by the French themselves. The railroad station at the Porte Maillot had been blown entirely away. The rail tunnel under the Avenue de la Grande Armée had been destroyed. Houses were windowless, walls peppered with holes, the earth churned up "as if by an earthquake." Telegraph wires hung in strings; roads were choked with débris. The silence in the Champs-Elysées was eerie. The doctor proceeded to the Place de la Concorde. He found it a wreck: pavements torn up, the fountains dead, the eight statues honoring French cities chipped, shattered, headless. Through the gardens of the Tuileries he glimpsed the blackened walls and stark chimneys of the ruined palace, melancholy reminders of past splendors. The exact date of Dr. Evans's return is not known, but it must have been very soon after the last stand of the Federals in the Père-Lachaise cemetery, because smoke still rose along the Rue Royale, the air heavy with the acrid odor of charred wood and apartment varnish. In the Rue de la Paix the dentist could hardly find the door of his own office.[13]

"Dismayed and sick at heart, I returned home," Evans said. "It seemed to me that Paris would never recover from the ravages of two such fearful sieges." But he was mistaken.

> Hardly six months had passed before most of the traces
> of this destruction had disappeared . . . yet, for many
> long years one huge pile of blackened walls loomed up

in the very center of the city, solemn, grand, and mysterious, like a funereal monument, to remind the world of
the uncertain life of governments — in France. It was
only in 1883 that, becoming apparently ashamed of this
startling exhibition of the savagery of the mob . . . the
Government ordered the demolition of these ruins [the
Tuileries], and covered with fresh turf and with flowers
the ground on which had stood the home of the most
famous kings of France.[14]

The contractor in charge of the work invited collectors to take
what they would from the ruins. Worth, the reigning dressmaker
of the Second Empire, he of the rude mustaches and imperious
manners, who commanded the beautiful Parisians like a drillmaster,
came to look at the marble statues lying among the weeds, the
windows like empty eye sockets, and saw with emotion the ruined
pink, blue, and green salons. He carted away to his estate in Suresnes
statues and busts, cornices, pediments, and Corinthian columns, all
souvenirs of the spacious days when the great ladies of the Empire
came to his atelier as suppliants, grateful for his attentions.

To modern eyes, grown accustomed to global violence, to geno-
cide, atrocities, and atomic weapons, France's Terrible Year appears
a remote episode, now overshadowed by the greater terrors of the
twentieth century. Not so, of course, to those who lived through it.
When Dr. Evans saw little republican children and their nurses on
the terraces where royal princes and the sons of Napoleon I and
Napoleon III once played, a bird charmer setting up on the grass
beside the laurel where the Tuileries had stood, where indeed he
himself had found the palace a stately pleasure dome during the
Second Empire, the doctor reflected somberly, "The place that has
been the scene of so many great events in French history no longer
even suggests continuity with the past."[15]

So far as his professional life was concerned, Dr. Evans adjusted
to the Third Republic with smoothness and aplomb. Surely, the
tortured St. Apollonia, patron saint of dentists (whose jaw was
smashed and teeth yanked out in Alexandria in A.D. 249), had the
capable American under her special tutelage during the flight of the
Empress, the siege, and the civil war. True, there were no more
brilliant court functions for the doctor. His role as a diplomatic go-

between had ceased with the fall of the Empire. But he was still the famous American dentist and a man of fortune, still held his annual Fourth of July party in the garden of Bella Rosa, entertaining such prominent American figures as former President Grant and James G. Blaine, the powerful Maine Republican, twice Secretary of State; and on the mornings of the Fourth, he always went to place flowers on the grave of La Fayette. At Bella Rosa nothing was changed except the name of the street. The Avenue de l'Impératrice had become first the Avenue Genéral Uhrich, after Jean Jacques Alexis Uhrich, who had made a heroic defense of Strasbourg during the late war, then changed again in 1875 to the Avenue du Bois de Boulogne, and finally, if anything is final in the evolution of place names, to the present designation, Avenue Foch. It was all a part of the determination of the Third Republic to remove every name or symbol or architectural feature or icon that could possibly remind France that the Second Empire had ever existed.

In dentistry, Dr. Evans was as busy, as sought after, as ever; republicans, except those who were edentulous, desired as expert care as had the imperialists. French dentists engaged in much anguished thought and self-flagellation over the vogue for the Americans. Was it based on some kind of chic, like the style of dresses or hats as dictated by the *Mode illustrée?* Surely, a writer in *L'Art dentaire* reflected, the American dentist does not draw his celebrity from the soil like the vine, the olive tree, or turnips, but rather from his knowledge and skill developed in special colleges, the sharing of experience in surgery and prosthesis through specialized journals, dental societies, and professional meetings where knowledge is exchanged, whereas in France these fruitful opportunities for personal growth are absent.[16]

Dr. Evans still had the appearance and presence of a young man, despite the passage of years, the distinction he had attained in his profession, and his many honors. It often amused him, when a visitor arrived, to hear the caller say, "Oh, I wish to see your father — the old doctor!" In his social relations Evans continued to be, as a writer described him in 1874, "the agreeable and elegant gentleman, a hospitable host, a faithful friend, and a kind and devoted husband."[17]

The Third Republic was firmly established by Adolphe Thiers as President, a self-made man and astute master of the French political game, who destroyed the Commune and would have preferred a constitutional monarchy to the Republic he headed. The Bonapartists pinned their hopes for a return to power on nostalgia and myth, which had once served them well, and on the personable Prince Impérial. There were two Bourbon pretenders to the throne of France: the Comte de Paris, grandson of Louis Philippe, representing the younger or Orléanist line, which was willing to merge its royal hopes with those of the elder and childless Legitimist pretender, the Comte de Chambord, known to his supporters as "Henri V," who was fat, lazy, liked to hunt, and knew no history after 1788. Chambord killed all monarchical expectations by insisting on the restoration of the Bourbons' white standard powdered with fleurs-de-lis and positively refusing to accept the Tricolor. To him France was apparently not worth a flag. Monarchism died when he died in 1883. Thiers said ironically that Chambord ought to be called the French Washington, because by his obstinacy he became the father of the Republic.

The loss of Alsace and part of Lorraine, the heavy reparations exacted by the Germans, the presence of occupation troops, a certain puritanism that infected French republicanism, all suggested, somewhat prematurely, that Paris and Parisians would never smile again. But France paid off the war indemnity in a remarkably short time, and the Germans went home. Once more Paris became the fascinating, multilayered City of Light and a heaven for the light in heart.

Dr. Evans's past associations with the Empire were offset in the eyes of the Republic by his humanitarian activities during the Franco-Prussian War, which started as an imperialist war but ended as a republican conflict. The official attitude softened to the point where President Thiers, himself a patient of Evans's, promoted the doctor, on October 15, 1871, to the rank of commander in the Legion of Honor. A curious footnote to the history of bureaucratic police fumbles: at the very time when Evans received the Legion's cravat, and for the three following years, the police were zealously compiling an extensive and largely irrelevant dossier on the dentist, finding, despite what they called *les difficultés insurmountables,* that he was an American, about fifty years old, had a considerable fortune, an expensive way of life, and that in April 1873 he talked with a German banker in Hamburg. But the clumsy surveillance that produced such trivialities was like bringing on the mustard after the dinner was over: Dr. Evans was solidly re-established in Paris, although, according to one account, he rode down from his house to his office with a rifle sticking out the window of his coupé.

In 1883 the dental profession and the interested public got a glimpse of just how successful in a monetary sense Dr. Evans had been. A man named William Williamson, who, it was learned, had been stealing from Dr. Evans, was extradited from Belgium. A former clerk and cashier in the dental office, he admitted that he had stolen three hundred thousand francs from the doctor over a period of ten years. The case came to trial in the Seine Assizes.

"How much, then, sir, do you earn per annum, if you have been robbed at such a rate without discovering it for ten years?" demanded the prisoner's counsel.

The doctor replied that the question was hardly fair, "but I have no objection to saying that my income is large enough to prevent my missing the loss of 100,000 francs a year."[18] The jury gave a verdict of guilty but took the view that there was no excuse for Evans's remaining for so long unaware of what was going on. Williamson got off with three years' imprisonment.

Under the Third Republic, Americans were not received with as much enthusiasm as formerly. Invitations to official receptions were extended only to accredited diplomats or persons on special missions, and French society itself was fragmented, broken up into cliques whose relation to one another, Evans noted wryly, was "determined solely by mutual repulsion."[19] Contacts between the doctor and American diplomats were frequently of the same character. Washburne had been irritated — the dentist said it was because of envy — by Evans's easy access to the previous imperial government officials. Among Washburne's successors, Levi Parsons Morton has been described as "no friend of Evans," though he was successful with the French because he overlooked the various contretemps that had arisen between the two countries over the years and wisely clung in his public utterances to such safe topics as Yorktown, La Fayette, and Bartholdi's statue. Robert M. McLane, who followed Morton as Envoy Extraordinary and Minister Plenipotentiary — to give the full, formal title of a minister heading a legation — once wrote an angry letter, definitely not a thank-you note, after dining with Evans, because he thought he should have been seated in the place of honor on the right hand of his host, where Blaine sat, instead of the left side. As the representative of the United States government, he felt he had been "insulted." It did not help matters that Dr. Evans entertained in a luxurious setting, whereas the modest American Legation was housed in two third-story rooms over a grocer's shop and was reached by steep stairs; or that the doctor assumed he occupied a permanent, not a temporary, position of leadership in the American colony; or a tendency on the part of the dentist to drop famous names.

Perhaps it would be fair to say the social leadership was divided. When former President Grant visited Paris in October 1877 on his trip around the world, he was received as a figure of international importance, though he came as a private person. General Edward Follansbee Noyes, the American minister at the time, who had left a leg in Georgia, and leading members of the American colony greeted General Grant and his party at the railroad depot when they reached Paris. The visitors saw the sights, scaled Montmartre, inspected the Latin Quarter, looked down the Champs-Elysées to the vista of the Concorde, the blackened, scorched remains of the Tuileries, the massive buildings of the Louvre, and the façade of Notre-Dame. Noyes gave a brilliant dinner at his residence in the Avenue Joséphine, as did Evans at Bella Rosa, and a member of the Grant party, surveying the Paris scene, commented, "The American dentist becomes an institution almost royal in its relations and appliances."[20] At a ball given by Evans's artist friend G. P. A. Healy, Mrs. Julia Ward Howe, author of "The Battle Hymn of the Republic," danced a quadrille with General Grant, M. Gambetta, and Mrs. Healy, and particularly noticed Mrs. Evans, then a tall, aristocratic-looking woman of gracious presence who wore in her white hair a diamond necklace "said to have been given to her by the Empress."[21]

The doctor enjoyed a relationship of some intimacy with Grant, for he told his nephew Theodore that he "felt from what the General . . . told me that he was in danger of being drawn into speculation" and warned him that "retired military men have too many advisers."[22] Evans's cautionary remark, had it been heeded, would have spared General Grant bankruptcy and public humiliation a few years later. An editor of *Le Figaro* recounted how "an amiable

and intelligent American, Dr. Evans, who is known to the whole
of Paris," coached him on how to approach Grant for an interview:

> You are going to see General Grant. He will certainly
> be glad to receive an editor of the *Figaro*, but do not
> expect to make him talk . . . I will tell you the best
> means of opening his mouth. Search Paris through, if
> necessary, for two of the very best cigars to be had; put
> them in your pocket; and when you find yourself in the
> presence of the General, and when he has shaken hands
> with you, according to the American custom, you will
> draw the cigars from your pocket, and say "General, I
> know that you are a connoisseur of cigars; permit me to
> offer you some of the best to be had in Paris." The Gen-
> eral will examine your cigars, and if he finds them of an
> absolutely superior quality, you will put him in a fine
> humor, his tongue will wag as if by enchantment upon
> everything, politics excepted.[23]

No doubt Dr. Evans may sometimes have been a bit of a bore
as he retold and perhaps embellished the dramatic story of the
Empress's escape, for he never applied to himself the wisdom of
the successful concert musician — always play one less encore than
the audience wants. He knew what had happened to Louis XVI
and Marie Antoinette, and that "where Count Ferson had failed,"
as an article in the *American Legion of Honor* magazine pointed
out, "he, Thomas Evans, American dentist, had succeeded." The
rôle of raconteur grew on him with the passing years. The doctor
was a fast eater, up on his feet as soon as Agnes Evans folded her
napkin, saying, "Gentlemen, let us withdraw to have a smoke in
the library." There, seated on a sofa, left leg curled under him,
he told the story of his success or his impressions of an illustrious
patient, his face animated, drawing on his cigar like a boy, a long
pull, then a short puff. He spoke of how a Russian grand duke
came to see his pets and stroll in the garden; of how he had known
and treated two Sultans; of the large punch bowl given him by
the Prince of Wales, which he kept in the buffet of the dining
room, "for as you know I never drink, outside of wine at meals."[24]
When official delegations came to Paris, such as the American

commissioners to the Paris exposition held in 1878, they were entertained at Bella Rosa. A large dinner party given by Dr. Evans for the Americans who were in Europe as representatives on the Geneva Tribunal, for settling claims against Great Britain for British-built Confederate raiders, was marked by an incident that everybody in Paris heard of at the time and that became part of the *ana* of the Geneva experience. It appears the doctor spoke at such length about the intimate remarks made to him by this or that royal personage, that William B. Evarts, who served as counsel in the Geneva arbitration, thought the dentist was unduly monopolizing the conversation. "Leaning forward," wrote Frank W. Hackett, then private secretary to Caleb Cushing, another American counselor, "in that smiling, half-quizzical manner that betrayed his own keen enjoyment of the bright saying that was about to be uttered, Mr. Evarts remarked: 'Well, Doctor, we certainly owe you a debt of gratitude. For us it is a great thing even to see a king or prince; but it seems that they all have opened their mouths to you.' "[25]

Dr. Evans had literary aspirations but no facility as a writer; "he told me so," Labouchere wrote after the doctor's death, "the last time I saw him."[26] He could, however, become a publisher, and added another facet to his career when he founded the first American newspaper to be published at Paris, the *American Register,* a weekly that first appeared in 1868. It was edited and largely written by Dr. Crane at 12 Rue d'Antin "to facilitate the intercourse between Americans on the continent," and told of "their movements throughout Europe."[27] For example: Parke Godwin of New York and Edward Pepper of Philadelphia are in Paris. Charles A. Dana, the brilliant editor of the *New York Sun,* is in Florence, staying at the Casa Guidi. The paper published book and theater reviews and art notes from both sides of the Atlantic. News from America included ship news, and such cultural and business items as a farewell dinner for Charles Dickens at Delmonico's restaurant in New York and a wreck on the Erie Railroad. Advertisements reflected the interests of tourist readers — hotels, dressmakers, laces and ribbons, banking houses, jewelers and perfumers, notices of where to find champagne.[28] Dr. Evans sometimes contributed a column called "Paris Local." It consisted of personal items about notables he knew, especially the remnants of Bonapartist society, including such names as General Fleury, Prince Joachim Murat, Princess Mathilde, the Empress Eugénie and the Prince Impérial. But in the articles about his noble clients he was always the soul of discretion.

Occasionally Evans's name appeared in the paper, as when a dinner was offered at the banquet hall of the Hotel Continental to the actors of the Comédie-Française when they performed *Hamlet*. McLane, the American minister who had had the sulks after a dinner at Evans's residence, presided and handled the oratory. The guest list included Dr. Evans; his friends Stéphane Mallarmé and Healy; United States Senator Eugene Hale of Maine; a Roosevelt; and Nathan Appleton, wealthy Boston textile manufacturer and merchant, whose son Tom encouraged Bostonians to be virtuous because "all good Americans when they die go to Paris."[29] The *Register* broke even financially but lost ground after 1887 to an aggressive daily competitor, when James Gordon Bennett, Jr., launched the Paris edition of the *New York Herald,* universally known as the *"Paris-Herald"* or more colloquially as *"le New York."* It had been started in 1887 by Bennett as his very personal toy, and became the bitter rival of Dr. Evans's journal, matching the *American Register* in its respectful attention to princes, monarchs, or visiting Vanderbilts, passing along titillating oddments about the famous or notorious, together with practical travel information useful, say, to a grain elevator operator from Iowa.

To dentistry, philanthropy, and journalism, Dr. Evans added another dimension to his participation in the life of Paris — the church. As a boy he had attended the Sunday school of the Mantua, later Northminster, Presbyterian Church at Baring and 35th streets in Philadelphia. In Paris he saw the growth and future importance of the American colony and became the leading layman of a union church representing all shades of evangelical Protestantism, the oldest nongovernmental American organization in Europe. In 1850 he had taken an option on a Church of England chapel, but the English members opposed the sale. Queen Victoria was quite displeased by the idea and asked the British ambassador, Lord Cowley, to intervene, so the offer was withdrawn. Aware of population trends and advancing real estate values, Dr. Evans persisted, kept looking, and finally chose 21 Rue de Berri, just off the Champs-

Elysées, quite far west at the time. The doctor helped raise the money for the building, and held the first meeting of the executive committee at his home. The church was built in 1857 and dedicated on May 2, 1858. It flourished for years at that location. The site was later the setting for the bright doings of the staff of the *Paris Herald*.

After returning to Paris in 1871, the Evanses moved up, or over, to a new liturgical church with a wealthy congregation, the fast-growing American Protestant Church of the Holy Trinity. The doctor again made available his expertise in real estate matters by finding a suitable location for expansion, at a bargain price, in the Avenue de l'Alma. And he demonstrated the sincerity of his conversion to the Thirty-Nine Articles and the governance of bishops by purchasing bonds to help finance a costly edifice in the English Gothic style.[30]

Although in the years of the Third Republic Dr. Evans's kingly patients sometimes came to his office, as the Queen of Spain did in 1885, simply announcing the day and hour of their arrival and having no fears of waiting because of overbooking, it was more common for him to make regular visits to the royals. One can see in imagination the bustling doctor, handsome, mannerly, kindly of countenance, self-respecting yet respectful, his figure thickening, though he was still full of vitality, lugging his foot-powered dental engine and trunk filled with the other tools of his profession — forceps, ivory-handled excavators, articulators and extraction keys, pluggers, foil carriers, mouth mirrors, inhalers for nitrous oxide, and dentifrice powder of his own prescription. These swings around Europe took Evans to most of the northern courts and to Belgium, whose King Leopold II regretted, in a letter, that he had been forced several times since Dr. Evans's last visit to turn to a local dentist. Even a king, one notes, felt it necessary to offer Evans an explanation. In closing he expressed the hope "that you & your Family are quite well and that we shall soon have the pleasure of seeing you this May again." There was always a stop to see the Empress Augusta of Germany, who once remarked that she didn't want to be a queen, but that Evans wanted to be exactly what he was.[31]

The German Empress depended on Dr. Evans for medical advice that went beyond his own specialty. Once, when she was about to have a serious surgical operation, Augusta insisted that the dentist be called in to "hear all they had to say in regard to the necessity of the operation and the chances of her getting over it for it was a question of life or death . . . I came from Paris to Baden Baden" — this is Evans himself speaking. He advised that she have the operation. On the day before the surgery the Empress gave Dr. Evans a ring with a large cabochon emerald, the emblem of hope. *Espérance* was the word she used. The Empress did recover, and her first words were "Inform Dr. Evans — all is right. I feel sure he wore the ring." He did, but noticed in Augusta, whose intelligence he always praised, "a slight feeling of superstition."[32]

A striking instance of service to the German royal family on the part of Dr. Evans occurred early in 1888, when Crown Prince Frederick, heir to the throne of Germany, was at San Remo on the Italian Riviera, suffering from cancer of the throat. He could no longer speak, and had to write on a slate to make himself understood. Dr. Evans was present, at the insistence of the family, simply as a supportive friend, to observe the treatment being followed by Sir Morell Mackenzie, the leading London throat doctor, to smooth out medical disputes, which took on a nationalistic edge, between Mackenzie and the German doctors, and to report privately to the Empress Augusta and Frederick's wife, the Crown Princess Victoria. When the Crown Prince was about to strangle, a tracheotomy was decided on. After the operation, a cannula, or metal tube to facilitate breathing, was required, but there was no one in the little Italian village capable of fashioning such a tube — except Dr. Evans.

"I walked down with him to a little jeweler's office in San Remo and saw him put on his workman's apron and begin with a blowpipe and a hammer upon a five-franc piece," wrote T. C. Crawford, whose account was read and confirmed by Evans. "He worked there all night," Crawford continued, "and the next morning a beautifully made silver tube was ready and the life of the Prince was prolonged, where suffocation would probably have set in in the next twenty-four hours." The Prince, under the title of Frederick III, succeeded to the throne on the death of his father, William I, but lived to rule only ninety-nine days. When the Empress Augusta died, her daughter, the Grand Duchess Louise of Baden, told the dentist that among her mother's last words were "Has Dr. Evans arrived . . . ?"[33]

Often Dr. Evans returned from his swing around Europe with unusual gifts from his patients. Augusta prepared for him an elegant book of royal autographs, explaining that she had made the gift because he hadn't asked for it, and on her death she left him a portrait of herself. Another expression of esteem came from Russia and was observed and recorded by young Frederick Van Wyck, a scion of the old New York aristocracy. He visited Paris in 1874 and was welcomed warmly by Dr. Evans, who declared that "the fresh young Americans kept him in trim for his work at the chair." The doctor had just returned to Paris after taking care of the Czar Alexander II and his family. The Czar had presented him with a beautiful pair of black Russian Orloff stallions, with flowing manes and tails that almost reached the ground. They were a magnificent sight, and the doctor said:

> "Fred, it's too bad we cannot have them out on the Champs-Elysées tomorrow, Grand Prix Day, because my coachman is afraid to drive them." With the assurance of one and twenty I said, "I'll drive them!"
>
> So the following day, after we had been to the races . . . the stallions were harnessed to the Russian drosky with all its Russian trappings. These included the ornamental yoke which arched over the horse's neck between the shafts. The other stallion was attached only by the inside trace to the drosky, thus giving him freedom to prance and caper to his heart's content . . . When we turned into the Champs-Elysées, the stallions gave their call of announcement . . . They screamed to their mates in Paris that they had arrived.[34]

The story of this exciting drive and an amorous adventure that followed appears in the next chapter.

Remaining always an "enthusiastic American," Dr. Evans had the satisfaction of receiving recognition from his native land. Quite early in his career the Baltimore College of Dentistry conferred on him the honorary degree of Doctor of Dental Surgery (1850), as did, soon afterward, the Philadelphia College of Dental Surgeons (1853). In 1870 the Board of Directors of Lafayette College, at Easton, Pennsylvania, after prayer, bestowed the honorary degree of Doctor of Philosophy on the Paris dentist. Subsequently — it does not appear to have been a *quid pro quo* — Dr. Evans presented to the college a copy by Healy of a full-length portrait by the French artist Ary Scheffer of La Fayette at his château La Grange. In making the gift Evans said he "wished to express my interest in the cause of liberal education in my native state." The board gratefully accepted the picture and, after exhibiting it in New York and at Earle's galleries in Philadelphia, hung it in one of the halls of the college. It may still be seen at the top of the stairs leading to the second floor of Kirby Hall of Civil Rights.[35]

About the time of this exchange of amenities honoring the doctor's professional achievements and the cause of liberal education in Pennsylvania, Dr. Evans tangled romantically with a beautiful and elegant *originaire* of Nancy, recently arrived in Paris, who rose not out of the foam of the sea, like Aphrodite, but jumped in her splendid altogether from an enormous silver-mounted seashell in an apotheosis of fairies at the theater of Le Châtelet.[36]

13

"Handsome Tom": A Doctor's Fling at Gallantry

No one knows now precisely when Dr. Evans met Marie Laurent, the vivacious and delicious blond Venus of the Gaieté, the Variétés, Le Châtelet, and the smart cafés where gold was turned into champagne. Perhaps it was during those heady days, and nights, when the fading Second Empire was caught up in that frenzy of pleasure-seeking which announces the end of régimes. To the censorious, Paris was "a gas-lit Gomorrah." A friendlier observer, Comte Emile Félix Fleury, could say in recollection, "It was not exactly a proper empire, but we did have a damn good time."[1] An ambitious and well-endowed girl could début at the Variétés and have her own carriage by the end of the month, lose all at the gaming tables, recoup by writing her spicy memoirs, and go once again from a dinner of five sous' worth of Italian cheese to a rendezvous with a prince at the Grand Seize, the very private room at the restaurant Anglais, all done with style and insouciance.[2]

Robert Goffin, the poet and critic whose researches regarding Dr. Evans and Marie Laurent grew out of his studies of their friend Stéphane Mallarmé, the Symbolist poet, concluded that Evans met and was captivated by the beautiful young actress, who loved life, laughter, and luxury, in the spring of 1872, when she had a walk-on part in Offenbach's operetta *Le Roi Carotte,* a smashing success under the Third Republic. One night she received a gorgeous basket of white roses with the card of Thomas W. Evans, dentist, who was waiting at the stage door. He carried her off into the warm April night in a handsome carriage, he a whiskered fiftyish gentleman with courtly manners, to see a show and later sip champagne in a cabaret. The next year Marie appeared in a grand blaze of gaslight at the Châtelet theater. The dancers parted, and Marie made her spectacular nude leap out of the silver shell.[3]

The extent to which Dr. Evans was a habitué of the green room is not known. It is not a subject on which a cautious man would be loquacious. At any rate, about this time Marie accepted the offer Evans made of a luxurious apartment at 52 Rue de Rome, within easy walking distance of the doctor's office. There, Evans visited Marie, or Méry, as he Anglicized her name, every day at lunchtime. Méry was not prospering on the stage; acting was not her métier. She was seen in *Les Braconniers (The Poachers)* at the Variétés, and enjoyed a passing notoriety for her performance at Le Châtelet. It is not as a lightly equipped actress, then, that Méry is remembered, but as an alluring woman who early mastered the ABCs of gallantry, as the admired *amie* of artists and writers, the favorite model of Edouard Manet, and as a fastidious demimondaine, something of a queen among the modistes who dressed her, and finally as the official mistress of the most famous dentist in Europe.

Mlle. Laurent was born on April 29, 1849, at Nancy. Her name was recorded at the mairie as Anne Rose Suzanne Louviot, her mother described euphemistically in the register as being "without profession." The father was unknown, though he may have been *"un certain Lapierre,"* who remembered Anne Rose in his will. The child's manners were carefully supervised, and her education was above that of young girls of her day. She studied singing and diction, and soon after her first communion little Anne Rose was performing creditably on her mother's rosewood piano. She was precocious in other ways, too, and at fourteen her reddish-blond beauty attracted the eye of Marshal Certain Canrobert, then governor of Nancy, a good fellow, brave officer, and something of a lady-killer. Shortly afterward, a marriage was hastily arranged with a young grocer named Laurent, who needed money and received a considerable dowry along with the hand of a very pretty girl.

But young Madame did not remain long behind her counter with her spices, her jars, her casks of prunes, and her pickle barrel. The marriage did not last. Neither did the shop. The wife demanded a judgment of separation with a division of goods and abandoned her grocer and the ennuis of life in the provinces. At sixteen, with some furniture and part of her dowry, she advanced on Paris to become successively Marie of the theater and Méry of the bohemian world. So by her early twenties Méry had been a grocer's clerk, had known intimately a general of the Empire and the dentist of the Empress, had entered the life of the Left Bank, and inspired in succession or simultaneously such creative talents of the Third Republic as Stéphane Mallarmé, Edouard Manet, François Coppée, Théodore de Banville, Edouard Dujardin, Philippe Auguste de Villiers de l'Isle-Adam, and several others.[4]

There were in Paris about a hundred courtesans who stood, or reclined, at the top of their profession; they were the *lionnes* of the period. Notable within this caste was Anna Deslions, who looked like an Italian choir boy but threw velvet glances "like warm caresses" and made wise investments; Adèle Courtois, who set fashions in clothes and conversation and when full of years received only ecclesiastics at dinner; Marguerite Bellanger, who had the smallest feet in Paris and once gave Napoleon III a picture of a naked woman tempting St. Anthony; Alphonsine Duplessis, who wore a camellia in her hair and inspired Dumas to write *La Dame aux Camélias* and Verdi to compose *La Traviata;* and the Marquise de Paîva, who, when it became prudent for her to leave France quickly, carried off as a souvenir a necklace that the Empress Eugénie had worn at the great balls in the Tuileries. First among equals was perhaps Cora Pearl, an English odalisque who once had been Prince Napoleon's exclusive property and later bestowed on her lovers, as a special privilege, the right to wear Prince Napoleon's nightshirt during a nocturnal tryst.[5]

When Frederick Van Wyck, the young sophisticate from New York mentioned in the previous chapter, who had seen his first stag show in Greenwich Village at the age of seventeen, put Dr. Evans's stallions through their paces on the Champs-Elysées, Cora Pearl passed the Evans turnout three times in her victoria with coachman and footman on the box. The first time she raised her eyebrows. The next time she smiled. The third time she smiled again and gave three little nods.

"Fred," said Dr. Evans, "I see your finish."

"No," the sapient youth replied. "She has no lure for me. We will have a quiet dinner, go to a show and then to the Mabille where the girls can kick our hats off dancing the can-can!"

At the Jardin Mabille, Van Wyck picked up a beautiful woman wearing widow's weeds and sitting with her maid.

"Doc, that one's for me!"

"You're crazy! She's the mistress of Count X!"

The next time Dr. Evans saw his enterprising young friend, and heard the details of his adventure, was at Bella Rosa when he was eating breakfast. "I was trying to decide," the doctor remarked amiably, "whether to look for you at the morgue or the police station." The dentist, too, was a man of the world.[6]

Méry Laurent was one of the select company of *grandes hori-zontales* who have been referred to. She was tall, with an exquisite tea-rose complexion, blue eyes, and fair hair with hints of red, a laughing beauty with arched eyebrows and a wide-eyed gaze that gave her a bewitching expression of surprise. Her mouth was sensual, her bosom formidable, and she excited artists, especially Manet, through whom Méry as model achieved the recognition denied her in the theater. There were a number of highly placed admirers, including Prince Metternich, but before she was vulgarized, Méry escaped to a stable, orderly, almost bourgeois relationship with Dr. Evans. It lasted for three decades. The doctor was generous. He provided his elegant conquest with a monthly allowance of five thousand francs, later raised to ten thousand, which hardly supports the proposition that sin does not pay.

In addition to the apartment and its amenities, Evans provided a second home, the Villa des Talus, an agreeable cottage at 9 Boule-vard Lannes, then an unspoiled country setting opposite the turfed slopes of the fortifications. To this pleasant retreat Mallarmé once sent a letter with the address in the form of a quatrain:

> *A Mademoiselle Méry*
> *Laurent qui vit loin des profanes*
> *En sa maisonette* very
> Select *du neuf boulevard Lannes.*

To Mademoiselle Méry
Laurent who lives far from the vulgar
In her cottage *very*
Select at 9 Boulevard Lannes.

To the eternal honor of the postal service of France, the letter was delivered. The English words "very select" serve as reminder that the author of *L'Après-midi d'un faun,* which suggested Debussy's musical interpretation, earned his living as a teacher of English. It is a fair assumption that clever Méry, so closely associated with an American, was also English-speaking.[7]

The villa, which was not far from Bella Rosa, had small rooms and a low ceiling. It was furnished with pleasant rustic furniture covered in flowered cretonne, curtains of Turkey-red cotton or flowered chintz at the windows, and on the wall Manet's portrait of Méry with the toque she used to wear, perhaps the very same one that appears in *A Bar at the Folies-Bergère.* Outside there were climbing vines at the windows, a charming little garden where the hostess and her friends walked in the evening, and lilacs blooming in the dooryard. It was at this countrified little house that Marcel Proust first encountered Whistler.

Méry Laurent appreciated good conversation and good cooking, and her faithful *femme de chambre,* Eliza Sosset, also from Nancy, provided a table that was a glory of French cuisine. Men of letters, novelists and poets, painters and sculptors, soon gathered in Méry's salon; to some of them, wrote Henri Perruchot, biographer of Manet, "she was prepared to give the quasi-marital favours she sold Evans at so high a price."[8] Everything worked well. The wealthy and generous doctor was busy with his dental office and his rich clientele, his aviary and his horses, and made no difficulty about Méry's leisure hours.

As to Dr. Evans's side of the arrangement, the possession of a beauteous and welcoming mistress who could make him the friend or the acquaintance of artists of stature was simply a part of the good life for an ambitious man of talent. Proudly the doctor urged his steppers into a brisk trot around the lakes of the Bois, with the handsome Méry seated beside him in a sumptuous toilette, knowing that she was as elegant, as coquette, as well turned out, as such expensive enchantresses as Caroline Tessier or Blanche d'Antigny.[9]

It was a way of life led by many of Dr. Evans's noble clients. With his regular features, well-tended whiskers worn à la Jockey Club, and suave personal charm, the former court dentist was a gallant not immune to the attractions of gay, decorative, and broad-minded ladies, despite solid evidence that he was devoted to Mrs. Evans and that she was unstinting in her admiration of her celebrated husband. There is a problem of social mores here that some wiser writer will have to elucidate.[10] But perhaps there is a slight nuance to be recognized in a beautiful, dressy, high-spirited mistress such as Méry being looked on favorably in the doctor's circle as a status symbol. The opinion of men of fashion on this point would weigh heavily with the dentist.

Evans was away from home a good deal in the course of his professional life. Did Agnes Evans think he was caring for royal Hohenzollern or imperial Romanoff bicuspids when he was attending the revels at the Anglais with "Bertie," the Prince of Wales, or when he was taking the cure at Royat, the pleasant spa in the Auvergne, with Méry and their guest Stéphane Mallarmé?[11] We do not know whether there was deceit or accommodation. Dr. Evans's *Memoirs* do not help us to understand. If there were tiresome, lonely hours at Bella Rosa as Mrs. Evans sat in her spacious salon done in red silk, she could at least turn for consolation to her piano or look at the doctor's array of foreign decorations on display in their rosewood cases.

In her own inconstant way Méry Laurent was very much attached to the doctor. She was kindly by nature and grateful for the stability of their relationship and the bourgeois comfort he provided. But she could be flighty and could yield to temptation. Something of a wit herself, Méry once remarked that to leave Dr. Evans "would be a wicked thing to do. I content myself with deceiving him."[12]

It was a shock to Evans when he discovered her transgressions, but he became surprisingly tolerant. Henri Mondor, a leading student of the life and oeuvre of Mallarmé, described the relationship between the dentist and the model as a "munificent attachment which was complicated neither by authoritarianism nor sullen jealousy."[13]

Laurent's superb talent for handling men appears to advantage in an anecdote that was told by George Moore, the Irish-British author who was admitted to Méry's circle. Wishing to be free of

Evans after dinner, the lady pleaded a migraine headache, oldest of feminine stratagems. As soon as the doctor had departed, she threw off the dressing gown that hid her ball dress and signaled to Manet, who was waiting at the street corner, perhaps to take her, as he often did, to an intimate supper at Tortoni's or the Café Madrid. But as the couple descended, whom should they meet on the staircase but the dentist, who had forgotten his appointment book! Dr. Evans was very angry, but it took his wayward mistress only three or four days to coax him out of the sulks.[14]

The apartment in which Méry received those who enjoyed her friendship, platonic or otherwise, was overstuffed with bric-a-brac, house plants, stools and gilded consoles, Oriental rugs, puffs and cushions, beads and trimmings and tapestries. Heavy folds of draperies framed doors and windows. Walls were densely hung with ornately framed paintings. A rosewood piano reflected satyrs painted on the ceiling that seemed to wink at Méry. The bedroom was furnished with a profusion of mirrors and a majestic bed ornamented with braid trimmings. The total effect was monied and heavy. But the same could be said of the private apartments of the Empress Eugénie and other tastemakers. Expensive clutter expressed the materialism of the times.

Dr. Evans was attracted to Méry Laurent's circle, and his *chère amie* paid him in good coin by introducing him to her bohemian friends, whom she received at her "Tuesdays" in the winter when she was in town and in summer at the cottage near the Bois. Among them, in addition to those already mentioned who dined at Méry's table, were Henri Becque of the theater; Catulle Mendès, also a playwright; J.-K. Huysmans the novelist; Henri Dupray, who painted a picture of the escape of the Empress; Henri Gervex, friend of Renoir and Monet, who exhibited portraits of both Méry and Dr. Evans at the Salon in 1892; James McNeill Whistler, the influential and sharp-tongued American painter and etcher; and George Moore, who, noting that Laurent was at one time or another the mistress of so many distinguished men in the creative arts, called her *toute la lyre*.[15] Méry's entertainments were marked by laughter and fun, light gossip and serious talk, and genuine, uncomplicated affection. There was in her a gentle skill for decelerating grand passions, and she offered generous support when the bright days were over. For instance, when Villiers de L'Isle-Adam, the novelist and playwright, fell ill and was dying in abject poverty, Méry Laurent saw to getting a good doctor without fee, the distinguished professor Edouard Charles Albert Robin, Legionnaire and member of the Academy of Medicine. She sent Villiers fruit, wine, a pigeon, and shared to the end the anxieties and grief of Mallarmé and Huysmans. And after Manet died, each spring she took the first lilacs to lay upon his grave in the little cemetery at Passy.

Under the guidance of Méry Laurent, Dr. Evans developed contacts. He came to know Mallarmé well and served his family professionally; he also made the acquaintance of Whistler. His position as proprietor of a newspaper helped. When Whistler published a scorching letter in the London journal *Truth*, accusing Oscar Wilde of plagiarism, Whistler asked Mallarmé to have it inserted in Dr. Evans's *American Register*. It appeared under the heading "Mr. Whistler's Latest Scalp," and Evans in turn inquired where he could buy a copy of Whistler's *The Gentle Art of Making Enemies*, which Mallarmé also asked him without hesitation to have reviewed in the *Register*. Since it is beyond dispute that Mallarmé was passionately in love with Méry Laurent, though whether the love was ever consummated involves questions that can never be resolved, it is worth noticing that the poet felt at ease in asking favors of Dr. Evans; and when Evans's brother and professional associate, Dr. Theodore Sewell Evans, died, Mallarmé wrote to Dr. Tom a warm letter of condolence. Whistler's requests for publicity were frequent; he often asked Mallarmé to have some item, letter, or clipping printed in the doctor's newspaper, sometimes with a punning "aside" in his covering letter addressed to "Mistress Mary." What he wished to be done was usually done promptly. Evans — Méry — Manet — Mallarmé — and Whistler. One gets the feeling almost of a minuet, though the doctor once vexed his friends by bargaining somewhat too sharply over some Whistler etchings.[16] But that is often the disposition of men who are very rich.

Beyond contributing to dental journals, and collecting loosely his recollections of Napoleon III, Eugénie, and the spacious days of the Empire, Dr. Evans ventured only once into a literary effort. He obtained the rights to the English version of some autobiographical writings of Heinrich Heine and published them with a long, rambling introductory essay on the Francophile German poet who called Paris "my beautiful and kind Lutetia." There has been some speculation that the doctor employed Mallarmé to write the introduction that Evans signed. This seems questionable on two grounds. The French scholar praised the introduction extravagantly, calling it a "subtle aesthetic piece of analysis," which scarcely fits with his having written the piece himself.[17] And he would have written it better.

It was inevitable that Dr. Evans would become a collector of art. He built up a collection of some hundred and thirty canvases, and his taste improved as the collection grew, covering completely, as was the style of hanging then in vogue, the walls of his residence and office, frame to frame. The doctor began with anecdotal subjects, such as *A Bone Is Stuck in His Throat,* or, most suitably, *A Visit to the Dentist,* or a river scene that could have been his native Schuylkill. It is true that the doctor had his dog painted and that he liked pastoral treatments of sheep and cows, but condescension toward Evans's preference in domestic animals hardly becomes us, since we today applaud Jamie Wyeth's pigs.

When the doctor acquired a Caneletto and a Meissonier, one cannot determine now whether they reflected his considered taste or were esteemed by him as a proof of wealth. He did, whatever the case, come to own three Corots, a Jan Steen, a Teniers, and many paintings following various masters in a style described as "copy of" or "school of." Under the intuitive guidance of Méry Laurent, Evans came to appreciate Whistler, and he purchased several Manets, two of them long lost to view but authenticated in the 1970s, both still-life paintings of engaging charm.[18] Their acquisition by a collector who once would have been content with a chromolithograph of Niagara Falls is a reminder of personal growth in Evans, and of the intricate overlapping social circles of the wealthy dentist and the Impressionist artist through the person near to both, the remarkable Méry Laurent.

The blond mistress, the social intercourse with celebrated and gifted men, the role of publisher and patron of art, rounded out for the beribboned doctor his lifetime aspiration to be recognized by royalty, whether of blood or of talent.

14

The Tragic Empress

PAULINE DE METTERNICH had smuggled most of Eugénie's jewels out of France and returned them to her friend, together with the offer of a temporary loan. In addition, the Empress owned the Villa Eugénia at Biarritz and had considerable property in Spain. The real estate and the sale of the jewels placed Eugénie in a position of "liberal comfort." After Marshal Marie Edme Patrice MacMahon, also the Duc de Magenta, a soldier by profession, a royalist in sentiment, assumed the presidency of the Republic in 1873, he returned a great deal of the Empress's private property, including rental property in Paris, and the priceless gold reliquary containing Charlemagne's fragment of the True Cross.[1]

At a later time, after she had left Camden Place for a new home at Farnborough, it was believed that, thanks to more property inherited from her husband, to good financial judgment on the part of her London bankers, and to a turn she herself had for mathematics, the Empress Eugénie could touch about twenty-five thousand pounds a year.[2] At the time of the fall of the Empire, it was rumored that the imperial family had a large fortune carefully removed from France, including well-chosen investments in New York real estate, made under the guidance of Dr. Evans. His astuteness as an investor and his close connection with the imperial family lent a degree of plausibility to this idea, but the doctor firmly denied all such surmises and pointed to Eugénie's diamonds as the basis for the family's moderate-sized fortune.[3] So once again in history, diamonds proved to be the ideal asset for those who may require a sudden change of venue.

A small court of faithful Bonapartists gathered around Eugénie, some of whom she supported. The Duc de Bassano acted as high chamberlain, and when the maître d'hôtel announced dinner at seven, Bassano offered his arm to the former sovereign as her little retinue fell into place to maintain a shadow of the formalities of the past. The Duc de Mouchy and his beautiful duchesse, the former Anna Murat, were there, the Conneaus, faithful Francheschini Piétri, Eugénie's private secretary, and Augustin Filon, tutor to the Prince Impérial. Dr. Evans was a frequent guest, especially after Napoleon III returned from Germany.

Determined to share the fate of the French army, Napoleon had refused offers of liberation until the Germans set free the French prisoners of war. He was released in March 1871, landed at Dover, and proceeded to Camden Place. In their common misfortune, the causes of the estrangement between Louis Napoleon and Eugénie disappeared and the couple were reconciled. Each had something to forgive, and their hopes came together in the future of Louis, the young prince. The family lived quietly. Napoleon occupied himself with educating his son to be Napoleon IV. Dr. Evans remembered often finding the Emperor seated at his desk in a small room off his bedchamber, surrounded by books, maps, papers, and documents, just as he had encountered him in his study at the Tuileries. Louis Napoleon spoke with Evans of his humiliation over French social discord, of the violence of the Commune, carried on by Frenchmen in the presence of the German army of occupation, and he discussed without rancor his political opponents, some of whom, he said, had principles, and some of whom had none.[4]

After dinner the men went to the billiard- or the smoking room, the ladies did needlework, and the young people gathered around the grand piano in the hall. Dr. Conneau and the Duc de Bassano played cards while Napoleon sat in a big armchair near the fireplace, wrapped in cigarette smoke and his thoughts. Sometimes after lunch the dining room was transformed into a fencing gallery, or the three o'clock train from London brought friends. One day Mme. Nilsson sang, and Sir Arthur Sullivan improvised on the piano; in fair weather tea was served on the lawn. There were occasional holidays, for a change of scene, at Torquay, Brighton, or Cowes. But sometimes the monotony, the daily pacing up and down the gallery, the life of an exile in an island kingdom notable for its fogs, grave statesmen, constitutional government, and the homely virtues of a strong middle class, made the once-gay Empress recall vividly the last painting she had noticed as she escaped through the Louvre. "This is the raft of the *Méduse*," Eugénie commented. "Every now and then we feel like eating one another."[5]

Hopes rose briefly for a restoration of the Empire, based on the belief that France, shocked and destabilized by revolution and anarchy, would turn away from republicanism. Napoleon counted on a revival of personal sympathy and declared, "I am the only solution," as he bent over his charts, received encouraging messages from abroad, and tested his ability to ride, since it was obligatory for a savior to arrive on a horse. A "return from Elba" was in the air, but two developments intervened.[6] The Republic, a form of government that M. Thiers declared "divides Frenchmen least," grew stronger, and Napoleon's health became critical because of the concretion in his bladder.

Once more Dr. Evans was called in, as he had been at San Remo when the Crown Prince Frederick was about to strangle, to consult on a medical problem far removed from his own specialty, further evidence of the extraordinary confidence his patients and friends felt in his balance and judgment. Evans advised on the choice of a surgeon to undertake the preliminary examination, and managed the necessary arrangements. Several operations to crush the stone were undertaken, but after initial successes the Emperor fell into delirium and died on the morning of January 9, 1873. Dr. Evans describes the illness and death in his *Memoirs* and was present at the funeral.

What, one wonders, may have passed through the disordered mind of Louis Napoleon as he sank toward his end? The years in prison and exile? His sudden rise to head the French nation? The shouts and tumult when he made his triumphal tour of the south of France? His ardent courtship of the beautiful, elusive Eugénie? The Queen of England bending to fix the Order of the Garter to his knee? Hearing Mrs. Moulton sing the Agnus Dei at High Mass in the court chapel? The assignation at Compiègne with the goddess of love, Virginia Castiglione, in her cambric and lace nightgown?

Or such solid accomplishments of his reign as the completion of the rail network, the beautifying of Paris, the industrialization of France?[7]

No, none of these, judging by his last, faintly uttered words, dimmed by chloral. They were whispered to his faithful friend, Dr. Henri Conneau: *"N'est-ce pas, Conneau, que nous n'avons pas été des lâches à Sedan?"* ("Isn't it true, Conneau, that we weren't cowards at Sedan?")[8] Sedan, Sedan; his life was haunted by the memory of the defeat and the harsh reproaches that followed him to his grave. Eugénie and the Prince Impérial knelt at the bedside, she prostrated with grief, he reciting in a strong voice the Pater Noster.

Louis Napoleon was buried across the common in Chislehurst at the Church of St. Mary's, which Queen Victoria described in her journal as "a pretty, rural little place, quite like a village church." The body was laid out in the undress uniform of a French General of Division, with the broad, red Grand Cordon of the Legion, the Star of a Grand Officer, the Military Medal, and the Italy Medal, a sword by his side. Immediately behind the members of the imperial family in the funeral procession a man wept as he looked at the coffin covered with purple velours and imperial violets. The man was Evans. The Queen of England, too, sincerely mourned the passing of a faithful ally, and the London press was respectful. The will was political in that it enjoined the Prince Impérial to preserve the memory and protect the tradition of "the Emperor, my uncle," and expressed the hope "that after I am dead she [Eugénie] will forget whatever sorrow I may have caused her," which is as close as Napoleon III could come to an apology for his offenses against their marriage.[9]

The Empress forgave. But the French people could never bring themselves to pardon Louis Napoleon and his Empire. Failure, as Eugénie once remarked, is never forgiven in France. The Third Republic, so durable by French standards, largely determined how we see the Second Empire and its leading figures, for history is written by the victors. Napoleon III was not an evil man, but when ambition called, virtue hesitated. Mme. Hortense Cornu, the only woman who ever loved Louis Napoleon as a sister, put it this way: conscience never caused difficulties for the Bonapartes. Jean Baptiste Carpeaux, the French sculptor, carved a marble bust of the Emperor that presents a powerful psychological characterization, showing "the troubled inwardness of a man whose goals were thwarted." Modern historians have found more enduring qualities in Louis Napoleon than did the men of the Third Republic, or have concluded, at the least, that the intricacies of his character cannot be easily categorized; and a society in England, the Souvenir Napoléonien, has presented a revisionist view of him as "a beneficent and far-sighted man" who one day "will find true justice."[10]

Eugénie, as is so often the way with widows, raised her husband to sainthood after he was gone, and when she pronounced the words "the Emperor" one would have thought she was invoking a deity. But as she readjusted her life she turned to politics. The wife and son would finish Napoleon's work. She dreamed of Lou-Lou wearing a crown and governing the French under a program giving the people freedom, but with *order*. It was not to be. Louis was bold, eager to the point of rashness to prove himself, and he had been stung by stories circulated in France that he had fled before the Prussians. He died on June 1, 1879, as a soldier, wearing a British uniform — in the artillery, of course, as befitted a Bonaparte — in a small, miserable guerrilla war in South Africa. His patrol, imprudently desaddled, was surprised in a donga by the Zulus and fled, every man for himself. His horse, named Fate, bolted when the Prince tried to mount. Louis, facing the enemy, one against forty or so, revolver blazing, fell under eighteen wounds from assegais, a victim of Sedan and the obligations of his name. Thus, in a strange and tragic fashion, the Bonaparte legend was finally put to rest in a dry ravine far from France.[11]

It fell to the Duc de Bassano to tell Eugénie. She thought at first that Louis was ill, then that he was wounded. She would go to him at once. Then Bassano, with tears in his eyes, had to say "Your Majesty *would arrive too late*." There was a terrible cry as Eugénie understood, and she wished that she, too, could die. "For her," Dr. Evans said, "there is no to-morrow."[12] In less than a decade, she had lost her country, her husband, her son, and all hope for the restoration of a Bonaparte dynasty.

The remains of the Prince Impérial were brought back to England on a slow steamer, the *Enchantress*. The body could not be identified because of the lapse of time and poor embalming. Dr. Evans was invited by Dr. Conneau to be present at Camden Place on July 11, 1879, when the coffin was opened, and to "visit the mouth" in an effort to establish the identity of the body. Evans took a small glass from his pocket. "Gentlemen," he said, "if this is truly the remains of the late Prince Louis Napoleon, we will find . . . in the upper lateral left, a gold filling which I made . . . in 1869, also another gold filling in the first upper small molar right." Both were found. Later the doctor said, "I am the first who had the idea of proving the person by their teeth . . . where the identity after death was uncertain."[13]

Dr. Evans was, however, in error about this. Dental identification has been made from time to time throughout recorded history. Perhaps he meant that he was the first *dentist* to practice forensic odontology; but there had been celebrated instances, American in origin, that he may have forgotten or not known about because of his long sojourn in Europe. Paul Revere, the versatile silversmith, engraver, and Revolutionary patriot, practiced dentistry from 1768 to 1778 and identified the body of Dr. Joseph Warren, the hero of the battle of Bunker Hill, when he was reburied in 1776, from bridgework he had made for Warren. Again, in 1850, John White Webster, a Harvard University professor, was convicted of the appalling crime of murdering a colleague, Dr. George Parkman, on the testimony of a dentist, Dr. Nathan C. Keep; and, finally, legends that John Wilkes Booth, assassin of President Lincoln, still lived were scotched in 1869, when his body was exhumed and definitely identified by the family dentist, who recognized his fillings.[14]

Guns boomed at the funeral of the Prince Impérial. The band of the Royal Artillery marched to the sound of muffled drums, and Louis was laid beside his father in a chapel attached to St. Mary's Church. It was a soldier's funeral. The Prince of Wales was a pallbearer, and Queen Victoria knelt before the coffin. Dean Stanley, a broad-church ecclesiastic greatly esteemed by the Queen, preached a sermon on the character of the Prince, Cardinal Manning came to Chislehurst to praise him, and the Queen continued to offer such solace as she could to her "dear sister," Eugénie. Because looseness in the British chain of command made the ambush possible, France bristled with the Anglophobia that always lurked beneath the surface of political life in the hexagon.

Departing from his rule not to write for his own newspaper, Dr. Evans published an emotional tribute to the Prince over his own signature. He reaffirmed his faith in what he called "the Imperial idea": "There is immense vitality in the principle . . . the thought of some strong man — of an Emperor who shall again lead the legions of France to victory is not easily abandoned by a brave and patriotic people," and he described the death of Louis as the most profound shock he had experienced since the assassination of Abraham Lincoln.[15]

After the death of her son, a number of reasons impelled the Empress Eugénie to leave Camden Place. She wished to buy a meadow beside the church for an imposing mausoleum, but the owner, a wealthy German toy manufacturer and a strongly anticlerical Protestant, refused to sell. Furthermore, Camden Place was a house of too many sorrows. In 1880 the Empress bought an extensive property in Hampshire known as Farnborough Hill. There she built an imposing structure, the Church of St. Michel. Dom Fernand Cabrol, an erudite Benedictine, became prior, later abbot, and made the abbey a center for scholarly investigations of the origins of the Mass and liturgy. There was also an enormous mausoleum, which received the sarcophagi of Napoleon III and the Prince Impérial, with space left for the Empress. These moves accomplished, Eugénie reached a level of emotional stability and a measure of peace. Though she said, "My rôle in this world ended in 1879," she had in fact an almost incredible forty-one years of life ahead of her.[16]

Settled in at Farnborough, Eugénie knitted, read, played patience, occupied herself with her far-flung correspondence. "Every morning a flood of letters," Dom Cabrol wrote, came "from all over France and the whole world."[17] There were, of course, many begging letters, ranging from the ingenious to the impudent. Perhaps the most outstanding example of this latter genre was one from a retired tax functionary in Brittany named Trochu, a son of the general who, at some risk to himself, to be sure, might have saved her life and her authority, but who preferred to be a live dog rather than a possibly dead lion. The Empress kept busy with her rosaries, her teas, the arranging of her papers, some of which, regrettably, she destroyed. Sympathetic visitors were received in the main residence, its interior filled with portraits and busts of Napoleon III, with uniforms, robes, and flags; with her various Winterhalters; with portraits of Queens Marie Antoinette and Hortense; and a library of books on the Franco-Prussian War, paper battles still being "fought with ink and venom." The Prince Impérial's personal effects were assembled in a special room: unopened letters, his cradle, a plaster cast of a little hand, the first uniform and sword, a blood-stained shirt, and a gold chain the superstitious Zulus had spared.[18]

Dr. Evans was frequently invited to come and see the Empress for nonprofessional visits. Carefully preserved among his papers are telegrams sent to him when he was in London: IMPERATRICE VOUS VERRA AVEC PLAISIR DEMAIN POUR LUNCH AVEC DEUX TRAINS LE MATIN — PIETRI (The Empress will see you with pleasure for lunch tomorrow. There are two morning trains — Piétri). Or, sometimes in English: WILL YOU COME AND DINE TODAY ROOM READY FOR YOU IF CONVENIENT CAN COME AT FIVE-FIFTY FROM WATERLOO — COMTESSE PIERREFONDS. And sometimes the message was simply to forward quickly six bottles of his elixir and two of his tooth powder.[19]

After the Empress was deemed to be politically harmless, she was allowed to visit republican France without hindrance or harassment, the sequestration of her French property having been lifted. Her fortune was now more than adequate for traveling and, under skillful management, still growing. Once she stayed at the Hôtel du Rhin in the Place Vendôme, only a few yards from the mansion where she had received the Emperor's formal request for her hand. Once she visited the ruins of Saint-Cloud. The château, having been used by the Prussians for the direction of artillery fire, was bombarded and destroyed by the French. In the débris she recognized a slab of marble from the fireplace of a drawing room where she had presided in the radiance of youth, power, and beauty. Again, she picked a flower in the Tuileries gardens. An attendant rebuked her sharply, but her escort whispered, "It is the Empress," and the guard, an old soldier with the Italy Medal, came stiffly to attention and saluted. She visited the palace of Compiègne, an anonymous old lady in black, with a veiled black hat tied under her chin, leaning heavily on a stick. There she saw again the pencil marks behind a shutter where she had recorded Lou-Lou's height, with the lines and dates still visible; and on this visit she was warned not to touch the furniture, much of which was hers.[20]

Friends and old adversaries were dropping off, and sometimes she had to suffer the merely curious. "People," she complained, "come to see me like a fifth act." The one reproach that roused her ire to the end of her life was any suggestion that cast doubt on her feeling for France. "I have only one country," she insisted, "France." When the great Allied offensive was launched in October 1918, Eugénie whispered, "If Foch could only catch them at Sedan!" She thought once more of the summer of 1870, of Wissembourg, Forbach, Gravelotte, Metz, and Sedan, and buried her face in her hands.[21]

Eugénie left no memoirs and engaged in no polemics regarding the Second Empire or herself or the complex maneuverings that accompanied the settlement of German-French relations at the conclusion of the war. Dr. Evans, however, undertook, with Dr. Crane's collaboration, to prepare a defense of the French sovereigns, entitled *The Fall of the Second Empire: Fragments of My Memories* and published in Paris in 1884 with specially commissioned gravure illustrations depicting the flight of Eugénie. She read the volume, appreciated the doctor's motives, but requested that he not publish the apologia during her lifetime. He therefore destroyed all copies except one, which exists in the Library of the University of Pennsylvania School of Dental Medicine. But some of the material in the *Fall* was incorporated in Evans's *Memoirs* after his death.

From the 1890s on, Eugénie's life had three centers, Farnborough Hill, a small steam yacht, the *Thistle,* and a villa that she built at Cap Martin, between Monte Carlo and Mentone. At this time Dame Ethel Smyth, the English composer and a friend of the Empress in her later years, described her as "straight as a dart, equal to a ten-mile walk, and has always looked at least twenty years younger than her age," and she quoted the Duchesse Anna de Mouchy as saying that in some ways she was more beautiful than when she was young "because years and sorrow have done away with the accidents of beauty . . . and revealed the exquisiteness of design."[22] Dr. Evans's last visit with Eugénie was at Farnborough, only a few months before his death, an occasion when they returned from a long walk that had exhausted the doctor more than it had the redoubtable lady. When she was eighty, she rode a camel in Egypt. In her eighty-second year she visited Ceylon, where a very young Leonard Woolf, then a cadet in the Ceylon Civil Service, had the honor of showing her the most sacred of Buddhist relics, known as Buddha's Tooth, which Woolf, the product of a skeptical age, describes in his autobiography as being definitely of canine origin.[23]

Release came at last for Eugénie on July 11, 1920, during a visit to Spain. Mourners at her funeral ceremony at Farnborough Hill included the Kings and Queens of Spain, Portugal, and England. When the coffin was lifted off the gun carriage the band played the "Marseillaise," unaware that its performance had been banned for most of Napoleon III's reign and that it had been sung by the rioters who forced the Empress to flee from the Tuileries. Her memory was at least spared one last rendition of "Partant pour la Syrie." British regimental bands had long ago forgotten how to play it. Dr. Evans was not present. He had been dead for over twenty-two years.

Between the ages of twenty-six and forty-four Eugénie touched the heights and depths of human experience, then in the winter of her days lived on for almost another lifetime, bearing her memories with tact and dignity. A century after her fall from power and her personal bereavements, two historians, both women, offered modern perspectives on Eugénie's character. First, Cecil Woodham-Smith, the late Anglo-Irish writer, who said of the Second Empire, "It is impossible to imagine its gaslit splendours without her beauty, her charm, her chic," and added that when misfortune came, she displayed a courage "which won her universal respect." Nancy Nichols Barker, professor of history at the University of Texas, touched appreciatively on the same qualities and emphasized her superb courage in the presence of physical danger and her generosity of spirit, but was severe in judging her influence on events. She was poorly prepared for her imperial rôle. Her views were passionately held but never sorted out. Her secret longing — not very secret, actually — was for getting back to an absolute, dynastic monarchy, purged of liberal nonsense. But all of her appealing personal attributes, according to Professor Barker, "did not add up to statesmanship."[24]

15

An Ending
and a Beginning

IN HIS LATER YEARS Dr. Evans enjoyed the cabarets, the life of
the boulevards, and reminiscences with old Bonapartists. He continued to be an industrious writer and produced a considerable
body of professional literature and materials for his memoirs, as
well as preparing the volume referred to earlier, *The Fall of the
Second Empire*. It is doubtful whether any American of the period
ever equaled Dr. Evans in his attachment to Napoleon III's imperial
system or held on more tenaciously to the hope of a restoration.
Loyalty, one of his most admirable qualities, was reinforced by
self-interest. Posterity's view of him, by which he set great store,
has been largely dependent on his Bonapartist relationships. The
death of the Prince Impérial ended all hope of reversing the politics
of the times, and by the decade of the 1880s Evans was reconciled
to the French Republic. He continued his support of the American
presence in Parisian life through the American Dental Club,
founded at his home and still flourishing, the *American Register,*
his church activities, the American Charitable Association, which
he organized to aid Americans who needed temporary relief or
money for a ticket home, the American University Committee,
which worked for reforms that would smooth the way for American
medical students seeking degrees in France, and the Lafayette Home
for Girls. This was a nonprofit residence for young American

women who came to Paris to study art. It was sponsored by the doctor and had a board of directors representing American and European society.

Around 1885 the elegants of Paris, who had never thought of living otherwise than in imposing residences with courts and gardens, began to move into flats, which they found more convenient than their hôtels; so a trend developed toward construction of apartment houses of some six stories with impressive façades and porte-cochères, which reduced the occupants' expenses without lessening their social dignity. In 1892 Dr. Evans followed the trend. Mrs. Evans was not well, owing to a chronic inflammation of the kidneys. There were stairs to be considered and the responsibilities of maintaining a small palace. So Evans gave his birds to the Zoological Gardens and built an apartment house just across the street from Bella Rosa on the Rue de la Pompe, retaining the first floor for his own use. Bathrooms imported from New York and central heating introduced Paris to the wonderful world of American plumbing.

Dr. Evans's last years were clouded by several controversies. A dispute erupted between Evans, the manager of the Lafayette Home, whom the doctor had dismissed, and Mrs. Walden Pell, a wealthy American matron who was the largest single financial supporter of the women's residence. The *New York Herald* happily jumped into the fray. It published certain complaints against Dr. Evans in connection with the affairs of the Lafayette Home written in the spicy Gordon Bennett style of reporting. Bennett's newspaper said that the home had no real organization; that the doctor spent an inordinate amount of time among the young ladies even if he was a genial old gentleman; that he housed stablemen and footmen in part of the building he could not rent; that he "wanted to be the hero of the whole concern"; and that at a board meeting held in the drawing room of Mrs. Pell the doctor had become heated and called his lady associates "a lot of liars and fishwomen." This, said the *Herald* slyly, was "the American millionaire dentist, who has a certain reputation in Paris as regards refinement."[1] Evans sued Bennett for defamation of character, but failed to get satisfaction because of the loose French libel law. The court, however, did reprimand the *Herald* for "the violence of its language."[2]

In another incident, touching his professional life, Dr. Evans learned how sharper than a serpent's tooth was the bite of a thankless nephew. He had wanted, as he once explained to his parents, "to build up a name and family — I may say to found a dynasty — that I should be no less proud of than Napoleon was of his." He had brought John Henry Evans, son of his eldest brother, Rudulph, to grow up in his Paris office, be shaped by him, and presumably succeed to his practice. But John Henry departed in the 1870s to establish his own office. Even worse, he attracted the same clientele that Dr. Tom regarded as his own preserve, including Pope Pius IX, who created John Henry a hereditary marquis of the Holy Roman Empire, under the name d'Oyley, confected from Doyle, his mother's family name. By the eighties John Henry was prospering mightily through the sale of tooth powder and mouthwash under the label *Evans*.[3]

Socially he was d'Oyley. In the dental world he was Evans. Confusion was inevitable, and no doubt intended. The "famous American dentist" was furious at the prospect of an ungrateful nephew having the best of two worlds. The doctor used the columns of the *American Register* to inveigh against "counterfeit" titles of nobility, and there was litigation. John Henry failed to get a judgment for damages, but Dr. Thomas was required by the court to give space in his newspaper for a reply from John Henry. Dr. Tom counterattacked, trying to have the marquis-cum-dentist deported under the immigration law as well as restrained from using the name Evans in connection with the sale of his dental products. Both of these efforts failed, leaving Dr. Thomas Evans angry and frustrated.

A line of descent for the Evans dental practice did develop, however, though it was not based on kinship. During the boyhood of the Prince Impérial, Lou-Lou had a playmate, born in the Tuileries and often, though mistakenly, rumored to be a natural son of Napoleon III and — perhaps — the beautiful Italian Countess of Castiglione. His name: Arthur C. Hugenschmidt. His mother was in fact a sewing woman of the palace, his father a major-domo, and they were husband and wife. The boy must have been attractive and intelligent, for both the Emperor and the Empress took an interest in him and urged Dr. Evans to supervise his education. As a dentist, naturally. Hugenschmidt proved to be an apt pupil. He later came to the United States and graduated from the School of

Dentistry at the University of Pennsylvania, Class of 1885, and returned to Evans's office in Paris. In time, Hugenschmidt took over the Evans practice, which he carried on for fifty years with something of the same celebrity, charm, discretion, and influence with personages in positions of power as his mentor had exercised.[4]

On June 17, 1897, Mrs. Evans died of Bright's disease after a lingering illness. Thus the ample provisions for her that Dr. Evans had made did not come into effect. In his first visit to the United States since the Centennial Exposition at Philadelphia in 1876, Dr. Evans returned with the body of his wife and placed her remains in a vault until the family mausoleum he planned for Woodlands Cemetery in West Philadelphia could be built. Evans stayed in America for some four months, showing still, in the words of a Philadelphia reporter, "the same vigor and activity which are the marvel of all who know him."[5]

He was entertained by Dr. William Pepper, recently retired provost of the University of Pennsylvania, and a leader in modernizing and revitalizing higher education in this country. It was a congenial meeting, since Dr. Evans, representing the University Committee of Paris, was making strenuous efforts to obtain the recognition of American college degrees in France and especially to change existing regulations so that American-trained dentists could practice on the same terms as the French.[6]

Being childless and now without a legatee, the doctor, like other wealthy and lonely potential donors, derived considerable solace, and possibly amusement, from encouraging the hopes of willing recipients of his fortune of approximately five million (gold) dollars. He had often expressed his appreciation for the lifetime opportunities that France had afforded him and was widely known for his generous support of philanthropic endeavors in Paris. There were expectations, then, that he would leave his estate to the City of Paris, and some remarks the doctor dropped gave encouragement to this idea. Or, again, perhaps the native son would remember the City of Philadelphia. Dr. Evans visited around. There was a stop in Cincinnati, where he was accompanied by a friend and attorney, Arthur E. Valois, of Paris and New York. A school for boys in Cincinnati might be a suitable project. One interviewer who found the dentist at the St. Nicholas Hotel conjectured that he was thirty times a millionaire and went on, in the luxuriant journalistic prose for which the Queen City was famous, to describe him as "the marvel of dentists of this age," the father of gold fillings, the friend of European royalty, the celebrated savior of the Empress Eugénie, noted for his culture, and so forth. Moving on to Chicago, Dr. Evans thought of leaving his assets to the Chicago College of Dental Surgery. He gave some thought to a romantic scheme for a colony in Minnesota for French nobility, especially those aristocrats whose homeland was the French territory annexed by Germany after the Franco-Prussian War.[7]

In St. Paul, Dr. Evans visited with two friends, both nationally known ecclesiastics, Bishop Henry Benjamin Whipple, Protestant Episcopal Bishop of Minnesota, and the Roman Catholic Archbishop, John Ireland. The *St. Paul Pioneer Press* gave a word portrait of Evans at this time. He was seventy-four years old, rather portly, with a high forehead, brown hair tinged with gray and combed straight back from the forehead in a single wide curl. His face was full and almost ruddy, eyebrows thick, eyes dark. He had a large Roman nose. The doctor talked readily in agreeable tones, somewhat in the manner of a professor, waving his hands for emphasis. In the lapel of his black broadcloth jacket he wore the rosette of a commander of the Legion of Honor, though the newspaper noted that he could have worn similar insignia conferred by most of the courts of Europe. Summing up, the writer concluded, "He has the whiskers of a German, the accent of an Englishman, the manners of a Frenchman [but] he has creditably clung to the nationality that permitted his success."[8]

The reporter tried to lure the doctor into some piquant revelations about the reactions of royal personalities when they, like ordinary mortals, had a loose filling. But Evans was too experienced in dealing with the press to be drawn out. "All my relations with them," he said rather formally, "are sacred."[9]

Dr. Evans, having returned to Paris, where he lived alone, resumed his practice on October 19. He spent a week at Baden visiting the Grand Duchess Louise and meditated on the establishment of a museum that would house his art collection, his gifts from European royalty, the ribbons and medals signaling the honors that had been bestowed on him. The museum might be located in Paris, he confided to his loyal nephew Theodore, who had shown a respectful interest in his uncle's career. "Philadelphia," Dr. Tom told him, "can never build what I have wished, and then, here I can overlook its installation, whilst living give directions."[10]

But it didn't work out that way. Dr. Evans attended a public dinner in Paris on November 13 — the year is still 1897 — at which he experienced severe chest pains. The doctors, recognizing angina pectoris, held a consultation, but Evans died at his home the morning of the fifteenth. When the will was opened it was found that there was to be a museum *and* a dental school in Philadelphia, after all. Various family bequests were made. There were a hundred thousand francs for Americans stranded in Paris, and a considerable fortune was left to Méry Laurent. Dr. Crane was named Evans's literary executor and received the *American Register,* which was sold in 1901 and ceased publication in 1915. The Evans residence was willed to the City of Philadelphia and was rented to the French government for the entertainment of foreign sovereigns during the exposition of 1900. It was demolished in 1907. The marquis, born Evans, who had snatched some of Dr. Tom's patients was cut off in the will "for reasons as well known to the said John Henry Evans as to me."[11]

The Empress Eugénie lived on . . . and on . . . as described in the previous chapter, but Méry Laurent died on November 26, 1900. Adolphe Tabarant memorialized Méry as an *amiable femme* who had been passionately loved, who had stirred many hearts without ever condemning them to despair. She was, he wrote in summary, both beautiful and good. Referring to Méry's relations with Manet and Mallarmé, who had died respectively in 1883 and 1898, Josette Raoul-Duval has finely said, *"Ces princes de l'art lui ont rendu en gloire ce qu'elle leur avait donné en plaisir"* ("These princes of art gave back in glory what she had given them in pleasure").[12] Méry made bequests of money to Dr. Evans's coachman, his secretary, René Michel, and his nephew Theodore; also money and her silverware to Mallarmé's daughter, in memory of the affection her father had shown to Méry. Eliza Sosset, Méry's maid and cook, was well looked after, and Dr. Arthur Hugenschmidt received a valuable painting and a tapestry representing the apotheosis of the First Consul.[13]

∽

What has informed opinion concluded about the life and character of Thomas Evans? Throughout his career, Evans demonstrated his interest in the advancement of his profession and in military hygiene on the battlefield. He is remembered for his successful experiments with vulcanized rubber, innovative procedures for straightening irregular teeth, the introduction of nitrous oxide in Europe as a general anaesthetic. Evans's technical resourcefulness was brilliantly exhibited when he fashioned the tracheotomy cannula for Crown Prince Frederick. Altogether, Dr. Evans contributed a special distinction to American dentistry in Europe, which it still retains. Speaking in more general terms, the *New York Times* described Dr. Evans when he died as "a man of graceful manners and many accomplishments [who] was in love with his profession"; his coolness and devotion when Eugénie was menaced were recalled by *Le Figaro* in a page-one story.[14]

There were — need one add? — nay-sayers. One British dental journal scoffed at Dr. Evans's diplomatic activities and complained because he did not acquire his fortune by the practice of dentistry. This censorious view was both ungenerous and inaccurate, since his successes rested on his professional attainments, exceptional for the period, and would not have been possible without that firm underpinning. Certain French dental journals, but not all, held that Evans stood aside from the development of purely French dentistry. There is an element of truth in this, as well as jealousy. Looking at the matter from the opposite side, Dr. Evans must have been amused or affronted when a French "brother" claimed to be *dentiste américain*. However, inside and outside of the dental world of France, England, and the United States, it was remembered that Dr. Evans had managed the escape of Eugénie, which made the doctor a sympathetic and somewhat romantic character.[15]

"To his great honour . . . his affection and his allegiance to his Imperial patrons suffered no diminution after Sedan . . ." *The Academy* (London) observed in reviewing the doctor's *Memoirs*. "What a pleasant man Thomas W. Evans must have been, and what a pleasant country the America of the Victorian era must have been to have produced such a pleasant man."[16]

There was in Evans a great sensitiveness to the verdict of succeeding generations on his career. He wished for an outward and visible sign of his inward worth at his place of interment, Woodlands

Cemetery. So he arranged for the raising of a shaft of granite, soaring a hundred and fifty feet upward from a granite platform, towering above his neighbors in the marble orchard, including such notables as the naval heroes Charles Stewart, brilliant commander of the *Constellation* in the War of 1812, and the Civil War commodore, David Porter, Anthony J. Drexel, the banker and philanthropist, and Eli Kirk Price, the quintessential Quaker lawyer and philanthropist, whose public services included the establishment of Philadelphia's jewel, Fairmount Park.[17] Still today, the monument under which Thomas W. Evans lies with his wife and parents remains by far the most imposing monolith in Woodlands.

Dr. Evans would be pleased to know that.

The Evans Museum was to be housed in its own new building, a fireproof, burglar-proof memorial to the doctor's varied accomplishments, preserving such visible evidences as the art collection, his books and manuscript papers, his royal autographs, the gifts from persons of high consideration, busts, swords, tankards, vases, repoussé silver bowls, the gold box in which Marie Antoinette kept her beauty patches, ladles, inkstands, silver candlesticks, snuff boxes, a pair of buffalo-horn cups from the Prince and Princess of Wales, a blaze of gems, even the carriage in which Dr. Evans spirited the Empress out of Paris. The dentist's own instruments, mounted on ivory handles, include his favorite extraction key, and a whole museum case full of royal teeth or bridgework that Evans kept individually wrapped, each sealed with wax, under such labels as "Manuela, Countess of Montijo, October, 1865." She was, the reader will recall, the Empress Eugénie's mother.

Turning now to the Evans Institute: this institution was conceived to be a great dental school; in the language of the will, "not inferior to any already established."[18] The location the doctor prescribed was the corner of Fortieth and Spruce streets, where his parents had lived and died, a location then beyond the western boundary of the University of Pennsylvania but now part of the campus. Delay was inevitable. Disappointed and determined relatives, in all sixteen persons, led by the disinherited John Henry Evans, brought proceedings to upset the will. The legal struggle, complicated by French inheritance laws whose technicalities the doctor did not understand, dragged on for twelve years. It is strange indeed that Dr. Evans, who had earned a reputation for his shrewd conduct of business affairs, never took the time to be explicit and tidy in his arrangements for carrying out his wishes after death. One can only hypothesize that the doctor, like other men of strong ego, did not really believe in his own mortality.

A settlement was finally arrived at. After the payment of enormous legal fees, court costs here and abroad, the satisfaction of miscellaneous bequests, and an agreement with the Evans clan to obtain their surrender of all claims against the estate, there remained approximately $1.75 million in 1897 dollars, the first liberal endowment for dental education. Yet it was a sum deemed insufficient to carry out Dr. Evans's plans for an independent institution. Thus the Evans trustees were faced with an inadequate endowment and the prospect of establishing a new institution close to the University of Pennsylvania, which since 1878 had had a strong School of Dentistry. Affiliation was chosen over unnecessary competition, through an agreement with the university by which the university's School of Dentistry was merged in 1912 with the institute under the cumbersome but accurate designation, the Thomas W. Evans Museum and Dental Institute School of Dentistry University of Pennsylvania.[19]

On the site of the old Evans home, and adjoining properties that were acquired, a building in the collegiate Gothic style, with Dr. Evans's name displayed over the main entrance, was erected for teaching, graduate training, scientific research, and as a home for what became one of the most complete collections of dental literature in existence. And, of course, the doctor's memorabilia. The entrance to the museum was flanked by two busts of Carrara marble, representing Dr. Evans on one side and Napoleon III on the other. The museum was dispersed some years ago under pressure of the need for more classroom space. The doctor's Manets are on loan at the Philadelphia Museum of Art. The Evans jewels, greatly enhanced in value and called by the *Philadelphia Inquirer* "the crown jewels of the University of Pennsylvania," repose in the vault of a Philadelphia bank and are exposed to public inspection only on very special occasions, such as the centennial of the formation of the university's Dental School.[20] Some of the doctor's better paintings grace the walls of the dean's office. The Evans manuscripts and royal autographs, including the remarkable studio register of the photographer Nadar, are deposited in the library. Clocks, jardinières, porcelains, bibelots, articles technically known to archivists as three-dimensional objects, are stored in a warehouse, and the historic carriage that transported the Empress Eugénie out of Paris is preserved at the New Bolton Center of the University of Pennsylvania School of Veterinary Medicine, in Chester County.

The cornerstone of the building that was to bear Dr. Evans's name was laid on May 3, 1913, in the presence of civic, religious, and dental dignitaries. The Empress, who was then eighty-seven years old and lived on the Côte d'Azur, was invited to attend but declined with a graceful reference to Dr. Evans: "I am reminded of his sincerity, the proof of which he gave me in the darkest hours of my life."[21] The completed building was dedicated two years later, with clinics, exhibits and demonstrations, academic exercises, dinners, and speeches in which the beneficence of Dr. Evans was not overlooked. The end of his useful and brilliant life had meant, it was emphasized, a new beginning for the University of Pennsylvania Dental School.

Seven years later, as already noted, Eugénie, friend of Dr. Evans, Empress and Regent under the Second French Empire, who said she had already died three times, followed Thomas W. Evans — dentist, hedonist, staunch American, unofficial diplomat, generous philanthropist — in the death of the body if not of the spirit. We forgive Napoleon III much because he brought France unparalleled prosperity and departed from the world scene as one of history's most conspicuous scapegoats for the culpability of a whole nation; Eugénie, despite her political stumbles, because she was brave and beautiful; Thomas W. Evans, though too occupied with shallow honors, because he showed grace under pressure and became an inspiration to his profession. Each — Louis Napoleon, the nominal Catholic, Eugénie, the true believer, and the Quaker-bred doctor who died an Episcopalian — could reasonably rest on almost the last words of the poet Heine, with whose thought Dr. Evans was familiar. *"Dieu me pardonnera,"* Heine had whispered, *"c'est son métier."* ("God will forgive me — that's His business.")[22]

Acknowledgments

Notes

Bibliography

Index

Acknowledgments

MANY LIBRARIES AND INDIVIDUALS have helped in large ways and small to shape this book, extend its reach, or verify matters of fact, and my warm thanks go out to all. But first among equals is John M. Whittock, Jr., Librarian of the University of Pennsylvania School of Dental Medicine, for endless courtesies in opening up unique materials under his charge, in loaning books and photocopies, scanning periodicals for long-buried items, and providing most of the illustrations appearing in the book. I am also grateful for the interest of D. Walter Cohen, Dean of the School of Dental Medicine, University of Pennsylvania, and Associate Dean James F. Galbally, Jr., in following the progress of the work.

Other institutions whose resóurces and helpful staffs have contributed notably to the book include the French Embassy Cultural Services (New York); the Library of Congress; Mid-Hudson Libraries, Poughkeepsie, New York, and its affiliate, the Millerton Free Library; the New York Public Library; Princeton University Library; and Vassar College Library. I also acknowledge correspondence, interlibrary loans, and photocopies from the Bibliothèque nationale, the library of the American Dental Association, from the British Tourist Authority, Bucks County Free Library (Pennwood Branch), Cornell University, the Historical Society of Pennsylvania, the Edsel Ford Memorial Library of the Hotchkiss School, Lafayette College, Lancaster County Historical Society, Massachusetts Historical Society, Minnesota Historical Society, New York Academy of Medicine Library, Presbyterian Historical Society of Philadelphia,

Ulysses S. Grant Association, University of Rochester Library, School of Dental Medicine of Washington University, Wesleyan University Library, and the Library of the University of Wisconsin.

I have had the benefit of a careful reading and editorial suggestions from Mme. Annette Harispe Emgarth, a long-time student of Dr. Evans's career, and also from the historian J. C. Furnas. Louis I. Grossman, D.D.S., answered professional questions, made important emendations, and generously made his personal collection of Evans material available to me. Charles J. Hill, in a rigorous examination of the text, contributed invaluable stylistic suggestions that enhanced the euphony and flow of the narrative.

An incomplete list of other individuals from whom I received many different kinds of assistance — a letter, a conversation, a check on my French, a photocopy, a clipping, or a courtesy hard to classify — includes le Docteur René Beck, le Président, Ordre National des Chirurgiens-Dentistes, Madeleine Berry, Dean Anthony D. Branch, Eleanor and Louise Campion, Michael Clark, Sally Forden, Professor Louis M. Greenberg, Professor Anne Coffin Hanson, Jane Heimerdinger, Ruth Hill, Dr. William Krogman, the late Germaine Lafeuille, Professor Harry Levin, Dr. Lester L. Luntz, Jean McPherrin, Jean-Marie Moulin, Conservateur en chef, Musée national du Château de Compiègne, Dr. Edward P. Rich, Dr. Malvin E. Ring, and the late Margaret E. Taylor. My editor, Ruth K. Hapgood, impeccable copy editor, Frances Apt, and my agent, Willis Kingsley Wing, all skilled professionals and warmly appreciated friends, were ever helpful in bringing this project to a happy conclusion. My wife, Lettie Gay Carson, often busy with other concerns, was ever responsive and supportive and quickly stopped, looked, and listened when help was needed.

Notes

Abbreviations

Academy	New York Academy of Medicine Library
Baker's	*Baker's Biographical Dictionary of Musicians,* fifth edition
Bénézet	Bénézet, E., *Dictionnaire des peintres, sculpteurs* . . .
Bibliothèque	Bibliothèque nationale (Paris)
Biographie	*Biographie Universelle*
Congress	Library of Congress
Cornell	Cornell University Library
DAB	*Dictionary of American Biography*
Dictionnaire	*Dictionnaire de biographie française*
DNB	*Dictionary of National Biography*
Herald	*New York Herald*
Herald (Paris)	*New York Herald* (Paris)
Lafayette	Lafayette College Library
Notable	*Notable American Women*
NYPL	New York Public Library
Penn State	Pennsylvania State University Library
Princeton	Princeton University Library
Register	*The American Register* (Paris)
Rochester	University of Rochester Library
Times	*New York Times*
U. Penn	University of Pennsylvania School of Dental Medicine Library
Vapereau	*Vapereau's Dictionnaire universel des contemporains*
Vassar	Vassar College Library
Wisconsin	University of Wisconsin Library

For full identification of sources cited, see the bibliography. Locations of manuscripts and of rare or unique printed materials are given in the bibliography.

1: Golden Dreams in West Philadelphia

Biographical information about Dr. Thomas W. Evans begins with his own writings: the *Memoirs;* a manuscript entitled "Some Remembrances"; reminiscences recorded in a manuscript left by his nephew Theodore Evans, "To the Memory"; family letters and manuscripts entitled "Prince of Wales" and "My Relations . . . with this personage." Other works that add details are Asbell; Branch; Charenton; Hahn; Jones, "Who Was Theodore Evans, Paris, France?"; Baudet, "Autour de la Famille Impériale: le Docteur Evans et les dentistes"; Carr, "Thomas W. Evans, His Life and Influence on the Development of Dentistry as a Learned Profession"; MaHeu; Bernard Veillet; and Maurice Veillet.

Dr. Evans's person and appearance: Crawford, "Dr. Thomas W. Evans," *New-York Tribune,* December 28, 1890, quoted in *Items of Interest,* and Talbot, "Dr. Thomas W. Evans — Dentist to the Crowned Heads of Europe." Both Crawford and Talbot were personally acquainted with Evans, who read and revised the Crawford article.

Descriptions of the Tuileries palace and court life: Gesztesi; Gosseln [G. Lenôtre, pseud.]; [Ernest Alfred Vizetelly], *Court of the Tuileries.*

Dental history: Stein, "The Teeth and Dentists of Some Monarchs of France"; Guerini, citing an eighteenth-century German work; Branch, citing an unpublished thesis on dentistry in France; Proskauer and Witt; and Taylor.

1. Maurice Veillet, p. 88.

2. Evans, *Memoirs,* 1:20; Evans, "Some Remembrances"; Baudet, "La Famille Impériale," p. 436; Soyer, "Le dentiste Thomas Evans et l'histoire du Second Empire," pp. 1136–1137.

3. Theodore Evans, "To the Memory," pp. 4–6; Thomas W. Evans, "Some Remembrances"; Crawford, "Dr. Thomas W. Evans," p. 207; Hahn, pp. 23–24; MaHeu, p. 9; Talbot, "Dr. Thomas W. Evans," p. 850; Maurice Veillet, p. 88.

4. *DAB,* s.v. "Evans, Thomas Wiltberger"; Evans, "Some Remembrances"; Carr, "Thomas W. Evans, His Life and Influence," p. 95; *Lancaster* (Pa.) *Sunday News,* January 31, 1954; Lufkin, pp. 177, 232; Taylor, pp. 60, 101.

5. Asbell, p. 47; Theodore Evans, "To the Memory," pp. 7–8; Jones, "Who Was Theodore Evans?" p. 4; Taylor, p. 101.

6. Asbell, p. 48; Theodore Evans, "To the Memory," pp. 9–12.

7. Jones, "Who Was Theodore Evans?" p. 4.

8. Charles Godfrey Leland to Frank Fisher, April 28, 1840, quoted in Hanscom, p. 304.

9. Simpson, pp. 17–25.

10. Charlatanism in Paris: Charenton, pp. 53–56, 65–67; Stein, "Teeth and Dentists of Some Monarchs," p. 58; Guerini, p. 216; Jarves, pp. 28–29; Lufkin, p. 88; Proskauer and Witt, plates 133, 134, 135, and p. 198.

11. Evans, "Some Remembrances."

12. Ibid.

13. Ibid.

14. Branch, pp. 13–19; Evans, "Some Remembrances"; Guerini, pp. 255, 259; Lufkin, pp. 103, 108–109.

15. Dr. Progrès, "Les dentistes américains," pp. 530–534; Branch, pp. 10–13; Lufkin, p. 109; Branch, pp. 17–19.

16. Evans, *Memoirs*, 1:17–18; Ridley, p. 33.

2: *A Versatile American Meets a Man of Destiny*

Theodore Evans, "To the Memory"; Evans, *Memoirs;* and Baudet, "Autour de la Famille Impériale," are important sources for Evans's relations with Napoleon III.

Biographical material about Louis Napoleon: Burnand; Cornu, "Louis Napoleon Painted by a Contemporary"; Evans, *Memoirs;* Legge; Osgood; George [Robert Sencourt, pseud.]; Vizetelly, *Paris and Her People.*

The question of Louis Napoleon's paternity is reviewed and dismissed in Corley, Thompson, and major biographical works of reference. The coup d'état: Briggs; Jarves; Osgood; Williams, *French Revolution;* and Williams, *Gaslight and Shadow.*

1. Theodore Evans, "To the Memory," p. 10.

2. Ibid., p. 86.

3. Evans, *Memoirs*, 1:16.

4. King Jérôme's gibe at Louis Napoleon appears in Evans, *Memoirs*, 1:64, and in the *Memoirs of Count Horace de Viel Castel*, 1:117.

5. George, p. 20.

6. Cowley, p. 8.

7. Van Deusen, *Thurlow Weed*, p. 188.

8. A highly critical contemporary view of Louis Napoleon from the perspective of a conservative New York lawyer appears in Strong, 2:78.

9. Bicknell, pp. 3, 13, 31–33. The legend of the Little Red Man is explained in [Vizetelly], *Court of the Tuileries*, p. 6.

10. Theodore Evans, "To the Memory," p. 35.

11. Evans, *Memoirs*, 1:54.

12. Osgood, p. xi.

13. Jarves, p. 264.

14. Evans, *Fall*, part I, p. 122.

15. Theodore Evans, "To the Memory," p. 60.

16. Du Camp, 1:130; George, p. 69; Williams, *Gaslight*, p. 41. Cabanel's luscious *Nymph* can be seen in *The Second Empire 1852–1870: Art in France under Napoleon III*, p. 263.

17. Evans, *Memoirs*, 1:45.

18. Welch, "Dr. Thomas Evans: An American Knight in Paris," p. 32; Evans, *Fall*, part I, p. 142; Maurice Veillet, p. 111.

3: Miss Howard: Love's Labour's Lost

Principal sources: Decaux, *Amours second empire;* Dansette; and especially Maurois.

1. Maurois, p. 57.
2. Dansette, pp. 95, 101–103.
3. Ibid., p. 106–107.
4. Kracauer, pp. 121–122, 203.
5. Dansette, p. 96; Evans, *Memoirs,* 1:3; Stoeckl, *When Men Had Time,* p. 14.
6. Legge, p. 270.
7. Maurois, p. 37.
8. Ibid., p. 29.
9. Ibid., p. 37.
10. Du Camp, 1:107; Evans, *Memoirs,* 1:6.
11. Maurois, pp. 51–52; Ridley, p. 236.
12. Maurois, pp. 67–68, 198–199.
13. Ibid., pp. 63, 116, 118, 120–122, 126, 154–155, 157. Maurois, clearly a sympathetic biographer, wrote of Harriet, "She was a woman purified by solitude and devoted to the remembrance of her lost love," p. 200. The quotation from Jane Austen appears in *Persuasion,* p. 106.

4: An Emperor Needs a Wife

For Louis Napoleon's matrimonial maneuvers, and the entrance of Eugénie de Guzman Montijo, my principal sources are Dansette; Evans, *Memoirs;* and Kurtz.

1. Evans, *Memoirs,* 1:73, 75.
2. "The Imperial Dentist," p. 1309; Dansette, pp. 116–121, 123–125; Evans, *Memoirs,* 1:80–82.
3. Duff, pp. 86–87, 90–91, 93–94; Woodham-Smith, pp. 347–348.
4. Encomiums to Eugénie's beauty: Aubry, pp. 39–40; Evans, *Memoirs,* 1:91.
5. Aubry, p. 31; Barker, pp. 7–9.
6. Simpson, p. 223.
7. Dansette, p. 137.
8. Aubry, pp. 48–50; Decaux, *Amours,* p. 34.
9. Brodsky, p. 141.
10. Branch, 1:32 footnote; Evans, *Memoirs,* 1:90.
11. Conway, p. 146.
12. Kurtz, pp. 29, 372.
13. Ibid., p. 29.
14. Ibid., p. 39.
15. Dansette, p. 136; *Dictionnaire,* s.v. "Eugénie (-Marie) de Montijo"; Lacour-Gayet, p. 12; Maurois, p. 73.
16. Kurtz, p. 50.
17. Aubry, p. 76; Stoeckl, *When Men Had Time,* pp. 14–15.

5: The Wise Virgin

The marriage of Louis Napoleon and Eugénie and the establishment of a brilliant court life: the Evans *Memoirs*, supplemented by Aubry, Dansette, Cowley, Vizetelly, Woodham-Smith, with additions cited in the notes that follow.

1. Dansette, pp. 151, 185–186; Duff, pp. 98–101; Evans, *Memoirs*, 1:95ff.

2. Brodsky, p. 147; Duff, pp. 100–101; Evans, *Memoirs*, 1:96; Saunders, pp. 32–33, 35; Simpson, p. 215.

3. Strong, 2:118; Woodham–Smith, p. 349.

4. Washburne, 1:35.

5. For a favorable judgment on Eugénie's character and intelligence, see Legge, p. 64; for a severe estimate, Du Camp, 1:147. The deficiencies in her education were regretted by Cornu, "Louis Napoleon Painted," p. 611.

6. Evans, *Memoirs*, 1:117.

7. Ibid., 1:94. Lacour-Gayet also tells the story, p. 20.

8. Descriptions of the palace functionaries and their costumes: Arnaud, pp. 92, 126; Evans, *Memoirs*, 2:366; and [Vizetelly], *Court of the Tuileries*, pp. 38, 42–43.

9. Evans, *Memoirs*, 1:98–99.

10. Ibid., pp. 99–100.

6: Years of Splendor

General history of the Second Empire at its apogee: Arnaud, Barker, and Seignobos. Dr. Evans in mid-career: Theodore Evans, "To the Memory"; Evans's own recollections in *The Fall* and his *Memoirs*. Stoeckl, *When Men Had Time*, gives an intimate view of Dr. Evans by one of his patients. His innovative contributions to dentistry can be traced in Asbell, Branch, and in an excerpt from a letter of Dr. Evans to the Odontological Society of Great Britain. See also W. D. A. Smith, "T. W. Evans — Before and After"; Carr, "Thomas W. Evans," pp. 93–94; Thomas W. Evans, *Report on the Instruments and Apparatus of Medicine, Surgery and Hygiene . . .* pp. 22–23; Soyer, "Le Dentiste Thomas Evans."

The social environment: Aubry; Bicknell; Decaux, *Amours;* Filon; Gesztesi; Hegermann-Lindencrone; Kracauer; Maugny; de Wissant.

1. Evans, *Memoirs*, 1:34–35.

2. Lufkin, p. 209; Taylor, pp. 136–139.

3. Welch, "Dr. Thomas Evans: An American Knight," p. 31; Theodore Evans, "To the Memory," pp. 20–30; Evans, *Memoirs*, one-volume edition, p. 10; Thomas W. Evans to Rudulph H. Evans, January 20, 1860. Some fifty-four folders of letters and telegrams in the Evans Papers testify to the doctor's busy practice.

4. Labouchere, "Notes from Paris: A Diplomatic Tooth-Doctor," p. 1367.

5. Stoeckl, *When Men Had Time*, pp. 65–66.

6. Arnaud, p. 121.

7. Aubry, p. 101; Decaux, *La Castiglione,* p. 84; Gumpert, pp. 32–34; Ridley, p. 356.

8. Saunders, p. 43; Simpson, pp. 367–370.

9. Evans, *Fall,* part II, p. 118.

10. Aubry, pp. 108–112; Du Camp, 1:180, 2:324.

11. Guedalla, p. 250.

12. Evans, *Memoirs,* one-volume edition, p. 11; Fleury, 1:195; Simpson, p. 327; Woodham–Smith, pp. 359–360.

13. Arnaud, p. 155; Brodsky, p. 213.

14. When the Empress Eugénie returned to the Tuileries she opened her Bible and her eyes fell on Isaiah 54:15, where she read, "Whosoever shall gather together against thee shall fall for thy sake," according to the Abbé Puyol in his "Journal de l'Abbé Puyol," p. 306.

15. Evans, *Memoirs,* one-volume edition, pp. 18–19; Cowley, p. 146 and footnote.

16. Arnaud, pp. 180–181; Barker, pp. 35–40; Seignobos, pp. 112–113.

17. Evans, *Memoirs,* 1:133–134; Thompson, pp. 192–195.

18. Arnaud, p. 349; Dansette, p. 362; Maurois, pp. 127–128.

19. Kransberg, "An Emperor Writes History . . ." pp. 80–100. The promotions of Maury and Dr. Evans were announced in *Le Moniteur universel,* January 13, 1866.

20. Lévêque, p. 426; Salomon, pp. 153–155; Whiteing, pp. 76, 91.

21. Hurley, "Thomas W. Evans — Dentist and Diplomat," p. 557.

22. Grimmer, *Cinq essais nadariens . . .* pp. 4–5; Primet, pp. 119, 126; de Wissant, p. 230. Everyone of importance in Paris sat for Nadar, including Dr. Evans. Nadar's guest book, filled with famous autographs, sentiments, drawings, poems, epigrams, bars of music, was a part of Evans's estate and is now in the archives at U. Penn.

23. Kracauer, p. 187.

24. Evans, *Memoirs,* 1:106.

25. Carette, p. 165; Kracauer, p. 187.

26. Johnston, 2:451. I give Johnston's figure for the cost of the dresses but do not vouch for it.

27. Ibid., 2:505–506.

28. Evans, *Memoirs,* 1:120–121.

29. Kurtz, p. 217.

30. Allem, p. 66; Bicknell, p. 43; Perruchot, p. 81.

31. Evans, *American Ambulance,* p. 35; Evans, *Memoirs,* 1:61–62; Gesztesi, p. 217; Matthews, p. 79; Queen Victoria, *Letters of Queen Victoria,* second series, 1:384–385.

32. Evans, *Memoirs,* 2:432–433. According to Agnes Carey, *The Empress Eugénie in Exile,* pp. 295–297, writing of "only what I positively *know*," when the Empress was rowed across the Bosphorus in the Sultan's private caïque, she gave the alarm that saved a small rowboat from being run down. Its occupant was Dr. Evans. However, Evans does not mention the incident. It is incredible that he would not have recorded it. Lady Mary Meynell, who

is often full of misinformation, picks up the story but says, in her *Sunshine and Shadows,* pp. 124–125, the man was an Englishman. Duff, pp. 191–192, accepts Meynell's version but changes her Englishman back into the American dentist. Too bad it isn't true.

33. Ibid., 1:122–123.
34. *NYH,* November 17, 1869.
35. Paléologue, p. 23.
36. Aubry, p. 98; Malmsbury, 2:321, quoted in Ridley, p. 517.

7: *Rebuilding Paris*

Pinkney is the standard work. I also consulted Boucher; Doniol; Theodore Evans, "To the Memory"; Evans, *Fall* and the *Memoirs;* Fouquières; George; Rochegude; and Bernard Veillet, among other works.

1. Vizetelly, p. 165; Whiteing, p. 87.
2. Couperie; Ridley, p. 351; Zeldin, 1:553.
3. Evans, *Fall,* part I, pp. 141–142; Evans, *Memoirs,* 1:42–43; Bernard Veillet, pp. 6–8; Maurice Veillet, p. 81.
4. Theodore Evans, "To the Memory," p. 65; Pinkney, pp. 98–99; Bernard Veillet, pp. 6–9. Veillet, p. 25, says that the new avenue was the doctor's idea, as does Boucher, p. 25, and Fouquières, p. 236, but Evans's own account does not support this.
5. Theodore Evans, "To the Memory," p. 66.
6. MaHeu, pp. 12–13.
7. Ibid.
8. Hegermann-Lindencrone, pp. 137–138.
9. Doniol, pp. 78, 413; Crawford, "Dr. Thomas W. Evans," p. 204; Pinkney, p. 11.
10. Theodore Evans, "To the Memory," pp. 65–66; Baguenier-Désorimeaux, "L'Hôtel Evans," p. 246; Bernard Veillet, p. 15.
11. Theodore Evans, "To the Memory," pp. 66–67, 69; Bernard Veillet, p. 16; Washburne, 2:224.
12. Boucher, pp. 25, 97; *Dictionnaire,* s.v. "Delaunay, Auguste-Joseph"; Doniol, pp. 58, 122; Fouquières, 1:253; Hahn, p. 38; Bernard Veillet, p. 17; Washburne, 1:135.

8: *The American Civil War — As Fought in Paris*

My survey of life in the American colony: Champceix; Evans, *Memoirs;* Hegermann-Lindencrone; de Laurière; and Young.

Diplomatic history of the period: correspondence between John Bigelow and William H. Seward and between Seward and Dr. Evans. Printed sources: Case and Spencer; Evans, *Memoirs;* and Jordan and Pratt. Useful biographies: Clapp; Ross; Van Deusen, *Seward;* and Van Deusen, *Thurlow Weed.*

1. Champceix, pp. 3–4; Evans, *Memoirs,* 1:128–129, 135, 137; and the one-volume edition of the *Memoirs,* pp. 111–113.

2. Champceix, p. 6.

3. Ibid., pp. 4–6.

4. Ibid., p. 5. Champceix's remark about beautiful American shoulders calls to mind the famous statement of Eugène Lami, painter of the social scene during the Empire: "Sovereigns may change but the shoulders of women remain," *Second Empire: Art in France*, p. 393.

5. *St. Paul Pioneer Press*, September 28, 1897.

6. Conway, p. xi; Evans, *Memoirs*, 1:129.

7. Grandeffe, p. 85; Young, 1:136–137, 140, 142.

8. Gesztesi, p. 122; de Laurière, pp. 13–17.

9. Hegermann-Lindencrone, p. 41; de Laurière, pp. 23–24.

10. Hegermann-Lindencrone, pp. 42–43.

11. Saunders, pp. 138–139.

12. Evans, *Memoirs*, one-volume edition, p. 115; Weed, p. 274; Young, 1:137, 146–147, 153.

13. Young, p. 137.

14. Ibid., p. 153.

15. John Bigelow to William H. Seward, February 6, 1863, Bigelow Papers; Case and Spencer, pp. 181–182.

16. Evans, *Memoirs*, one-volume edition, p. 122.

17. Willson, pp. 36–37.

18. Clapp, p. 169; *DAB*, s.v. "Slidell, John"; Willson, pp. 43, 57.

19. Willson, pp. 59–60.

20. Washburne, 2:248.

21. Branch, pp. 85–87; Case and Spencer, pp. 253, 256–257; Van Deusen, *Weed*, pp. 275–278; Weed, *Mission Abroad*, p. 174, quoted in Branch, pp. 86–87.

22. Case and Spencer, pp. 412–413.

23. Branch, pp. 80–81, 89; Clapp, pp. 150–151, 173–174; Evans, *Memoirs*, 1:147, 149. Evans's favorable estimate of Dayton is shared by the *DAB*, s.v. "Dayton, William Lewis."

24. Evans, *Memoirs*, one-volume edition, pp. 121–122.

25. John Bigelow to William H. Seward, November 21, 1862; Bigelow Diary, October 14, 1863, quoted in Branch, p. 89.

26. Clapp, p. 202; William H. Seward to Thomas W. Evans, December 6, 1862.

27. Seward to Evans, December 6, 1862.

28. Seward, *Travels*, pp. 760–761.

29. Evans, *Memoirs*, one-volume edition, p. 129.

30. Ibid., pp. 129–130.

31. "Frederick Gutekunst," Oberholtzer, 2:334–335. Gutekunst was regarded as the dean of American photographers at the time. Among his sitters who touch on French affairs were Bishop Charles Pettit McIlvaine, of Ohio, and Mlle. Rachel, the celebrated actress who taught Eugénie to curtsy.

32. Evans, *Memoirs*, one-volume edition, p. 131.

33. Ibid., p. 132.

34. Ibid., p. 133; *Herald,* September 10, 1864.
35. Evans, *Memoirs,* one-volume edition, p. 136 footnote.
36. Ibid., p. 137; U. S. Grant to Julia Grant, September 25, 1864. Evans refers to his offer to supervise the education in Paris of one of General Grant's sons in a manuscript, "Prince of Wales," but Mrs. Grant was unwilling to have a son so far away in wartime.
37. Evans, *Memoirs,* one-volume edition, p. 138.
38. Evans to Seward, December 3, 1864.
39. Evans, *Memoirs,* one-volume edition, p. 139.
40. *Notable,* s.v. "Greenhow, Rose O'Neal"; Ross, pp. 246, 250–253.

9: *Mercy on Europe's Battlefields*

Primary materials: Dr. Evans's own extensive writings: *History of the American Ambulance;* Evans, *La Commission sanitaire;* Evans, *Report on the Instruments and Apparatus of Medicine;* Evans, *Sanitary Institutions During the Austro-Prussian-Italian Conflict.* I have also consulted Branch; Dulles, *American Red Cross; Paris Universal Exposition, 1867;* Jane Gray Seaver, "Thomas William Evans," in *Our Representatives Abroad;* and Baguenier-Désorimeaux, "L'Hôtel Evans." A concise summary of Dr. Evans's philanthropic activities appeared after his death in "Obituary: Dr. Thomas W. Evans." Details of the critical attitude of U.S. Sanitary Commission leaders toward Evans can be found in Maxwell, *Lincoln's Fifth Wheel.* Dunant was a witness to the tragic scenes at Solferino, and his *Origin of the Red Cross* made a deep impression on European opinion. Dunant's biographer, Gumpert, reports on his mission and battlefield experiences.

1. Evans, *Memoirs,* 1:171–172; Baguenier-Désorimeaux, "L'Hôtel Evans," p. 248.
2. Branch, p. 144; *Sanitary Institutions,* p. x.
3. Evans, *La Commission sanitaire,* pp. xiff, xix, 25, 44–49, 55–56, 65; Maxwell, p. viii.
4. Branch, pp. 117, 120, 122; Evans, *Sanitary Institutions,* p. vii.
5. Dunant, pp. 40, 57–58, 67–68; George, pp. 211–212, 216–217; Gumpert, pp. 43–44, 46–49, 59–60, 63.
6. Evans, *La Commission sanitaire,* pp. iii, v; Evans, *Report on Instruments* 5:23–24.
7. Dulles, p. 7; Dunant, p. vii; Evans, *Sanitary Institutions,* pp. 9–13; Maxwell, p. 230.
8. Dulles, pp. 8–9; Evans, *American Ambulance,* p. x; Evans, *Sanitary Institutions,* p. v.
9. Evans, *Report on Instruments,* 5:53; Evans, *Sanitary Institutions,* pp. 37–39, 61, 64, 66, 117–119, 121, 125–126.
10. Evans, *Sanitary Institutions,* pp. 132–133, 136ff.
11. Ibid., pp. 150, 169–171, 174–175, 177.
12. Branch, p. 129; Evans, *Sanitary Institutions,* pp. 8, 183.
13. Maxwell, pp. 289–290.

14. Strong, 4:164.

15. Branch, pp. 128–129, 131, 153; Evans, *Report on Instruments*, 5:16, 29–32, 39–42; Evans, *Sanitary Institutions*, pp. 216, 219; *Paris Universal Exposition, 1867*, p. 262; Johnston, pp. 505–506.

16. Theodore Evans, "To the Memory," pp. 47–48; Evans, *Sanitary Institutions*, pp. 185, 188, 205–206.

17. Evans, *Report on Instruments*, 5:45–46; Maxwell, p. 290.

10: To Berlin!

For the political events of the summer of 1870; the views of Eugénie and Dr. Evans; Napoleon III's health; the military disaster: I consulted principally, though not exclusively: Arnaud; Aubry; Theodore Evans, "To the Memory"; Dr. Evans's *Fall* and the *Memoirs;* Grandeffe; Kurtz; Ridley; Seignobos; Thompson; Washburne; Williams, *French Revolution*. The underpinning for the account of the American Ambulance: Branch; Theodore Evans, "To the Memory"; Dr. Evans's *American Ambulance*, the *Fall*, and the *Memoirs*. See also [Henry Labouchere], *Diary of the Besieged Resident*, and Piedagnel. The Abbé Puyol, in "Journal de l'Abbé Puyol," evokes vividly the scene at Saint-Cloud as Eugénie waits for war news.

1. Evans, *Memoirs*, 1:194; MaHeu, pp. 14–15.

2. Theodore Evans, "To the Memory," p. 62.

3. Evans, "My Relations . . . with this Personage," p. 8.

4. Ibid., p. 13.

5. Evans, *Memoirs*, 1:204. General Leboeuf's silly brag has given him posthumous fame of a sort.

6. Arnaud, p. 384; Seignobos, p. 219.

7. "The Imperial Dentist," *Academy*, p. 1309; Barker, pp. 202–203; Evans, *Memoirs*, 1:203; Seignobos, p. 223.

8. Dupuy, p. 46; Evans, *Fall*, part I, pp. 17–18; Ridley, p. 562; Saunders, p. 172.

9. Evans, *Fall*, part I, pp. 27, 117; Sarcey, pp. 7–11.

10. Evans, *Fall*, part I, pp. 7–8, 27; Fleury, 1:121–123, 125; George, p. 323.

11. [Puyol], "Journal de l'Abbé Puyol," pp. 307–308, 311, 315.

12. The general historical background summarized in this chapter is widely available, but a convenient, popular account is Thompson, Chapter X. For a description of the cavalry charge at Reichshoffen, see *France-Amérique*, February 19–25, 1981, and June 11–17, 1981. For the conduct of the Empress-Regent during the August crisis, I followed Aubry, p. 228, and Puyol.

13. Evans, *Fall*, pt. I, p. 12; Baguenier-Désorimeaux, "L'Hôtel Evans," p. 249.

14. Theodore Evans, "To the Memory," pp. 45–46; Evans, *American Ambulance*, pp. 3–4, 11; Evans, *Memoirs*, 1:213–216.

15. Theodore Evans, "To the Memory," p. 46; Evans, *American Ambulance*, pp. 23, 511–513; Keeler, "With the American Ambulance Corps at Paris," pp. 84–85.

16. Branch, p. 153; Evans, *American Ambulance*, pp. 13, 15–16, 34.

17. *DNB*, s.v. "Wallace, Richard"; Kransberg, *Siege of Paris*, pp. 66–67.

18. Evans, *American Ambulance*, pp. 36–40.

19. Bowles, *Defence of Paris*, pp. 172–173, quoted in Branch, pp. 163–164, 279; Evans, *American Ambulance*, pp. 36–37, 78–80, 450–451, 517.

20. Theodore Evans, "To the Memory," p. 47; Evans, *American Ambulance*, pp. 48–55; [Labouchere], *Diary of the Besieged Resident*, p. 91; Piedagnel, p. 57. A picture of the grounds and structures of the American Ambulance appears in *L'Illustration*, October 22, 1870.

21. [Labouchere], *Diary of the Besieged Resident*, p. 73.

22. Evans, *American Ambulance*, pp. 25–26.

11: The Dentist and the Empress

My principal source for the flight of Eugénie from France is Dr. Evans, since he managed it. Other accounts of the day the Second Empire fell differ, naturally, in details and perspectives. I have read extensively, though not exhaustively, in the writings of contemporaries and later historians who have been fascinated by the drama of September 4, 1870. Especially useful: Aubry; Bicknell; Bigelow's Diary; Du Camp; Fleury; Gorce; and Kurtz. I am also indebted to Bouscatel and Abbé Puyol's long article in *Le Figaro*. The stormy passage from Deauville to Ryde is described in "The Empress Eugénie's Flight to England: From the Log of the 'Gazelle,'" with emphasis on the part played by the yacht's owner, Sir John Burgoyne. Letters written by Mrs. Thomas W. Evans were helpful; see Dubbs, "The Flight of an Empress," and Soyer, "Le Dentiste Thomas Evans." Dr. Evans's emotional declaration that when he united Eugénie and her son his mission in life had been accomplished is recounted in Seward, *Travels*, p. 762.

1. Evans, *Memoirs*, 2:346–347, 351; the *Goncourt Journal*, p. 53.

2. Evans, *Memoirs*, 2:346, 359.

3. Ibid., 2:359.

4. Aubry, pp. 216, 228; Du Camp, 2:30–33, 66; Fleury, 2:273–277; Gorce, 7:395–396.

5. Du Camp, 2:94–95; Duff, pp. 211–212; Fleury, 2:398; Kurtz, p. 251.

6. Aubry, p. 228; Du Camp, 2:73, 100, 111; Fleury, 2:459; Legge, p. 233.

7. Bouscatel, p. 81.

8. Gower, 1:372.

9. *Biographie*, s.v. "Lamballe, Marie-Thérèse de Savoie-Carignan"; Bouscatel, p. 103; Louis-Philippe, *Memoirs*, p. 261.

10. Bouscatel, pp. 174, 186.

11. Ibid., p. 186.

12. Aubry, pp. 240–241; Kurtz, p. 252.

13. Aubry, pp. 241–242; Du Camp, 2:103; Duff, p. 217; Evans, *Memoirs*, 2:329–330; Stoeckl, *When Men Had Time*, p. 106; Washburne, 2:110.

14. Aubry, p. 242; Evans, *Memoirs*, 2:329–333; Lévêque, p. 408.

15. Bigelow Diary, October 11, 1870; Gorce, 7:422–423; Stoeckl, *King of the French*, pp. 189–190.

16. Aubry, p. 243; Evans, *Memoirs,* 2:334-336; *Le Figaro,* November 24, 1870; Fleury, 2:364.

17. Aubry, p. 243; Bicknell, pp. 229, 232-233; Bigelow Diary, October 11, 1870; Du Camp, 2:104; Evans, *Memoirs,* 2:335, 365-366; Fleury, 2:464-465; Loliée, pp. 209-210; Baguenier-Désorimeaux, "L'Hôtel Evans," pp. 250-251.

18. Allem, p. 11; Aubry, pp. 244-245; Du Camp, 2:105.

19. Aubry, p. 245; Bigelow Diary, October 11, 1870; Evans, *Memoirs,* 2:338.

20. One cannot know exactly what the Empress said to the doctor. My account combines the recollection of Evans in his *Memoirs,* 2:359-360, with the version given in Baguenier-Désorimeaux, "L'Hôtel Evans," p. 250. Variants appear in Aubry, pp. 245-246, and Stoeckl, *When Men Had Time,* pp. 106-108.

21. Evans, *Memoirs,* 2:384; Ridley, pp. 23, 32.

22. Evans, *Memoirs,* 2:384, 386; Kurtz, p. 253.

23. *Register,* October 17, 1897, quoted in Branch, p. 252; Evans, "The Empress Eugénie's Flight from Paris," pp. 852-853; Evans, *Memoirs,* 2:394, 397-398, 400, 631.

24. Lacour-Gayet, "L'Impératrice Eugénie: Les derniers semaines aux Tuileries, le quatre septembre et la fuite en Angleterre," p. 26.

25. Bicknell, p. 236; "Eugénie's Flight to England: From the Log of the 'Gazelle,' " p. 388.

26. Evans, *Memoirs,* 2:434-435; Kurtz, p. 253.

27. Evans, *Memoirs,* 2:436, 439-440; Dubbs, "Flight of an Empress," p. 52.

28. Soyer, "Le Dentiste Thomas Evans," pp. 1144-1145.

29. "The Empress Eugénie's Flight," p. 392.

30. Hunting, "The Empress at Chislehurst," p. 934.

31. Aubry, pp. 271, 277.

32. Ibid., p. 271; Queen Victoria, *Letters,* second series, 2:89, 92-93.

33. Evans, *Memoirs,* 2:501; Eugénie to Dr. Evans, September 4, 1871.

34. Labouchere, "Diplomatic Tooth-Doctor," p. 1366.

35. Anne Coffin Hanson to author, March 15, 1981; Seward, *Travels,* p. 762.

12: *The "Terrible Year" and the Third Republic*

The siege, the winter of 1870-1871, the psychological state of the people: Baedeker; Bowles; Branch; Gorce; Kransberg; Labouchere, *Diary;* and Sarcey. An extensive note, below, covers my sources on the starvation of Paris. The Commune: I follow the chapter "The Commune of Paris," in Williams's *French Revolution.* The *Goncourt Journal* is indispensable for one attempting to visualize daily life in Paris. Dr. Evans also gives a vivid description in his *Fall* and the *Memoirs.* The burning of the Tuileries: Bicknell; Gosseln; and [Vizetelly], *Court of the Tuileries.*

For Dr. Evans's intimacy with former President Grant, I drew on his manuscript "The Prince of Wales," Packard, and Young. His increasing renown as a practitioner: "A Remarkable Case Was Recently Tried"; Young; various communications from royal figures in the Evans Papers; and Van Wyck.

1. *Goncourt Journal*, pp. 87, 106; Gosseln, pp. 294–295; Dubbs, "Flight of an Empress," p. 53; Legge, pp. 241–243.

2. Bowles, p. 173; Branch, p. 168; Evans, *American Ambulance*, pp. 42–43; Keeler, "With the American Ambulance Corps," pp. 85–88.

3. Baedeker, p. 98; Bowles, p. vii.

4. Bowles, p. 92; Kransberg, *Siege*, p. 11; Maillard, pp. xi, 80–81, 216.

5. Claretie, p. 8; Evans, *Memoirs*, 1:283; Gorce, 7:206–207; Horne, p. 107; Labouchere, *Diary*, p. 81; Washburne, 1:171.

6. Labouchere, *Diary*, p. 26; Gorce, 7:206–207.

7. Kransberg, *Siege*, p. 114; Primet, pp. 119, 126; Sarcey, p. 129.

8. On the famine: Bowles, pp. 93, 148, 298; Champney, pp. 131–138; Claretie, pp. 50, 52; Dupuy, p. 91; Gautier, p. 162; *Goncourt Journal*, pp. 84–86, 88–90, 138; *L'Illustration*, December 17 and 24, 1870, and January 7, 1871; Kransberg, *Siege*, pp. 43, 46–47, 62–65, 105–106, 120–121; Labouchere, *Diary*, pp. 50, 76; Schlosser, "Siege Dinners 1870–71," pp. 210–215; Maillard, pp. 53–55; Sarcey, pp. 169, 173, 250–251; Washburne, 1:232, 235.

9. Kransberg, *Siege*, pp. 148–154; *NYT*, February 15, 1871; Williams, *French Revolution*, pp. 113–114.

10. Gibson, p. 287. The quotation from Baudelaire appears in Joseph Barry, "Paris Commune from a dream to bloody nightmare in ten weeks," p. 57.

11. Bicknell, pp. 247–248; Gosseln, pp. 301–305; *L'Illustration*, June 3, 1871; [Vizetelly], *Court of the Tuileries*, pp. 410–414.

12. Evans, *Fall*, part II, pp. 84–85; Evans, *Memoirs*, 2:582.

13. Evans, *Memoirs*, one-volume edition, pp. 479–483.

14. Ibid., pp. 483–484.

15. Simpson, p. 326; Evans, *Memoirs*, one-volume edition, p. 484.

16. Progrès, "Les dentistes américains," pp. 522–534.

17. Seaver, "Thomas William Evans," p. 447.

18. "A Remarkable Case Was Recently Tried," p. 128.

19. Evans, *Memoirs*, one-volume edition, p. 114.

20. Young, 1:128–129, 131, 134–135, 137.

21. Howe, p. 421. Healy twice painted the doctor's "beautiful wife" with "liveliness and geniality": Bye, "Evans Museum," pp. 9–10.

22. Evans, "Prince of Wales."

23. Packard, p. 129.

24. Theodore Evans, "To the Memory," pp. 1–3, 22.

25. Hackett, p. 103.

26. Labouchere, "Diplomatic Tooth-Doctor," pp. 1366–1367.

27. *Register*, May 3, 1868.

28. Ibid., May 9, 1868.

29. Conway, p. xi.

30. Branch, pp. 232–233; Riddle, "A Lighthouse of American Faith and Freedom Abroad," pp. 6–9; Cochran, *Friendly Adventures: A Chronicle of the American Church of Paris, 1857–1931*, pp. 16–17, 56 and footnote, 65, 96, 107; Laney, p. 146. Riddle lists Dr. Theodore S. Evans as a communicant,

but confuses him with his brother Thomas in saying that Theodore helped the Empress to escape.

31. Evans, "My Relations . . . with this personage," p. 10; Grand Master of the Queen of Spain to Dr. Evans, July 20, 1888; Charles Murray, secretary to Leopold II, to Dr. Evans, November 18, 1894.

32. Evans, "My Relations . . . with this personage," pp. 31–32.

33. Asbell, p. 48; Branch, pp. 208–214; Evans, "My Relations . . . with this personage," pp. 41–43; "Dr. Thomas W. Evans," *Items of Interest,* pp. 203–207.

34. Van Wyck, p. 254.

35. "Commencement Exercises," p. 399; Minutes of the Board of Directors, Lafayette College, June 1870 and July 1872; Rainey, p. 22; Ronald E. Robbins to author, May 15, 1980; Skillman, pp. 557–558.

36. Flament, p. 326; Perruchot, p. 215.

13: "Handsome Tom": A Doctor's Fling at Gallantry

There is no reference to Méry Laurent in Dr. Evans's published writings or his private papers, but I have traced their relationship through the lives of Méry's artist and writer friends: Hanson, "Tale of Two Manets"; Branch; Goffin; MaHeu; *Correspondence Mallarmé-Whistler;* Stéphane Mallarmé's *Correspondence;* Moore; Mondor, *Vie de Mallarmé;* Mondor, *Mallarmé plus intime;* Raoul-Duval, "Méry Laurent"; Perruchot; Regnier; Tabarant; Weintraub; and Bernard Veillet.

For my glance at the elegant demimondaines of Paris: Blyth; Kracauer; Stoeckl, *When Men Had Time;* and de Wissant. The *savoureuse anecdote* about Van Wyck and his evening on the town with Dr. Evans appears in his *Recollections.*

1. Brodsky, p. 154; Raoul-Duval, "Méry Laurent," p. 35; Perruchot, p. 215; Tabarant, pp. 426–427.

2. de Wissant, pp. 205, 227–228.

3. Goffin, pp. 44–46, 51–52.

4. Ibid., pp. 14–15, 27–33; MaHeu, pp. 30–35; Mondor, *Vie de Mallarmé,* 2:417; Raoul-Duval, "Méry Laurent," pp. 33, 37; Viel Castel, 2:298.

5. Blyth, p. 223; Brodsky, p. 189; Kracauer, pp. 219–220, 332; Stoeckl, *When Men Had Time,* p. 31.

6. Van Wyck, pp. 255–257.

7. Raoul-Duval, "Méry Laurent," pp. 35–37; Regnier, pp. 72–74, 76, 78–79; Tabarant, pp. 427, 434.

8. Perruchot, p. 215; Weintraub, pp. 348–349.

9. Goffin, pp. 69–70; Weintraub, p. 349.

10. For a discussion of marriage and morals in the upper levels of nineteenth-century French society, see Zeldin, 1:291–292, 303–305.

11. *Correspondence Mallarmé-Whistler,* p. 32 footnote.

12. Mondor, *Vie de Mallarmé,* 2:538–541; Moore, p. 62; Bernard Veillet, p. 36.

13. Mondor, *Vie de Mallarmé,* 2:416.

14. Moore, p. 59.

15. George Moore borrowed the phrase *toute la lyre* from posthumously published poetic collections by Victor Hugo.

16. Relations and transactions among Mallarmé, Whistler, Méry Laurent, and Dr. Evans: *Correspondence Mallarmé-Whistler,* pp. 35–36, 39, 46–47, 50, 53, 58, 64, 79–80, 82, 89–90, 158.

17. Hanson, "Tale of Two Manets," p. 60; Branch, pp. 242–243; Heine, *The Memoirs of Heinrich Heine and some newly-discovered fragments of his writings, with an introductory essay by Thomas W. Evans;* Mallarmé, *Correspondence,* 4: part 2, pp. 472–473. Mallarmé received an autographed copy of Evans's *Heine;* the Historical Society of Pennsylvania has one, too.

18. Hanson, "Tale of Two Manets," pp. 59–68; Bernard Veillet, pp. 46–47.

14: The Tragic Empress

Eugénie's fortune: Bicknell; Carey; Evans, *Memoirs;* and Vapereau. The atmosphere at Camden Place during Napoleon III's remaining two years: Brodsky; Dansette; Evans, *Memoirs.* Napoleon III's last days: Ridley discusses his illness, death, and the medical quarrels that followed. Evans's account appears in his *Memoirs.* George imagines, pp. 366–367, the scenes and events that may have passed through Napoleon III's mind at his end in a passage I have adapted.

The ambush of the Prince Impérial: Kurtz covers the attack at length, Legge briefly. Guedalla does justice to the drama of Lou-Lou's death. Dr. Evans told his nephew, in "To the Memory," of how he identified the body. Ridley surveys the controversies over British culpability. ,

The Empress's move to Farnborough Hill and her life there: Carey; Cabrol, "The Empress Eugénie in England"; Evans, *Fall* and the *Memoirs;* various telegrams from Eugénie in the Evans Papers; Kurtz; and Smyth. The Empress's last years: Aubry; Filon; Evans, *Memoirs;* Kurtz; Soyer, "Le Dentiste Thomas Evans"; Smyth; and Woolf. For estimates of Eugénie's character and final — well, semifinal — place in history, see Barker and Woodham-Smith.

1. Bicknell, p. 253; Carey, p. 34; Legge, p. 197; Stoeckl, *When Men Had Time,* p. 115. The provenance of the Charlemagne talisman and its eventual resting place are discussed in Paléologue, pp. 241–244.

2. Carey, p. 356.

3. Evans, *Memoirs,* 1:108–110.

4. Dansette, pp. 274–275, 278; Evans, *Memoirs,* 1:578–579.

5. Brodsky, p. 303; Osgood, p. 11.

6. Aubry, pp. 279–281; Bicknell, pp. 254–255; Burnand, p. 29; Kurtz, p. 269; Rothney, pp. 3, 9, 17. Dr. Evans vehemently denied that Napoleon III had any idea of another coup d'état.

7. Ridley, pp. 585–589; Evans, *Memoirs,* 2:595–604; George, pp. 366–367. And see Williams, *Mortal Napoleon,* p. 162ff.

8. Thompson, p. 318; Soyer, "Le Dentiste Thomas Evans," p. 1285.

9. Filon, p. 274.

10. Alan B. Spitzer, "The Good Napoleon," pp. 308–310, 315–316, 324–326; Philadelphia Museum of Art, *Second Empire*, p. 217; Price, *French Second Republic*, p. 324; Williams, *Gaslight and Shadow*, p. 198; Zeldin, 1:509.

11. Guedalla, pp. 438–440; Kurtz, pp. 296–315; Legge, pp. 306–307; Ridley, pp. 596–613.

12. Bicknell, pp. 276; Carette, pp. 81–85; Evans, "Death of the Prince Impérial."

13. Theodore Evans, "To the Memory," p. 36; Fleury, 1:167.

14. Luntz, "History of Forensic Dentistry," pp. 7–17; *DAB*, s.v. "Webster, John White"; ibid., s.v. "Booth, John Wilkes."

15. *Register*, June 28, 1879.

16. Aubry, p. 334; *Dictionnaire*, s.v. "Cabrol, Dom Ferdinand"; Kurtz, p. 321.

17. Carey, pp. 345–347; Cabrol, "Empress Eugénie in England," p. 188.

18. Carey, p. 21; Evans, *Fall*, part 2, pp. 168–169; Kurtz, pp. 330–331, 333.

19. Eugénie to Dr. Evans, various telegrams; Le Pelletier to Evans, February 6, 1886, Evans Papers.

20. Aubry, pp. 313–315, 321; Kurtz, pp. 340–341.

21. Ibid., pp. 320, 328, 337–339.

22. Evans, *Memoirs*, one-volume edition, p. 411; Filon, pp. 311, 313; Kurtz, p. 332; Soyer, "Le Dentiste Thomas Evans," p. 1286; Smyth, 2:81, 240.

23. Woolf, pp. 11, 144.

24. Barker, pp. 12–13, 113, 211; Kurtz, pp. 367–368; Ridley, pp. 643–644; Woodham-Smith, p. 349.

15: An Ending and a Beginning

Dr. Evans's last years: Branch; Burnand; Talbot, "Dr. Thomas W. Evans"; and Baguenier-Désorimeaux, "L'Hôtel Evans." Lafayette Home imbroglio: *Register*, Branch, and O'Connor. Difficulties with John Henry Evans: Branch, Dr. Evans to his parents, and Rainey. Dr. Arthur C. Hugenschmidt, his relationship with Evans and Méry Laurent: Asbell; Benard, "Bâtards de Napoleon III"; Decaux, *La Castiglione, dame de coeur de l'Europe;* Goffin; Monnier, "Necrologie. Arthur Hugenschmidt (1862–1929)."

Death of Mrs. Evans, disposition of Evans's wealth and last professional activities: "An Honored Practitioner"; Barrett, "Dr. Thomas W. Evans"; Theodore Evans, "To the Memory"; and *St. Paul Pioneer Press*. The death of Dr. Evans is recorded in many places but is easily accessible in the *DAB* and *NYT*. Goffin is the best source on the death of Méry Laurent. Judgments on the career of Dr. Evans appeared in the *British Journal of Dental Science, Dental Cosmos,* and *Dental Practitioner and Advertiser*. Labouchere meditated on the doctor's life in *Truth,* and *The Academy* (London) printed a notably affectionate farewell. Comment in French journals is referred to in the notes that follow. A modern estimate of Evans: Carr, "Thomas W. Evans." Asbell, Carr, Cheyney, and Rainey are sources for the merger of the Evans

Museum and Dental Institute with the University of Pennsylvania's School of Dentistry.

1. *Register,* March 10, 1894; *Herald* (Paris), February 10, 1894; O'Connor, pp. 184, 186, 188–189.

2. "Au sujet d'un proces en diffamation," Evans Papers; Branch, p. 236, and 237 footnote.

3. Branch, pp. 237–239; Evans to his parents, December 19, 1859.

4. Asbell, pp. 36–37, 280; Benard, "Bâtards de Napoleon III," p. 288; Monnier, pp. 794–796. Decaux made a careful investigation of the parentage of Dr. Hugenschmidt and concluded that he was the legitimate son of the Tuileries Hugenschmidts. See *La Castiglione, dame de coeur,* Appendix I, pp. 387–389.

5. *Philadelphia Evening Bulletin,* October 5, 1897.

6. "An Honored Practitioner," p. 222; *DAB,* s.v. "Harrison, Charles Custis"; *Philadelphia Evening Bulletin,* October 5, 1897.

7. Branch, pp. 266–267; unidentified, undated clipping from Cincinnati newspaper, Evans Papers.

8. *St. Paul Pioneer Press,* September 28, 1897.

9. Ibid.

10. Theodore Evans, "To the Memory," p. 94.

11. Ibid., p. 94; Fouquières, 1:236; Raoul-Duval, "Méry Laurent," p. 82.

12. Ibid., "Méry Laurent," p. 82; Tabarant, p. 445.

13. Goffin, pp. 283, 286–288.

14. *Le Figaro,* November 16, 1897; "Obituary: Dr. Thomas W. Evans," p. 73; "Resolutions on Death of Dr. Thomas W. Evans," pp. 156–158; Evans, *Memoirs,* 1:21; Carr, "Thomas W. Evans," pp. 87, 93–94; Bye, "The Evans Museum," p. 8; *NYT,* November 16, 1897.

15. An unfriendly notice, "Dr. Evans's Wills," was published in the *British Journal of Dental Science* in January 1898, p. 40. An indignant reply entitled "Desecration of the Grave" appeared in *Dental Practitioner and Advertiser* in April 1898, p. 94; it ended "But he is now the dead lion, and every ass must have his kick at him"; "Necrologie — Thomas Evans," p. 364; Soyer, "Le Dentiste Thomas Evans," p. 1288; "Nouvelles — Necrologie," pp. 527–528.

16. "The Imperial Dentist," *Academy,* December 16, 1905.

17. Memorandum to author from the Historical Society of Pennsylvania, December 3, 1981; Rainey, pp. 60, 62; Rosenthal, p. 13.

18. Carr, "Thomas W. Evans," p. 96; Rainey, p. 48.

19. Asbell, p. 53; Cheyney, pp. 356–357.

20. *Philadelphia Inquirer,* October 2, 1977, and November 3, 1978.

21. Rainey, pp. 67–68.

22. Browne, *That Man Heine,* p. 403.

Bibliography

See the key to abbreviations at the beginning of Notes

Manuscripts, Typescripts, Photocopies of Unpublished Material

"Au sujet d'un proces en diffamation." Unsigned, undated document. Evans Papers, U. Penn.

Beck, René, to author, September 22, 1982.

Bigelow, John. Diary. Bigelow Papers. Manuscript Division, NYPL.

———. Letters (Confidential 1862–1866). Bigelow Papers, NYPL.

Branch, Anthony Douglas. "Dr. Thomas W. Evans, American Dentist in Paris, 1847–1897." Ph.D. dissertation, University of California, Santa Barbara, 1971. U. Penn.

Eugénie to Dr. Evans, September 4, 1871. Evans Papers, U. Penn.

Evans, Theodore Wiltberger. "To the Memory of My Uncle," [April 1900]. Evans Papers, U. Penn. Theodore was a son of Dr. Thomas W. Evans's brother Rudulph Henry Evans. Pagination used in Notes is of a typewritten transcript of the original holograph. Evans Papers, U. Penn.

Evans, Thomas W. "I Write Some Remembrances of Early Life," [1893]. Evans Papers, U. Penn.

———. Manuscript Journals 1859–1862. Typescript. Evans Papers, U. Penn.

———. "My Relations and Long Continued Friendship with this personage during these changes first as Princess of Prussia — Queen of Prussia — Empress of Germany" (July 1, 1894). Evans Papers, U. Penn.

———. "Prince of Wales," August 16, 1885. Without new heading the manuscript shifts focus to General Grant. Evans Papers, U. Penn.

——— to William H. Seward, November 18, 1862. William H. Seward Papers, Rochester.

——— to William H. Seward, December 3, 1864. William H. Seward Papers, Rochester.

Grant, Ulysses A., to Julia Grant, September 25, 1864. Manuscript Division, Congress.

Hahn, Janine. "Researches sur le docteur Thomas W. Evans." Université René Descartes, Faculté de Chirurgie Dentaire, Paris, n.d. U. Penn.

Hanson, Anne Coffin, to author, March 15, 1981.

Inventory of Paintings in the Evans Museum. Evans Papers, U. Penn.

Jones, Oliver P. "Who Was Theodore Evans, Paris, France?" May 2, 1979. Typescript. U. Penn.

Lafayette College, Minutes of the Board of Directors, June 1870, and July 1872. Lafayette.

Macfarlane, S. "Thomas W. Evans and his connection with Dr. Samuel S. Macfarlane." Typescript. U. Penn.

MaHeu, René. "Doctor Thomas William Evans: Dentist to Napoleon III and Literature." Trans. by Annette H. Emgarth. University of Paris, Faculty of Dental Surgery, Paris, 1975. U. Penn. Major libraries and works of reference list Evans's middle name as "Wiltberger," his mother's maiden name, but he signed official documents as "Thomas William Evans."

Miscellaneous telegrams and letters from the secretaries of Eugénie, Leopold II of Belgium, Isabella II, Queen of Spain, Comte Louis Philippe d'Orléans. Evans Papers. U. Penn.

New York Public Library, Economic and Public Affairs Division, to author, March 21, 1977.

Robbins, Ronald E., to author, May 15, 1980.

Seward, William H., to Thomas W. Evans, December 6, 1862. Seward Papers, Rochester.

Veillet, Bernard. "Researches sur le docteur Thomas W. Evans: Son Hôtel Particulier," Université René Descartes, Faculté de Chirurgie Dentaire, Paris, n.d. U. Penn.

Veillet, Maurice. "Research on Doctor Thomas W. Evans: His First Years in Paris." Trans. by Annette H. Emgarth. Université René Descartes, Faculty of Dental Surgery, Paris, 1974. U. Penn.

Books

Among published works used extensively in this essay the two-volume edition of *The Memoirs of Dr. Thomas W. Evans* was indispensable. There is also a one-volume edition, entitled *Memoirs of Dr. Thomas W. Evans: The Second French Empire*. Both draw extensively on a volume privately printed by Dr. Evans, but withdrawn at the request of the Empress Eugénie, *The Fall of the Second French Empire: Fragments of My Memories*. One copy exists at U. Penn. In some ways rather artless, and possibly meddled with by Dr. Crane, Evans's literary executor, the *Memoirs* are notable for their expression of unshakable loyalty in good times and bad to the star-crossed imperial couple who in the end lost France. And they gain in value because they were written with a view to posthumous publication.

Allem, Maurice. *La vie quotidienne sous le Second Empire*. Paris: Hachette, 1948.

Arnaud, René. *The Second Republic and Napoleon III*. London: William Heinemann, 1930.

Asbell, Milton B. *A Century of Dentistry: A History of the University of*

Pennsylvania School of Dental Medicine 1878–1978. Philadelphia: University of Pennsylvania Press, 1977.

Aubry, Octave. *Eugénie, Empress of the French.* Trans. by F. M. Atkinson. Philadelphia: J. B. Lippincott, 1931.

Austen, Jane. *Persuasion.* Ed. with an intro. and notes by Andrew Wright. Boston: Houghton Mifflin, 1965.

Baedeker, Karl, *Paris and Northern France.* Coblenz, 1872.

Barker, Nancy Nichols. *Distaff Diplomacy: The Empress Eugénie and the Foreign Policy of the Second Empire.* Austin: University of Texas Press: 1967.

Beaconsfield, The Earl of. *Endymion.* New York, 1880.

Bicknell, Anna L. *Life in the Tuileries Under the Second Empire.* New York, 1895.

Bidwell, R. L. *Currency Conversion Tables: A Hundred Years of Change.* London: Rex Collings, 1970.

Bigelow, John. *Retrospections of an Active Life,* 5 vols. New York, 1909–1913.

Blyth, Henry. *Skittles: The Last Victorian Courtesan: The Life and Times of Catherine Walters.* London: Rupert Hart-Davis, 1970.

Bonaparte, Louis Napoleon. *The Political and Historical Works of Louis Napoleon Bonaparte, President of the French Republic, now First Collected. With an Original Memoir of his Life, Brought Down to the Promulgation of the Constitution of 1852; and occasional notes,* 2 vols. New York: Howard Fertig, 1972. First published in 1852.

Boucher, François. *American Footprints in Paris . . .* Trans. by Francis Wilson Huard. New York: Doran, 1921.

Bouscatel, Edouard. *L'Impératrice et le quatre Septembre.* Paris, 1872.

Bowles, Thomas Gibson. *The Defence of Paris: Narrated as it Was Seen.* London, 1871.

Briggs, Asa, ed. *The Nineteenth Century: The Contradictions of Progress.* New York: McGraw-Hill, 1970.

Brodsky, Alyn. *Imperial Charade: A Biography of Emperor Napoleon III and Empress Eugénie, Nineteenth Century Europe's Most Successful Adventurers.* Indianapolis: Bobbs-Merrill, 1978.

Browne, Lewis. *That Man Heine.* New York: Macmillan, 1927.

Burnand, Robert. *La vie quotidienne en France de 1870 à 1900.* Paris: Hachette, 1947.

Carette, Mme. A. *Recollections of the Court of the Tuileries.* Trans. by Elizabeth Phipps Train. New York, 1889.

Carey, Agnes. *The Empress Eugénie in Exile.* New York: Century Co., 1920.

Case, Lynn M., and Warren F. Spencer. *The United States and France: Civil War Diplomacy.* Philadelphia: University of Pennsylvania Press, 1970.

Champceix, Léodile. *The American Colony in Paris in 1867.* Boston, 1868.

Champney, Elizabeth W. *Three Vassar Girls in France: A Story of the Siege of Paris.* Boston, 1888.

Charenton, Maurice L. *Le Docteur Thomas W. Evans dentiste de Napoléon III et les dentistes de son époque.* Paris: E. Le François, 1936.

Cheyney, Edward Potts. *History of the University of Pennsylvania 1740–1940.* Philadelphia: University of Pennsylvania Press: 1940.

Clapp, Margaret. *Forgotten First Citizen: John Bigelow.* Boston: Little, Brown, 1947.

Claretie, Jules. *Paris Assiégé 1870–71.* Paris, 1898.

Cochran, Joseph Wilson. *Friendly Adventures: A Chronicle of the American Church of Paris, 1857–1931.* Paris: Brentano, 1931.

Conway, John Joseph. *Footprints of Famous Americans in Paris.* New York: John Lane Co., 1912.

Corley, T. A. B. *Democratic Despot: A Life of Napoleon III.* London: Barrie and Rockliffe, 1961.

Correspondence Mallarmé-Whistler: Histoire de la grande amitié de leurs dernières années. Ed. by Carl Paul Barbier. Paris: A. G. Nizet, 1964.

Couperie, Pierre. *Paris Through the Ages.* Trans. by Marilyn Low. New York: George Braziller, 1968.

Cowley, Baron Henry R. C. Wellesley. *The Paris Embassy During the Second Empire.* New York: Harper & Brothers, 1929.

Dagen, Georges. *Le dentiste d'autrefois: 60 reproductions annotées par Georges Dagen.* Paris: n.d.

Dansette, Adrien. *Les amours de Napoleon III.* Paris: Fayard, 1938.

Dayot, Armand. *L'Invasion, le siège, la commune.* Paris, 1901.

Decaux, Alain. *Amours Second Empire.* Paris: Hachette, 1958.

——. *La Castiglione.* Paris: Rombaldi, 1972.

——. *La Castiglione, dame de coeur de l'Europe.* Paris: Amiot-Dupont, 1953.

——. *La Castiglione, dame de coeur de l'Europe d'après sa correspondence et son journal intime inédits.* Paris: Librarie Académique Perrin, 1964.

Doniol, Auguste. *Histoire du XVIᵉ Arrondissement de Paris.* Paris: Hachette, 1902.

Dougall, Richardson, and Mary Patricia Chapman. *United States Chiefs of Mission 1778–1973.* Washington, D.C.: Historical Office, Bureau of Public Affairs, Department of State, 1973.

Du Camp, Maxime. *Souvenirs d'un demi-siècle: au temps de Louis-Philippe et de Napoléon III 1830–1870,* 2 vols. Paris: Hachette, 1949.

Ducourtial, Claude. *Ordres et Décorations.* Paris: Presses Universitaires de France, 1968.

Duff, David. *Eugénie and Napoleon III.* New York: William Morrow, 1978.

Dulles, Foster Rhea. *The American Red Cross: A History.* New York: Harper & Brothers, 1950.

Dunant, Henri. *The Origin of the Red Cross: "Un Souvenir de Solferino."* Trans. by Mrs. David H. Wright. Philadelphia: John C. Winston, 1911.

Dupuy, Aimé. *1870–1871: la guerre, la commune et la presse.* Paris: Armand Colin, 1959.

Englebert, Omer. *The Lives of the Saints.* New York: David McKay, 1960.

Evans, Thomas W. *La commission sanitaire des Etats-Unis: son origine, son organization et ses résultats; avec une notice sur les hôpitaux militaires aux Etats-Unis et sur la réforme sanitaire dans les armées européennes.* Paris, 1865.

——. *The Fall of the Second Empire: Fragments of My Memories.* Privately printed in Paris, 1884.

——. *History of the American Ambulance Established in Paris During the Siege of 1870–71, Together with the Details of its Methods and its Work.* London, 1873.

——. *History and Description of an Ambulance Wagon Constructed in Accordance with Plans Furnished by the Writer.* Paris, 1868.

——. *The Memoirs of Dr. Thomas W. Evans: Recollections of the Second French Empire.* Ed. by Edward A. Crane, 2 vols. London: T. Fisher Unwin, 1906.

——. *Memoirs of Dr. Thomas W. Evans: The Second French Empire,* 1 vol. Ed. by Edward A. Crane. New York: D. Appleton, 1906.

——. *Report on Ambulance and Sanitary Material: Class XI, Group II, Paris Exposition, 1867.* Paris, 1867.

——. *Report on the Instruments and Apparatus of Medicine, Surgery and Hygiene . . . by Thomas W. Evans, M.D., United States Commissioner,* vol. 5. Washington, D.C.: Government Printing Office, 1868.

——. *Sanitary Institutions During the Austro-Prussian-Italian Conflict.* Third ed. Paris: Simon Raçon: 1868.

Exposition Napoléon raconté par les decorations organisée avec la participation de la société des amis du musée de la Légion d'honneur 28 novembre, 1973 — 27 janvier 1974. Paris, n.d.

Filon, Augustin. *Recollections of the Empress Eugénie.* London: Cassell, 1920.

Flament, Albert. *La vie de Manet.* Paris: Plon, 1928.

Fleury, Count Maurice. *Memoirs of the Empress Eugénie,* 2 vols. New York: D. Appleton, 1920.

Fouquières, André de. *Mon Paris et ses Parisiens.* Paris: Pierre Horay, 1953.

Gautier, Théophile. *Tableaux de siège: Paris, 1870–1871.* Paris, 1871.

George, Robert Esmonde Gordon [Sencourt, Robert, pseud.]. *Napoleon III: The Modern Emperor.* New York: D. Appleton-Century, 1933.

Gesztesi, Jules. *Pauline de Metternich Ambassadrice aux Tuileries.* Paris: Flammarion, 1947.

Gibson, William. *Paris During the Commune.* New York: Haskell House, 1974. Reprint of 1895 edition.

Goffin, Robert. *Mallarmé vivant.* Paris: A. G. Nizet, 1956.

Gorce, Pierre de la. *Histoire du Second Empire,* 7 vols. Paris: Plon-Nourrit, 1905.

Gosseln, Louis Léon Théodore [Lenôtre, G., pseud.]. *The Tuileries: The Glories and Enchantments of a Vanished Palace.* Trans. by Hugh Barnes. London: Hebert Jenkins, 1934.

Gower, Lord Ronald. *My Reminiscences,* 2 vols. London, 1883.

Grandeffe, Comte Arthur de. *Paris sous Napoleon III: mémoires d'un homme du monde de 1857 à 1870.* Paris, 1879.

Grimmer, Georges. *Cinq essais nadariens; Nadar . . . la famille, les debuts, l'oeuvre littéraire, l'homme Nadar . . .* Paris: Jammes, 1956.

Guedalla, Philip. *The Second Empire.* New York: Putnam's, 1923.

Guest, Ivor. *Napoleon III in England.* London: British Technical & General Press, 1952.

Gumpert, Martin. *Dunant: The Story of the Red Cross.* Garden City, New York: Blue Ribbon Books, 1938.

Hackett, Frank W. *Reminiscences of the Geneva Tribunal of Arbitration, 1872, the Alabama Claims.* Boston: Houghton Mifflin, 1911.

Hanscom, Elizabeth, comp. *The Friendly Craft: A Collection of American Letters.* New York: Macmillan, 1908.

Hegermann-Lindencrone, L. de. *In the Courts of Memory 1858–1875: From Contemporary Letters.* New York: Harper & Brothers, 1912.

Heine, Heinrich. *Heinrich Heine's Memoirs: From his Works, Letters, and Conversations.* Ed. by Gustav Karpeles, trans. by Gilbert Cannan. New York: Arno Press, 1973. Reprint of the 1910 edition.

Horne, Alistair. *The Fall of Paris: The Siege and the Commune 1870–1.* Pan Books, paperback, 1965.

———. *The Terrible Year: The Paris Commune 1871.* New York: Viking, 1971.

Howe, Julia Ward. *Reminiscences 1819–1899.* New York: Negro Universities Press, Division of Greenwood Publishing Corp., 1969. Reprint of 1899 edition.

Hugo, Victor. *The History of a Crime: The Testimony of an Eye-Witness.* London, n.d.

———. *Les Misérables.* Garden City, New York: The Literary Guild of America, 1954.

Hunt, Gaillard. *Israel, Elihu, and Cadwallader Washburn: A Chapter in American Biography.* New York: Macmillan, 1925.

Ingram, J. S. *The Centennial Exposition . . .* Philadelphia, 1876.

Jarves, James Jackson. *Parisian Sights and French Principles, Seen Through American Spectacles.* New York, 1856.

Johnston, William E. *Memoirs of "Malakoff."* Ed. by R. M. Johnston, 2 vols. London: Hutchinson, 1960.

Jordan, Donaldson, and Edwin J. Pratt. *Europe and the American Civil War.* Boston: Houghton Mifflin, 1931.

Kracauer, Siegfried. *Orpheus in Paris: Offenbach and the Paris of His Time.* Trans. by Gwenda and Eric Mosbacher. New York: Knopf, 1938.

Kransberg, Melvin. "An Emperor Writes History: Napoleon III's *Histoire de Jules César,*" in *Teachers of History: Essays in Honor of Lawrence Bradford Packard.* Ed. by H. Stuart Hughes. Ithaca, New York: Cornell University Press, 1954.

———. *The Siege of Paris, 1870–1871: A Political and Social History.* Ithaca, New York: Cornell University Press, 1950.

Kurtz, Harold. *The Empress Eugénie 1826–1920*. Boston: Houghton Mifflin, 1964.

[Labouchere, Henry]. *Diary of the Besieged Resident in Paris*. New York: Harper & Brothers, 1871.

Lacour-Gayet, G. *L'Impératrice Eugénie*. Paris: Albert Morance, 1925.

Laney, Al. *Paris Herald: The Incredible Newspaper*. New York: D. Appleton-Century, 1947.

Laurière, Y. H. de. *Une américaine à la cour de Napoléon III*. Paris: Calmann-Levy, 1938.

Legge, Edward. *The Comedy & Tragedy of the Second Empire: Paris Society in the Sixties Including Letters of Napoleon III, M. Piétri, and Comte de la Chapelle, and portraits of the Period*. New York: Scribner's, 1911.

———. *The Empress Eugénie and Her Son*. London: Grant Richards, 1916.

Lévêque, André. *Histoire de la civilization française*. New York: Holt, Rinehart and Winston, 1949.

Loliée, Fréderic Auguste. *Les femmes du Second Empire*. Paris: Juven, 1906.

Louis Philippe. *Memoirs 1773–1793*. Trans. by John Hardman. New York: Harcourt Brace Jovanovitch, 1973.

Lufkin, Arthur Ward. *History of Dentistry*. Philadelphia: Lea & Febiger, 1938.

Maillard, Firmin. *Les publications de la rue pendant le siège et la Commune. Satires — Canards — Complaintes — Chansons — Placards et Pamphlets. Bibliographie Pittoresque et anecdotique*. Paris, 1874.

Mallarmé, Stéphane. *Correspondence*. Ed. by Henri Mondor and Lloyd James Austin, vol. 4. Paris: Gallimard, 1973.

Matthews, Brander. *These Many Years: Recollections of a New Yorker*. New York: Scribner's, 1917.

Maugny, Comte Charles Albert de. *Souvenirs of the Second Empire*. London, 1891.

Maurois, Simone André. *Miss Howard and the Emperor*. Trans. by Humphrey Hare. New York: Knopf, 1957.

Maxwell, William Quentin. *Lincoln's Fifth Wheel: The Political History of the United States Sanitary Commission*. New York: Longman's, Green, 1956.

McElroy, Robert. *Levi Parsons Morton: Banker, Diplomat and Statesman*. New York: Putnam's, 1930.

Meynell, Lady Mary. *Sunshine and Shadows Over a Long Life*. London: J. Murray, 1933.

Mondor, Henri. *Mallarmé plus intime*. Paris: Gallimard, 1944.

———. *La vie de Mallarmé*, 2 vols. Paris: Gallimard, 1941.

———. *La vie de Mallarmé*, 37th ed. Complete in one vol. Paris: Gallimard, 1941.

Moore, George. *Memoirs of My Dead Life*. New York: D. Appleton, 1907.

O'Connor, Richard. *The Scandalous Mr. Bennett*. Garden City, New York: Doubleday, 1962.

Osgood, Samuel M., ed. *Napoleon III: Buffoon, Modern Dictator, or Sphinx?* Problems in European Civilization. Boston: D. C. Heath, 1963.

Packard, J. F. *Grant's Tour Around the World* . . . Philadelphia, 1880.

Paléologue, Maurice. *The Tragic Empress: A Record of Intimate Talks with the Empress Eugénie — 1901–1919.* Trans. by Hamish Miles. New York: Harper & Brothers, 1928.

Paris Under Siege, 1870–1871: From the Goncourt Journal. Ed. and trans. by George J. Becker. Ithaca, New York: Cornell University Press, 1969.

Paris Universal Exposition, 1867. Reports of the United States Commissioners. General Survey of the Exposition; with a Report on the Character and Condition of the United States Section. Washington, D.C.: Government Printing Office, 1868.

Pearson, Hesketh. *Labby: The Life and Character of Henry Labouchere.* New York: Harper & Brothers, 1937.

Perruchot, Henri. *Manet.* Trans. by Humphrey Hare. Cleveland: World Publishing, 1962.

Piedagnel, Alexandre. *Les ambulances de Paris pendant le siège (1870–71).* Paris, 1871.

Pinkney, David H. *The French Revolution of 1830.* Princeton: Princeton University Press, 1972.

Price, Roger. *The French Second Republic: A Social History.* Ithaca, New York: Cornell University Press, 1972.

Primet, Jean. *Nadar, par Jean Primet et Antoinette Delasser.* Paris: A. Colin, 1966.

Proskauer, Curt, and Fritz H. Witt. *Bildgeschichte der Zahnheilkunde: Zeugnisse aus 5 Jahrtausenden.* Trans. by Phoebe Cave. Cologne: Verlag M. DuMont Schauberg, 1962.

Rainey, Henry. *Dr. Thomas W. Evans America's Dentist to European Royalty.* No city, n.d. U. Penn.

Régnier, Henri de. *De Mon Temps* . . . Paris: Mercure de France, 1933.

Ridley, Jasper. *Napoleon III and Eugénie.* New York: Viking Press, 1979.

Rochegude, Félix, Marquis de. *Promenades dans toutes les rues de Paris par Arrondissements. XVI Arrondissement.* Paris: Hachette, 1910.

Ross, Ishbel. *Rebel Rose: Life of Rose O'Neal Greenhow, Confederate Spy.* New York: Harper & Brothers, 1954.

Rothney, John. *Bonapartism After Sedan.* Ithaca, New York: Cornell University Press, 1969.

Salomon, Henri. *L'Ambassade de Richard de Metternich.* Paris: Firmin-Didot, 1931.

Sarcey, Francisque. *Le Siège de Paris: Impressions et Souvenirs.* Paris, 1871.

Saunders, Edith. *The Age of Worth: Couturier to the Empress Eugénie.* Bloomington: Indiana University Press, 1955.

Seaver, Jane Gray. "Thomas William Evans," in *Our Representatives Abroad.* Ed. by Augustus C. Rogers. New York, 1874.

The Second Empire 1852–1870: Art in France under Napoleon III. Philadelphia: Philadelphia Museum of Art: 1978.

Seignobos, Charles. "Histoire de France contemporaine depuis la révolution jusqu'à la paix de 1919," in *Le Déclin de l'Empire et l'etablissement de la 3ᵉ république*, vol. 7. Paris: Hachette, n.d.

Seward, Frederick W. *Seward at Washington, as Senator and Secretary of State*. New York, 1891.

Seward, William H. *William H. Seward's Travels Around the World*. Ed. by Olive Risley Seward. New York, 1873.

Simpson, F. A. *Louis Napoleon & the Recovery of France*. London: Longmans, 1960.

Skillman, David B. *Biography of a College*. Easton, Pennsylvania: Lafayette College, 1932.

Smyth, Ethel Mary. *Impressions That Remained: Memoirs*, 2 vols. London: Longmans, Green, 1919.

Stanley, Henry M. *The Autobiography of Sir Henry Morton Stanley . . . edited by his wife, Dorothy Stanley*. Boston: Houghton Mifflin, 1909.

Stoeckl, Agnes de. *King of the French: A Portrait of Louis Philippe 1773–1850*. New York: Putnam's, 1958.

—— and Wilfred S. Edwards. *When Men Had Time to Love*. London: John Murray, 1953.

Strong, George Templeton. *The Diary of George Templeton Strong*. Ed. by Allan Nevins and M. H. Thomas, 4 vols. New York: Macmillan, 1952.

Tabarant, Adolphe. *Manet et ses oeuvres*. Paris: Gallimard, 1947.

Taylor, J. A. *History of Dentistry*. Philadelphia: Lea & Febiger, 1922.

Thompson, J. M. *Louis Napoleon and the Second Empire*. New York: W. W. Norton, 1967.

Van Deusen, Glyndon G. *William Henry Seward*. New York: Oxford University Press, 1967.

——. *Thurlow Weed: Wizard of the Lobby*. Boston: Little, Brown, 1947.

Van Wyck, Frederick. *Recollections of an Old New Yorker*. New York: Liveright, 1932.

Victoria, Queen. *The Letters of Queen Victoria*. Ed. by George Earle Buckle, second series, 2 vols. London: Longman's, Green, 1926.

——. *Your Dear Letter: Private Correspondence of Queen Victoria and the Crown Princess of Prussia, 1865–1871*. Ed. by Roger Fulford. New York: Scribner's, 1971.

Viel Castel, Count Horace de. *Memoirs of Count Horace de Viel Castel*. Ed. by Charles Bousfield, 2 vols. London, 1888.

A Visitor's Guide to the Second Empire. Philadelphia: Philadelphia Museum of Art, 1978.

[Vizetelly, Ernest Alfred]. *The Court of the Tuileries 1852–1870: Its Organization, Chief Personages, Splendour, Frivolity, and Downfall, by Le Petit Homme Rouge*. London: Chatto & Windus, 1912.

Vizetelly, Ernest Alfred. *Paris and Her People Under the Third Republic*. New York: Stokes, 1919? Reprinted by Kraus Reprint Co., New York, 1971.

Washburne, E. B. *Recollections of a Minister to France 1869–1877*, 2 vols. New York, 1887.

Weed, Thurlow. *Letters from Europe and the West Indies 1843–1862.* Albany, 1866.

Weintraub, Stanley. *Whistler: A Biography.* New York: Weybright and Talley, 1974.

Whiteing, Richard. *My Harvest.* New York: Dodd, Mead, 1915.

Williams, Roger. *The French Revolution of 1870–1871.* New York: W. W. Norton, 1960.

———. *Gaslight and Shadow: The World of Napoleon III 1851–1870.* New York: Macmillan, 1957.

———. *The Mortal Napoleon III.* Princeton: Princeton University Press, 1971.

Willson, Beckles. *John Slidell and the Confederates in Paris (1862–65).* New York: Minton, Balch, 1932.

Wissant, Georges de. *Le Paris d'autrefois, cafés & cabarets.* Paris: J. Tallendier, 1928.

Woodham-Smith, Cecil. *Queen Victoria: From Her Birth to the Death of the Prince Consort.* New York: Knopf, 1972.

Woolf, Leonard. *Growing: An Autobiography of the Years 1904–1911.* New York: Harcourt, Brace & World, 1961.

Wright, Vincent. "The Coup d'Etat of December 1851: Repression and the Limits to Repression," in *Revolution and Reaction: 1848 and the Second French Republic.* Ed. by Roger Price. New York: Harper & Row, Barnes & Noble Division, 1975.

Young, John Russell. *Around the World with General Grant . . . in 1877, 1878, 1879,* 2 vols. New York, 1879.

Zeldin, Theodore. *France: 1848–1945,* 2 vols. Oxford: Clarendon Press, 1973.

Articles

Baguenier-Désorimeaux, H. "L'Hôtel Evans." *Bulletin de la Société Historique d'Auteuil et de Passy* 7 (January 1912).

Barrett, W. C. "Dr. Thomas W. Evans." *Dental Practitioner and Advertiser* 29 (January 1898).

Barry, Joseph. "Paris Commune from a dream to bloody nightmare in ten weeks." *Smithsonian Magazine,* March 1971.

Baudet, le Docteur Raoul. "Autour de la Famille Impériale — le Docteur Evans et les dentistes." *Journal de l'Université des annales Conferencia,* October 15, 1933.

Benard, Dr. R. "Bâtards de Napoleon III." *Chercheurs et curieux* 4, no. 39 (1954).

Bicknell, Anna L. "The Tuileries under the Second Empire." *Century Magazine* 47 (March 1894).

Burgoyne, John Montagu. "How the Empress Eugénie Crossed the Channel." *Century Magazine* 58 (October 1905).

Bye, Arthur Edwin. "The Evans Museum." *Journal of the Missouri Dental Association* 9 (November 1976).

Byron, Robert. "Winterhalter." *Country Life* (London), December 5, 1936.

Cabrol, F. "The Empress Eugénie in England." *Dublin Review* 167 (1920).

Carr, Malcolm Wallace. "Thomas W. Evans: His Life and Influence on the Development of Dentistry as a Learned Profession." *Journal of the American College of Dentists* 46 (April 1979).

Castelnau, Edouard de Curières de. "Sedan et Wilhelmshöhe." *Revue de Paris*, November 1, 1929.

"Commencement Exercises." *Lafayette Monthly* 2 (July 1872).

Cornu, Hortense. "Louis Napoleon Painted by a Contemporary." *Cornhill Magazine* 27 (January–June 1873).

Crawford, T. C. "Dr. Thomas W. Evans." *Items of Interest* 13 (April 1891).

Dayot, Armand. "Winterhalter — Painter to the Second Empire." *International Studio* 91 (October 1928).

"Desecrators of the Grave." *Dental Practitioner and Advertiser* 29 (April 1898).

"Dr. Evans's Wills." *British Journal of Dental Science*, January 1, 1898.

Dubbs, Joseph Henry. "The Flight of an Empress." *Lancaster County Historical Papers*, no. 2 (1906).

"The Empress Eugénie's Flight to England: From the Log of the 'Gazelle.'" *Temple Bar Magazine* 68 (July 1883).

Evans, Thomas W. Letter to Odontological Society of Great Britain. *British Journal of Dental Science* 11 (April 1868).

———. "Napoleon III After Sedan." *Appleton's Booklovers Magazine*, July 1905.

———. "Physiological Action of Nitrous Oxide Gas." *British Journal of Dental Science* 12 (February 1869).

Fish, Mabel. "Imperial Exiles." *In Britain*, September 1970.

"The Funeral of Dr. Thomas W. Evans." *International Dental Journal* 19, July 1898.

Genêt. "Letter from Paris." *New Yorker*, January 20, 1962.

Goelho, David H. "Thomas W. Evans (1823–1897) in the Cultural History of American Dentistry." *New York Journal of Dentistry* 36 (February 1966).

Hanson, Anne Coffin. "A Tale of Two Manets." *Art in America* 67 (December 1979).

"An Honored Practitioner." *Dental Practitioner and Advertiser* 28 (October 1897).

Hunting, Penelope. "The Empress at Chislehurst." *Country Life* 29 (March 1979).

Hurley, Marcella. "Thomas W. Evans — Dentist and Diplomat." *Oral Hygiene* 30 (May 1940).

"The Imperial Dentist." *Academy*, December 16, 1905.

"It has just leaked out . . ." *Dental Advertiser* 19 (April 1888).

Jaccard, René. "Evans et L'Impératrice." *Médicine et Hygiène dentaires,* March 1, 1947.

Keeler, Ralph. "With the American Ambulance at Paris." *Lippincott's Monthly Magazine* 12 (July 1873).

Knudtzon, Kermit F. "Doctor Evans: Confidante to Napoleon III." *Cal* 41 (July 1977).

Labouchere, Henry. "Notes from Paris: A Diplomatic Tooth-Doctor." *Truth,* November 25, 1897.

Lacour-Gayet, G. "L'Impératrice Eugénie: Les dernières semaines aux Tuileries, le quatre septembre et la fuite en Angleterre." *Académie des Sciences, Morales et Politiques,* July–August 1925.

"The Lindsay Club: Centenary of Nitrous Oxide." *British Dental Journal,* May 7, 1968.

Luntz, Lester L., D.D.S. "History of Forensic Dentistry." *Dental Clinics of North America* 21 (January 1977).

Monnier, Léon. "Nécrologie, Arthur Hugenschmidt (1862–1929)." *Revue de Stomatologie* 31 (November 1929).

"Nécrologie — Thomas Evans." *L'Odontologie* 18 (November 1897).

"Nitrous Oxide." *British Journal of Dental Science* 13 (February 1870).

"A Notable Centenary." *British Dental Journal,* April 2, 1968.

"Nouvelles — Nécrologie." *Revue Odontologique* 16 (November 1897).

"Obituary: Dr. Thomas W. Evans." *Dental Cosmos* 40 (January 1898).

"Obituary: Resolutions on Death of Dr. Thomas W. Evans." *Dental Cosmos* 40 (February 1898).

Progrès, Dr. "Les dentistes américains." *L'Art Dentaire* 9 (September 1866).

Puyol. "Journal de l'Abbé Puyol." *Revue des deux mondes,* July 15, 1929.

Rainey, Henry. "Personalities in Dental History: Thomas W. Evans." *Pennsylvania Dental Journal* 57 (November 1953).

Raoul-Duval, Josette. "Méry Laurent." *L'Oeil, Revue d'art,* no. 77 (May 1961).

"A Remarkable Case Was Recently Tried . . ." *Missouri Dental Journal* 15 (June 1883).

Riddle, Sturgis L. "A Lighthouse of American Faith and Freedom Abroad." *Cathedral Age* (Autumn 1955).

Schlosser, Frank. "Siege Dinners 1870-71." *Living Age,* series 7, vol. 46.

Smith, W. D. A. "T. W. Evans — Before and After." *British Dental Journal,* August 6, 1968.

Soyer, Gérard. "Le Dentiste Thomas Evans et l'histoire du Second Empire." *Revue Française d'Odonto-Stomatologie* 1 (October 1954).

Spitzer, Alan B. "The Good Napoleon III." *French Historical Studies* 2 (Spring 1962).

Stein, John Bethune. "The Teeth and Dentists of Some Monarchs of France." *Dental Cosmos* 56 (December 1914).

Talbot, Eugene S. "Dr. Thomas W. Evans — Dentist to the Crowned Heads of Europe." *Oral Hygiene* 11 (June 1921).

Welch, M. L. "Dr. Thomas Evans: An American Knight in Paris." *American Legion of Honor Magazine* 38 (1967).

Pamphlets

Agreement Between the Thomas W. Evans Museum and Institute Society and the Trustees of the University of Pennsylvania. Dated June 15, 1912 and the Will of Dr. Thomas W. Evans. Philadelphia, 1912.

Davenport, Dr. W. S., Jr. *The Pioneer American Dentists in France and their Successors: Speech Delivered October 8th, 1965 upon the Occasion of the 75th Anniversary of the American Dental Club of Paris 1890–1965.* No city, n.d.

Dental Products of Dr. Thomas W. Evans. Paris, n.d.

Johnson, William Branch. *The Siege of Paris, 1870–1871.* London: Oxford University Press, 1943.

Miscellaneous

American Church, 65 Quai D'Orsay. Post card, n.d. U. Penn.

Appraisal of Estate of Thomas W. Evans, J. E. Caldwell and Co., November 10, 1938. U. Penn.

Inventory after the decease of Doctor Evans. Closure. January 26, 1901. U. Penn.

Lafayette Buildings. Advertisement, no city, no date. U. Penn.

Nadar [pseud.], Tournachon, Félix. Photographic studio guest book of autographs. U. Penn.